FEATHER FALL

Laurens van der Post was born in Africa in 1906, the thirteenth of fifteen children in a family of Dutch and French Huguenot origins. Most of his adult life has been spent with one foot in Africa and one in England. His professions of writer and farmer were interrupted by ten years of soldiering – behind enemy lines in Abyssinia and also in the Western Desert and the Far East, where he was taken prisoner by the Japanese while commanding a small guerrilla unit. He went straight from prison back to active service in Java, where he was Lord Mountbatten's – and for a while the British government's – military/political representative and, finally, when the British forces withdrew from Java, remained behind as military attaché. Since 1949 he has undertaken several official missions exploring little-known parts of Africa. His independent expedition to the Kalahari Desert in search of the Bushmen and an effort sustained over many years to save them from extinction produced his famous documentary film *The Lost World of the Kalahari* and several books. In addition to this series, other television films include *All Africa Within Us* and *The Story of Carl Gustav Jung*, whom he met after the war and grew to know as a personal friend. In the 1930s he wrote *In a Province*, the first book by a native of Africa to expose the horrors of colour prejudice and racism. His other books include *Venture to the Interior* (1952), *Flamingo Feather* (1955), *The Heart of the Hunter* (1961), *The Seed and the Sower* (1963), *Journey into Russia* (1964), *The Hunter and the Whale* (1967), *A Story Like the Wind* (1972), *A Far-off Place* (1974), *A Mantis Carol* (1975), *Jung and the Story of Our Time* (1976), *Yet Being Someone Other* (1982), *Testament to the Bushman* (with Jane Taylor, 1984), *A Walk with a White Bushman* (with Jean-Marc Pottiez, 1986), *About Blady: A Pattern Out of Time* (1991), *The Voice of the Thunder* (1993) and this anthology. Most of these are published by Penguin. *The Seed and the Sower* was made into a film under the title *Merry Christmas, Mr Lawrence*, and, more recently, *A Story Like*

D0107990

the Wind and *A Far-off Place* were combined and made into the film *A Far-off Place*.

Sir Laurens van der Post is married to Ingaret Giffard. He was awarded the CBE in 1947 and received his knighthood in 1981. He now lives mainly at his home in Chelsea.

LAURENS VAN DER POST

FEATHER FALL

AN ANTHOLOGY

EDITED BY JEAN-MARC POTTIEZ
ASSISTED BY JANE BEDFORD

PENGUIN BOOKS

PENGUIN BOOKS

Published by the Penguin Group
Penguin Books Ltd, 27 Wrights Lane, London W8 5TZ, England
Penguin Books USA Inc., 375 Hudson Street, New York, New York 10014, USA
Penguin Books Australia Ltd, Ringwood, Victoria, Australia
Penguin Books Canada Ltd, 10 Alcorn Avenue, Toronto, Ontario, Canada M4V 3B2
Penguin Books (NZ) Ltd, 182–190 Wairau Road, Auckland 10, New Zealand

Penguin Books Ltd, Registered Offices: Harmondsworth, Middlesex, England

First published by Chatto & Windus 1994
Published in Penguin Books 1995
1 3 5 7 9 10 8 6 4 2

Printed in England by Clays Ltd, St Ives plc

Contents

Acknowledgements

To Laurens van der Post, the true author of *Feather Fall*, who has allowed me to try to distil into a single volume the essence of a lifetime's writing, a lifetime that contains so much personal experience, has such abundant breadth and scope, and spans almost the whole of the twentieth century, I am more grateful than I can find the words to express. That he should place his trust in me and give me unfettered freedom to carry out such a sensitive task is entirely characteristic of a man who has not sought recognition for himself, yet is always generous and imaginative in his response to others. I hope devoutly that in some measure I may have been able to repay his trust with this anthology.

I have been enormously helped in its preparation by Jane Bedford, who, with her careful and creative editing and her intimate knowledge of Laurens van der Post's books, has contributed to almost every aspect of my work – as much in the process of distillation as in the detailed presentation of the text. Her editorial support, painstaking and constructive as it has been from beginning to end, has been invaluable and most certainly deserves special mention.

Nor should I fail to thank John Charlton, who for the last decade or more has been Laurens van der Post's publisher, and to whom this anthology was first suggested. He took to the idea at once, nursed it along and steered it to the brink of fulfilment before his retirement in the summer of 1993. Even after that he continued to provide unstinting help and advice, all to very good purpose and all greatly appreciated by me.

His editorial successor at Chatto & Windus, Alison Samuel, has in turn been most helpful and supportive. More and more I have grown to feel that, like Laurens van der Post, who has publicly acknowledged his long, harmonious and still unbroken association with The Hogarth Press (now an imprint of Chatto & Windus), I have been fortunate with my publishers.

While working on this anthology, I was also fortunate at my home in Paris, where my daughter Claire-Yumi was more help than she can possibly know to her 'Papa Gorilla', with her clever fingers, her patience and her kind heart.

In the end, of course, responsibility for the anthology rests entirely with me as its compiler, but in all fairness to everyone who has helped me I have to say that mine was not the only moving spirit behind it. *Feather Fall* is the outcome of a shared commitment and endeavour, and is, I am quite certain, all the better for being so.

JEAN-MARC POTTIEZ

Introduction

Laurens van der Post has a unique capacity to inspire, to heighten awareness and fire the imagination. That, above all, is what I have tried to reflect in this anthology – not just in the passages I have chosen but in the manner of their arrangement; for, instinctive storyteller that he is, there is always a pattern in his writing, a flow and a continuity. My aim has been to convey this sense of movement and exploration, not so much as a chronological progression, but rather with a sense of how the many elements in Laurens van der Post's life and imagination link up and lead on and together form a trail of their own.

That trail could just as easily have been chronological because the essentials would have been the same. Indeed, one of the most striking features of the books he has written over the last sixty years is the constancy of his fundamental values. The boy who wrote in his diary, at the age of eight, that he would one day go to the Kalahari Desert, seek out the Bushman and 'beg for his pardon' duly fulfilled that promise forty years later, and has since done everything in his power to save these resilient 'first people' of his native Africa from extinction. The young man of twenty who rebelled in spirit, action and words against the canker of colour prejudice in South Africa became one of the truest and most influential opponents of apartheid when the Nationalist government enforced its policy of segregation after the Second World War. And the young writer who, in his first novel (*In a Province*), rejected 'the lure and blasphemy' of communism because of its disregard for the individual, thirty years later witnessed at first hand what life was like for ordinary Russian people under the Soviet regime, whose downfall he predicted (*Journey Into Russia*, 1964).

In none of these examples, though, is chronology the key factor. What matters is the message itself; the content rather than the timing of the story – which is why I have chosen a thematic approach for this anthology. Nevertheless, it is true that chronology provides a context which is often illuminating. Thus, van der Post's first visit to Japan, which was to prove such a vital experience for him, took place at a time when the Japanese people had only recently begun to emerge from centuries of cultural isolation, and his vivid portrayal of this complex nation in *Yet Being Someone Other* reveals it at a fateful turning point in its history.

History – this time colonial history – helps to explain why Laurens van der Post, who came from a French Huguenot family living in the Dutch Cape Colony of southern Africa, joined the British army at the start of the Second World War. He had been drawn to Britain as the engine room of the empire into which he had been born, a country, as he puts it himself, that 'I had come to love and whose story and great historical values correspond most to my own seeking'. Then, in 1939, he remembered the regiment which in earlier days had defeated his father and grandfather in battle, decided that it must be a good one, and applied to join.

Awareness of history is ever-present in van der Post's life and writing. It manifests itself in his commitment to the cause of the Kalahari Bushmen, among the purest and most authentic representatives of original life on earth, whose stories, dreams and ancient ways belong to a timeless tradition, older by far than all recorded history, and whose intimate partnership with nature, ruined only by the cruel intrusion of human foes and friends alike, exemplifies the sense of balance, proportion and harmony without which no civilization can endure. History, for van der Post as it should be for all of us, is a continuous, seamless process, and it is more of a matrix than a mould. Even ancient history, the world of Homer for example, is linked with our time by no more than a few spans of living memory.

There is much more to 'memory' than that, though, in van der Post's perception, and readers of this anthology will discover far deeper layers of meaning and patterns of experience which he, both in his life and in his writings, consciously and unconsciously, has done so much to explore.

Who, then, is this explorer? In whose footsteps will we be following as we set out on the trail of discovery which I hope this anthology will be – this anthology which the author himself has named *Feather Fall* after the elusive, but attainable, 'white bird of truth'?

Laurens Jan van der Post was born on 13 December 1906 in Philippolis in the Orange Free State, the thirteenth of fifteen children in a pioneer family whose forebears had taken part in the Great Trek. His maternal grandmother, born in an ox-wagon, was the daughter of one of the first of the trekkers to establish a farm north of the Orange River. It was called 'Boesmansfontein' (Bushman Spring), and Laurens had a half-Bushman nurse whom he remembers to this day as vividly as his own parents. The sense of companionship with the indigenous peoples of Africa, the shared storytelling, the respect for nature and the love of animals which he still feels deeply today, all stemmed from his grandfather's farm, as did the sense of Africa as an 'Old Testament country'. For his grandfather was a God-fearing man, and the collective readings from the Bible, accompanied each night by rousing hymns and prayers, nourished the imagination of young Laurens.

His mother, who had herself received the great gift of stories and storytelling from her own indigenous nurses and native companions, reinforced the craving of the young 'backveld' boy for tales of life at large. And in the library of his father (a barrister by training who rose to prominence in the old Free State parliament) Laurens found the books that fuelled his spirit and stirred his longing for adventure and travel. For hours on end he would read in his favourite hiding place, a giant mulberry tree in the family garden, or out in the hills as he kept an eye on the grazing sheep.

Laurens was barely seven when his father died. His family left the farm, and before long he went away to school where, over the next few years, he excelled in many subjects; not just in his gift for writing – he wrote his first poem, in High Dutch, at the age of six – but in mathematics, physics and languages (he speaks nine today) as well as in sports (rugby, hockey and tennis). So it was a shock to everyone when, at the age of sixteen, he broke with the family tradition by refusing to go to university and decided instead to make his way in the world.

His first job was in Port Natal (Durban), where he worked for an evening newspaper, the *Natal Advertiser*, quickly gaining experience as a journalist, and taking particular interest in the drama of courtroom stories and the exciting world of ships and the sea.

Then, in 1926, he was invited to join Roy Campbell and William Plomer as the Afrikaans editor of South Africa's first serious literary and cultural magazine, *Voorslag* (*Whiplash*). The magazine made a big impact in its short life, not least for its vigorous stand against racial discrimination, which aroused fierce opposition.

Also in 1926, and as a result of a spontaneous act of courtesy towards two Japanese visitors who were refused a cup of coffee because of their colour, van der Post accepted an invitation to go to Japan, travelling on board a tramp steamer, the *Canada Maru*, under the command of Captain Katsue Mori. The story of this long journey, which was to have such a profound influence on van der Post's life, is told in *Yet Being Someone Other*, perhaps the most autobiographical of all his books.

From Japan he travelled back to Port Natal, but reluctantly. The voyage out in the *Canada Maru*, the encounter with Japan itself and the voyage back to Africa had worked a great change in him. He felt he owed it to the newspaper which had sent him to Japan to continue working for it for another year, but he did so in an inwardly rebellious mood, and left as soon as his self-imposed sentence expired to make for England.

He arrived there in 1928 in one of the coldest winters and, as he records in *Yet Being Someone Other*, faced a 'battle for survival in a London dark with economic depression, with unemployed and unwanted lives and abysmal aimlessness around me'. He took to the streets with thousands of other discontented and unemployed men and women. 'I felt compelled to march with the unemployed in Hyde Park and join in passionately with the debate which shook my generation over the nature of the radical reform and renewal that the societies and nations and the institutions urgently needed if life itself were not to be imperilled.' At the same time, 'the same hand of chance . . . which had taken me to Japan directed me infallibly to a chain of acquaintanceships that took me to the heart of Bloomsbury, where I met among many others: the Bells, Duncan Grant, Roger Fry, Lopokova, Maynard Keynes and, most important of all for me, Virginia and Leonard Woolf.'

The Woolfs were to publish Laurens van der Post's first book, *In a Province*. In it he rejected the communist ideal which so many of his literary and artistic friends were espousing, and he had spent four years finding a publisher for it. The book was a sensation, and began his long association with The Hogarth Press, which the Woolfs had founded seventeen years before.

In a Province was recognized at once by some of the most distinguished critics of the day, notably Herbert Read and Ernst Robert Curtius, as well as by the younger generation of writers such as Stephen Spender, Cecil Day Lewis and W.H.Auden. But in spite of the acclaim it received, which built on the reputation he had already gained with a devastating attack on segregation in *The Realist* (the literary magazine edited by Gerald Heard and supported by Aldous Huxley), the 1930s did not advance his career as a writer.

Married by now, and with two children to bring up, he had bought a farm in Gloucestershire and tried to combine farming and writing at a time of continued economic recession, when food was often short. The experiment was not a success, although he made his mark as a farmer with an award for the best-run farm at the prestigious Three Counties Show.

His writing during this period took two forms: freelance dispatches as a foreign correspondent reporting on current affairs; and a book of warning – warning about the powerful mythological forces that were breaking loose in Nazi Germany and driving the world to war. The book, provisionally entitled *The Rainbow Bridge* and still unfinished when war eventually came, was destroyed by one of Hitler's bombs; but its message was not lost, because he used its themes later in *The Dark Eye in Africa*, written in the 1950s after another outburst of violence and conflict generated by what a reviewer called 'the supreme African problem – colour.'

In 1938, judging war to be inevitable, van der Post arranged for his wife and children to return to South Africa. He stayed on in England and, when war was eventually declared in September 1939, enlisted as a private soldier. He was soon sent on the officer-training course at Aldershot – where he passed out top of his battalion, and, once in active service, took part in commando missions in North Africa, the Middle East, Abyssinia (now Ethiopia) and Burma before joining General Wavell's forces in Java in

1942. His guerrilla activities against the Japanese ended in his capture, in dramatic circumstances, in the jungles of Bantam, and for the next three-and-a-half years he was a prisoner-of-war. These experiences he has described in his own books, in particular his collection of linked 'Christmas' stories, *The Seed and the Sower* (later dramatized by the Japanese director, Nagisa Oshima, in the film *Merry Christmas, Mr Lawrence*) and in *The Night of the New Moon* – a reference to the night of 6 August 1945, after the first atom bomb had been dropped on Hiroshima. This book drew a special tribute from Raymond Mortimer: 'I rank Colonel van der Post with the best living writers of English ... this book confirms my constant admiration, not just for his talent but for the force of his imagination and the nobility of his mind.'

Laurens van der Post has never dwelled on the treatment he suffered in the prison camps during those long years. Suffice it to say that, like many of his fellow prisoners, he endured deprivation, torture and repeated threats of execution, yet he never became embittered. More than that, he went to great lengths, in the most debilitating circumstances, to instil in others the level of under-standing and tolerance that enabled tens of thousands of his fellow survivors at the end to return home with their spirit intact and forgiveness in their hearts.

His own war continued for another two-and-a-half years as he returned to active service as Lord Mountbatten's political and military adviser in Indonesia and, later, as military attaché to the British minister in Java. By now he had been appointed Comman-der of the British Empire for distinguished and gallant service in the field, and a long-term career in the army was open to him. How-ever, he decided to resign, his instinct taking him to the peacetime roles of explorer, writer, film-maker, conservationist and political adviser to which destiny (if that is the right word) had, in some mysterious but unmistakable way that he came to recognize with increasing clarity, been directing him from the start.

In 1949, his war now over, he married for the second time and, through his new wife, Ingaret Giffard, was introduced to Carl Gustav Jung, the Swiss psychologist whose pioneering work in the field of human understanding had made him world famous. The rapport between the two men was instant and enduring, and in time van der Post was to write a book entitled *Jung and the Story of Our Time*, which went beyond biography into areas of instinct and imagination that both men knew to be at the core of human experience, yet which were still largely unexplored. Jung confirmed much that van der Post had felt instinctively for years: about the significance of dreams, the unseen links and subtle patterns that shape our daily lives, the need for wholeness, balance and proportion, the essential complementarity of the masculine and feminine in life, the unconscious forces that determine so much in both individual and collective behaviour, and the quest for higher meaning.

Meeting Jung and finding so much in common with him undoubtedly helped van der Post to explore these inner areas of personal experience just as he was setting out to explore unknown areas of the outer world. For that is what he now did; and in so doing, found the way to the rehabilitation he so badly needed after the long ordeal of war.

Over the following years he led a number of expeditions to remote parts of Africa, some of them for special government purposes. His mission to Nyasaland (modern Malawi) in 1949 formed the basis of his book, *Venture to the Interior* (1952), which established him overnight as a bestselling author. This was followed a few years later by *The Lost World of the Kalahari* (1958) which, together with his documentary film of the same title (whose television ratings for the BBC matched those of the Queen's coronation), drew to the attention of a vast public the extraordinary spirit, skills, vitality and wisdom of the aboriginal desert Bushmen, as well as their desperate plight. Both books have been in print ever since; both were translated into many languages; and both went far beyond the boundaries of conventional travel writing, touching on mysteries of mood and place and venturing into the primal world of dreams, symbols, imagery and legend.

In the thirty-five years since then Laurens van der Post has never stopped writing – stories of action and adventure, probing narratives of travel and exploration, reflections on life, war, history and human aspiration. Few of his books fall into the familiar categories of fiction, history, travel, psychology, biography or autobiography. Rather they reflect his own many-layered outlook on life: a mixture of the practical and the spiritual that comes naturally to a man who has always wanted to combine being and doing; a man who has proved himself as a farmer, soldier, explorer, diplomat and trusted adviser, but whose creative imagination is that of a poet, artist and philosopher. Like the whaler hero of his book *The Hunter and the Whale*, he is 'a poet in action and an incorrigible romantic at heart'; not a romantic with a vague and idealized vision – his life has been far too deeply embedded in the taut world of reality for that – but one who has an unfaltering faith in mankind and, more important still, a compelling awareness of a larger dimension in life beyond our understanding.

The sanctity of the human spirit and all that guides it is the essence of his faith. Though brought up in a religious household, he has never been confirmed in the church into which he was baptised. He has never accepted the severe, sexist, misogynist and intolerant Calvinist concept of God which prevailed in Africa in his youth, responding instead to a more universal, less personal God whose love smoulders at the core of the Bible, nowhere more ardently than in the writings of St Paul and the mystics.

Many reviewers have testified to the strong moral quality of van der Post's writing. To choose a recent example, Simone Guyé, reviewing in the *Journal de Genève* the French edition of his inspirational book of hope and healing, *About Blady: A Pattern out of Time*, described him as 'not only one of the great writers but also one of the greatest spirits of our time'. Rosamond Lehmann made a similar judgement: 'Laurens van der Post, citizen of the world. He lived through hell in Japanese prison camps and emerged to become a great spiritual thinker and writer.'

Not just a thinker and writer, however, but also a man who takes part, joins in, commits himself to causes – championing the conservation of nature and respect for animal life, backing the Capricorn Society in its aim to establish 'a new order of emancipation and multi-racial integration in Africa', or contributing in countless other ways with characteristic clarity of purpose, energy and generosity of spirit. He has always been discreet about his confidential role as a political and personal adviser, but the services he has given to the public life of his country were recognized with a Knighthood in the New Year's Honours List of 1981.

Sir Laurens van der Post, CBE, author of twenty-five exceptional books written over more than sixty years, is the man whose anthology I have been privileged to compile. For me and those who helped me on the way it has been a labour of love, but also a challenge – to ensure that the long, living, shimmering tapestry of his work is not reduced to patchwork. A sampler, rather, is what I had in mind; certainly not a substitute. My selection cannot begin to replace the books themselves – books of action and dream, dream and reflection, mystery and wonder, full of seed words and seed stories.

If you, my readers, should happen to share some or even all of the pleasure I have had in re-reading and travelling again with Laurens van der Post, this anthology will help you to discover, or rediscover, a writer whose work is that of sower, pathfinder, message-bearer and bridge-maker all in one – a bridge, as he says himself in *The Heart of the Hunter*, between 'the first pattern of things' and the world of our own time.

My hope is that, for readers everywhere, *Feather Fall* will be the start of a long and fulfilling quest, such as I myself experienced when I came across my first van der Post book, *The Seed and the Sower*. That inspiring story, soon followed by *The Lost World of the Kalahari*, set me on my own irreversible way to 'planet van der Post', as I have come to call the worlds, both those within and without, which he explores.

Gradually I have formed the impression, now a certainty, that Laurens van der Post is a member of a vast family which constitutes a community of spirit and heart that has existed throughout our history. Like those wells in the desert that are so difficult to find and so far apart, yet are linked beneath the ground and combine invisibly to quench one's thirst, this vast and ever-growing family of fellow travellers is the company in which, step by step, century after century, we can all join in the ultimate quest, following the flight of the great white bird of truth, ready in heart and mind for its eventual feather fall.

JEAN-MARC POTTIEZ
Paris, 16 October, 1993

Feather Fall

In the heat of the day a young hunter came to a clearing in the Forest of the Night, and there he knelt down by a pool of water, transparent with the blue of the African day, to quench his thirst. At that moment he was dazzled by the reflection in the pool of a great, white bird of a kind he had never seen before. Instantly he looked away and up, but the bird had vanished.

From that moment he was filled with a great unease and could not rest. His community, who valued him greatly, assured him that the restlessness would pass, but a conviction that he would not rest until he had seen the great white bird itself grew stronger in him by the day until one morning he left the place where he had been born and set out to search for it.

The journey lasted so long and took him so far and wide that he was an old man, feeling his end was near, when he came to a great mountain. There he had firm news of the bird at last. He was told that it nested on the summit of the mountain. Enfeebled as he was, he slowly climbed the mountain and, towards the end of a long day, as he came over the last of many false summits, he found himself confronted by a final cliff he knew he could not scale. At the end of his physical powers, sadly he prepared himself to face his end.

But then it was suddenly as if a voice within him was commanding him to look up at the forbidden summit and as he did so he saw, in the light of one of the greatest of mythological African sunsets, a pure white feather fluttering down from on high towards him. He put out his hand and grasped the feather and, they who told me the story said, he died content. When I asked them what the name of this great white bird was, they told me: 'The bird has many names but we believe it was the Bird of Truth.'

LAURENS VAN DER POST
1994

Chapter One
Africa as a Mirror

═══════

My Mother's Country

Africa is my mother's country. I do not know exactly how long my mother's family has lived in Africa; but I do know that Africa was about and within her from the beginning, as it was for me. Her mother, my grandmother, was cradled, if not actually born, in an ox-wagon driving in the thirties of the last century steadfastly deeper into the unknown interior of southern Africa. The ox-wagon was part of the small and ill-fated Liebenberg Trek. My mother's grandfather was its leader. This little caravan consisting of no more than seven or eight wagons, this small group of people numbering no more than forty or fifty souls, had moved in the far forefront of a vast exodus. They formed part of the Great Trek of Dutch farmers from British rule at the Cape.

They had crossed the Karroo safely; hauled their wagons laboriously through the boulder-strewn drifts of the Orange River; crossed the wide, melancholy plains of the Free State and forded the deep, yellow Vaal River. They had gone safely across the highveld of the Transvaal, which was plundered bare and still smoked after the raids of Zulu and Matabele, and were moving into the bushveld, somewhere near where the town of Louis Trichardt stands today, when they in their turn were attacked. We shall never know precisely what happened.

My grandmother was little more than a baby; she could just run about and speak. All that is known about the attack is what was gathered afterwards from the incoherent account in broken Afrikaans given by the half-caste maid, who looked after my grandmother and her baby sister.

[3]

According to the maid, the wagons, after a long and exhausting trek, had come to rest the night before on the banks of a fairly big stream. During the night the two little children were very restless and had kept their parents awake with their crying. As a result, the maid was ordered just before dawn to dress the children and take them out of earshot of the wagons. One gets a clear impression from this order of how little the sleeping laager suspected what fate had in store for it. The maid had collected the children and had taken them down to the stream, as she had some washing to do.

She had not been there many minutes when the quiet – that lovely musical, rhythmical quiet of the bushveld at dawn – was broken with the war-cries and yells of the attacking Kaffirs. She must have walked through a gap in the encircling *impi* [Zulu or Sindabile army or regiment, usually attacking in a crescent moon formation] just before it drew its horns tight around the sleeping wagons. She snatched the two little girls and, with one under each arm, ran ducking along the side of the stream until she came to a wide, shallow waterfall. The stream fell, as I myself have so often seen them do in Africa, over a wide, overhanging ledge of stone. Behind the water there was a dry hollow, and shelter. The nurse dodged in behind this curtain of water and sat there fearfully all day with her terrified, uncomprehending charges. Late that night she crept out. She found the wagons burnt out and the battered, disfigured bodies of all who had been in them strewn far around.

Somehow, sheltering behind the waterfall by day and going out to forage when it became dark, she kept herself and the children alive. Nearly a week later they were picked up by a party of horsemen, who were wisely patrolling the disturbed country ahead of a much bigger trek following in the Liebenberg tracks.

I have no intention of writing a family history, but this much appeared necessary because it shows, as nothing else can show, how much Africa is my mother's country.

Venture to the Interior, Chapter 1

My earliest memories of Africa seem to focus round the large dining-table in my grandfather's ample home near the Great River. The scene in this theatre of my past is almost invariably the evening meal. One waited for this meal with the kind of excitement I was to experience later as a dramatic critic before the raising of the curtain on the first night of a new play in London by a friend from whom one expected much. The excitement would start when the coloured maids began to light the heavy oil lamps in the darkening house: first in the long passage which led from the front door on the stoep which surrounded the homestead which my grandfather had designed and built, and last, the largest lamp of all, which hung in the centre of the dining-room. In the middle of this room was the family table made out of African wood so hard and so heavy that a piece would sink like iron if thrown into water. Suspended in massive chains from the ceiling over this table, hung an immense brass lamp that shone like gold. It took one person over an hour to polish it every week and to me it always looked like the kind of oil lamp referred to in some New Testament parable or, better still, a lamp which Solomon might have hung in his first temple in the Promised Land.

I used to watch the lighting of this lamp as one might watch the performing of a miracle. I would experience a great sense of reassurance as I observed the heavy shadows roll back into the darkest recesses of the old Cape-Dutch furniture and saw the lamplight fall, as in a Rembrandt picture, on the table set and ready for its full complement of guests. At the same time I would become aware of a subtle scent of spice drifting in from the kitchen, despite the solid doors and passage in between.

First Catch Your Eland, 'Prelude'

All who worked for my grandfather no matter whether Griqua, Hottentot, Bushman, Basuto, Bechuana, Cape-coloured or poor white, were ultimately held in equal affection as part of his family, and the relationship was nightly redeemed by calling them into his dining-room to share with his wife and children in his communion with his God. One can only realize how significant such an attitude was when one remembers that the descendants of men like my grandfather are today trying to exclude such people from common worship in the same churches. I concluded, therefore, that in a brutal age my mother's people might have been, perhaps, less brutal than most. That helped, though not overmuch, for I knew that with

[5]

their deep Calvinist addiction to what they thought right, they would have done their duty conscientiously. Human beings are perhaps never more frightening than when they are convinced beyond doubt that they are right.

The Lost World of the Kalahari, Chapter 3

It was significant that my grandfather never referred to it as the Bible but always as the Book. He had such a feeling for the Book (which had been almost his only reading because he had never been to any school) that he had a special ritual before reading. He would reverently lift the large, heavy leather covers of the book with their metal clasps that shone like silver and open it slowly on the first ivory pages, smooth them out with his long, brown hand and then let them lie there exposed on the table a brief moment. I think perhaps he did this so that he could survey the large, green family tree with its spreading branches painted across both pages, and seek out, among the leaves, the names of his forefathers recorded there from the time they had landed in Africa as refugees from persecution in Europe some two hundred and fifty years previously. I suppose this silent roll-call of family history was necessary to quicken in him his feeling of continuity which, as he became older, appeared increasingly threatened by the discord gathering in the spirit of his people.

Jung and the Story of Our Time, 'The Time and the Space'

I remember vividly the day when my grandfather's favourite monthly magazine arrived with the weekly mail. It was printed in High Dutch and was called *The Church Messenger*. It had a bright yellow cover which I found repulsive with its title and sub-titles printed in a massive and inelegant black type. But it did have one virtue in my young eyes – its illustrations. In this particular issue there was one of what I thought to be the most beautiful ships I had ever seen. However, to my amazement, my grandfather seemed to be far from impressed by the beauty of the vessel. Pointing at it with a finger trembling with indignation and speaking in a voice which sounded to me like an Old Testament prophet, he resounded, 'Laurens Jan, do you know what they say about this ship you are looking at? They say it is unsinkable. And mark my words, the

Almighty will have something to say one day about so arrogant and blasphemous a boast.'

The lesson learnt was to go deeper when, in a later edition of the magazine, the same illustration was reproduced with the news that the ship had sunk after a collision with an iceberg in the North Atlantic, together with a monstrous loss of life. The name of the ship, of course, was the *Titanic*.

Yet Being Someone Other, Chapter 2

Above all, there was my Bushman nurse, Klara. She said her name meant 'light', and, for me, she was bathed in wonder: the light of rainbow morning, a crystal day and magic lantern evening, playing on the bright blue beads of glass of a heavy necklace around the smooth apricot skin of her throat. I remember her face as one of the most beautiful I have ever known; oval, with a slightly pointed chin, high cheek-bones, wide, large and rather slanted eyes full of a dark, glowing light as of the amber of the first glow on earth shining through the brown of evening on man's first day. These features gave her an oddly Chinese appearance, especially as I never saw the thick, short, matted hair which was always wrapped in cottons of the brightest colours. No one ever shone more brightly in my emotions. She remained at the deep centre of the love of the feminine which has given me so much.

The Voice of the Thunder, 'The Great Memory'

Meetings between different cultures, particularly of so-called civilized and so-called primitive men, are events of the most traumatic and fateful consequences, as immense as they must be unforeseen and irreversible. Neither 'civilized' nor 'primitive' men can ever be the same again once they have met one another and started the process of being a part of one another's daily lives. No matter how much the exponents of one culture would like to limit participation, interpenetration or even partnership with other cultures, these are matters to which no human or conscious limits can be set.

Yet Being Someone Other, Chapter 1

I could remember the fear and the unbearable anguish which the drought of 1911 – when I was barely four years old – brought not only to the earth but into my own being. This drought was clearly not just part of the external world, hurting the land, killing sheep and cattle and the toughest of wild animals, and turning the veld into a Dead Sea of scorched land, but it was in my own blood and scorched spirit, and made me feel that I would die of a thirst beyond thirst myself, if the rain did not soon come.

When I heard the distant sound of the first thunder from below the horizon and saw it announce its presence in long sweeps of lightning through the dark, the inrush of hope and sense of promise brought back into a hopeless moment of life was almost unbearable and could have been overwhelming were they not immediately balanced by a fear that the clouds might vanish again as they had often done, and the rain still not come. By this time our sheep and cattle were so weak that they could no longer walk and move from the places where they lay, the sheep with muffled, moaning little bleats breaking from them from time to time, adding a bleak sound to a bleak scene. We had to take their ration of water and food to them, each and every one – a task which went on from dawn to dusk through those burning fiery days.

The Voice of the Thunder, 'The Other Journey'

He was surprised I had not heard of it because the main wagon road from the capital into the interior wound round and over the shoulder of this hill. It was famous among all transport men because the road was so steep there that the oxen hauling their wagons had to strain at their yokes so much that the holes in their behinds yawned like old men fighting their sleep: hence it was also called 'Make-the-oxen's-arse-holes-yawn': but its real, its ancient name was Icoco.

The Hunter and the Whale, Chapter 4

Van Bredepoel was just about to walk casually to the edge of the veranda, when there came the sound of an aeroplane flying towards the town. This was so unusual that even he hurried forward to look. Both natives immediately stood up, their backs to him, and scanned the sky.

'What is that?' he heard the old man ask his companion.

'An aeroplane,' replied the other.

'It is heavy. Why does not it fall?'

'It has a machine like a motor car which keeps it up.'

'But why does not a motor car fly like that?'

'Its machine does not go fast enough. You see, old father, the machine of that aeroplane goes so fast that before it can fall from one place it has already reached another.'

'Ah!' replied the old man, evidently satisfied.

In a Province, Book III, Chapter 3

There is always for us who are truly born of the earth of Africa a kind of drama in the sunset hours, which no contrived theatre can equal. They are not merely remote impersonal moments confined to the external world. They are events joining the wheeling systems of a universe beyond even the light-year limits of our discerning, in a single totality because they correspond to a pattern within the human spirit, charged with a natural mythological import as of participation at that precise moment in some kind of cosmological sacrament.

Yet Being Someone Other, Chapter 1

In the high street of our hushed little township, total darkness came over us, and the black snuffed out the light as utterly as the silence quenched the sound.

There is no black like that black left anywhere in the world today, because the busyness and unease which have deprived us of pure silence have robbed us of the same quality in the dark. For again, everywhere there are almost as many lights attacking the black over the earth as there are stars in heaven. Even below the remotest horizon of the deepest bush and desert there is a ceaseless vibration of light of all kinds, not illuminating any essential road for the human spirit or being, but depriving it of the healing rest which the perfect black over Africa gave it in my youth.

About Blady, Chapter 2

I know no land which matches so well the dark continent of the sky, with its fountains and pools and lakes and rivers of light and its deserts of darknesses, as does the vast and sombre earth of Africa. It takes the night to itself like a bride chosen from among equals. As the sun goes down it brushes the shy, virgin twilight impatiently aside, and then the two of them fly passionately into each other's

[9]

arms to be close together in an untroubled oneness. I have watched the scene all my life and I have never got used to the majesty and fitness of their dark mating. It has been in a way I cannot hope to describe an unfailing source of reassurance to me. I can only say this: as I watched from childhood, night after night, the familiar lights go up in the sky, the glittering constellations move into their appointed places, the vast Babylonian cavalcade of the sky start out for the dawn of renewal with such irresistible confidence that the far-off thunder of their advance set every star-beam a-tremble in our midst, and as I saw at that selfsame instant, Africa hurl its immense land swiftly at the distant horizon to salute one brave battalion after another as they passed, and send its great peaks soaring swiftly upwards and spread out its own rivers and lakes to hold the sky jewelled and alive in their deepest depths, at that instant something of oneness of being, longing, and destination of this cosmic occasion unfalteringly has been communicated to me. I have felt part of the same steadfast and unfailing rhythm and I have been without regret of the past or fear of the future.

The Face Beside the Fire, Chapter 2

One of the key factors certainly, when we are talking about the white South Africans who call themselves the Afrikaners, is their history which still has a half-Nelson hold on them and will not let go. They are not, as people tend to think, basically of Dutch origin. The core, the heart, the spirit of the Afrikaner is Huguenot, the extreme Huguenot of the right. The Dutch East Indies Company never had any intention of starting a colony in South Africa. All they intended was to have a kitchen-garden to grow food for their scurvy-ridden ships on their way to the East. But in 1685, when Louis XIV revoked the Edict of Nantes, and the persecutions of the Huguenots started again in the most brutal manner, they fled: they fled to England, to Holland, and the Dutch allowed them to come to South Africa. Practically all the best-known South African names are French Huguenot names.

Apart from a few retired and minor company officials who were scratching a living out of the soil there, and some tolerated deserters and mercenaries in the garrison who had taken discharge and been given a piece of land, there was no real settlement of people at the

Cape. Then suddenly came this great influx of Huguenots. They became the core of the Afrikaner people. They had no alternative but to make Africa their home. They had nowhere else to go in the world and, what is more, they were extremely badly treated by the Dutch. The Dutch gave them land in Africa but would not allow them to speak their native French in their schools. They would not allow them religious services in French, and made it clear it was to be Dutch, and Dutch customs throughout, or else. So they were, in essence, rejected again. They were rejected where it hurt most, in their culture and in their Frenchness, and no wonder they came out of this with a great inborn sense of injury and deception, and never wanted to have anything to do with Europe again, saying in their hearts, 'From now on we are African and nothing but African. We shall make this our home and be our own people.' And the less they were Huguenot and French in their customs, the more they became so in their spirit. Their spirit, always extreme, became more extreme still. So the key to the Afrikaner ethos is their own rejection, and their rejection in return of Europe, as well as their extreme, Huguenot stubbornness. Henceforth all was a matter of the Huguenot spirit and a growing, two-dimensional isolation, one geographical and the other, most important, psychological . . .

I think an enormous amount of the spirit of Africa has entered the Afrikaners by the back door. Unconsciously they love Africa with a passion that nobody else can understand. Their attachment to the land is really very deep because they are born of it and have suffered and sacrificed for it. They are white Africans, but they are Africans. To call them Europeans is a misnomer. You just have to compare them with the English-speaking South Africans who came there much later and remained in contact with Britain. In fact, when I was a boy, all English-speaking South Africans talked of Britain as 'home' – they never called it Britain – which used to annoy the hell out of the Afrikaners. They complained angrily, saying, 'They talk of it as home, but this is home!' It really was a very sore point with them, and is a measure of the distance between the two psychologies.

A Walk with a White Bushman

The Great Trek

As that historical and evocative call went up: 'Come on; Trek!' the women and girls in their brightly coloured head-cloths and dresses appeared not to climb back to their places on the wagons, so much as flutter over them like a swarm of butterflies. The little boys, standing at the ready between the great crescent horns of the huge oxen, confidently took up their leather leads and pulled the teams one after the other into following them. Seeing well-trained oxen bowing their heads to thrust their broad shoulders against their heavy yokes, while the long steel chains which connected them to the wagon came glittering out of the dust and went taut with strain, was as always a moving sight . . .

First came the magenta span of eighteen, to be followed by the brindled ones, the strawberry roans, the cream whites, the Cape-gooseberry yellows, the earth red and, last of all, the coal-black team. At that the Matabele, who love and know cattle as few men do, forgot all reservations and cheered the train on with a reverberating, '*Hamba Gashle!*' Go in happiness.

They were answered in dialect with a shimmer of voices chanting, 'Stay joyfully, you farmers there! Stay joyfully!' At the same time, the long whips flashed and crackled like lightning over the heads of the teams and the wagoners exhorted the oxen with cries like: 'Step up, Fatherland! Pull, President, you lazy devil, pull! We've drunk tiger-milk now and can do the job ourselves, if you won't!'

As each wagon pulled clear out into the road, a rag and tatter minstrel walked ahead, either strumming a guitar, playing a concertina or mouth-organ, with the people riding on the wagons accompanying him in song . . . everybody . . . watching could just hear the wagons creaking mournfully under their heavy loads like ships in a storm at sea. Also they heard the muffled pounding of the earth under the great feet of the long spans of oxen who, watered and well-fed, despite their phlegmatic natures, seemed to be responding positively either to the music or the crackling of the whips.

A Story Like the Wind, Chapter 8

Both of them came from a people who had left Europe centuries before and come to Africa. They came originally not out of any petty or selfish motives because had they conformed to the life of their time in their native context of Europe, they would have been rich and comfortable in the homes they were about to abandon. No, they came not in order to make life more safe and the material rewards of life more abundant but to find a new and better way of being. It was wrong to judge things out of the context of the time which gave them birth. He did not wish to imply that their ancestors had not been right and probably justified in following the truth as they saw it most clearly in their own day. But the truth of yesterday could be the lie of today. They had come to Africa on the assumption that by moving to a new world they would leave their problems behind and find a place where there were no such problems and no such hindrances. They seemed to have had no inkling that human beings, whether they liked it or not, carried their problems about with them wherever they went.

So in their three hundred and twenty years of a new life, even in the Africa of their promise, when this craving for a better way of being seemed thwarted, they had again and again renounced homes and possessions just as readily as any in Europe and moved deeper into the interior, looking once more for a place where their problems would not exist, where life would be innocent like a slate wiped clean, and they could write all over it perfect phrases and sentences of the perfect life on earth. They had of course found no such thing. They had not only not found it but had gradually begun to create a greater form of tyranny than they had opposed and fled from in the beginning, so unaware were they of the new heresy of believing in places where evil did not exist. Not only were there no such places in Africa but there were none anywhere else in the world. Man had run out of places, had run out of geographical solutions for his problems and changes of scene as a 'cure' for his restlessness. The journey in the world without as an answer to our searching and resolution of our failings was dismally bankrupt.

There was only one thing which could lead to an answer and that was to let the sense of journey expressed for so long in travelling the world without become a journey within the spirit of man.

A Far-Off Place, Chapter 15

I saw in my mind's eye my father, Oom Pieter, my mother, and the long succession of Afrikaner pioneering faces and figures I had

known in my boyhood, spare, generous, upright, fearing God but
no man, always venturing courageously on and on into Africa's
dark interior. Is this how the Great Trek for a better life is to end?
I asked myself passionately. Is there no one great enough to take
over the adventure and carry it on in some other dimension, to
carry it on from world without to world within?

Flamingo Feather, Chapter 18

People of Africa

The essence of all this was put to me once by a great hunter, who
was born in Africa, and who died there after having wandered all
over it for seventy years, from the trembling bushveld of the Transvaal to where the mountains of Abyssinia dwindle down in dead
hills to the Red Sea. Africa, he told me, was truly God's country –
the last in the world perhaps with a soul of its own; and the
difference between those born of its great earth and those who
invaded it from Europe and Asia was simply the difference between
being and *having*. He said the natural child of Africa *is*; the European or Asian *has*.

The Heart of the Hunter, Chapter 10

I have never known Africans, no matter how poor, who do not
offer to share their food even with strangers who happen to find
them eating.

The Hunter and the Whale, Chapter 6

Deep in every Bantu African is a belief that a man cannot eat the
meat of an animal without in some way incorporating the character
of the animal into his own self. He is convinced that you become
what you eat. One tribe will readily eat zebra meat and a neighbouring
one will not touch it. Antelope, which is a delicacy in one region,
will be strictly taboo in another . . . I knew of a Bantu tribe who
had never seen crocodiles but who none the less called themselves:
'*Bakwena*' – Men of the Crocodile. It was a startling illustration of
the oneness of Africa, the underground telepathy which continues

to exist in spite of the social and political forces that work against it on the surface.

First Catch Your Eland, Chapter 4

Matter which is inanimate to us, is never mere matter to Africans but manifestations overflowing with the power of the spirit. Sickness is never just a physical infection but an invasion of the human spirit by another spirit of malign intent.

The Hunter and the Whale, Chapter 9

Then the voices rose again in the oldest 'Takwena chant I know.

'Yes! Oh! Yes. Yes. Yes!
We go one of the three ways:
The three ways a man and his brothers go:
The way to battle in the breaking morning;
The way from victory in the red of evening;
The way of dust to the last sleep at nightfall,
By the great Flamingo Water.
Guess, oh guess, guess, guess,
You who hear me,
Which of the three ways do we go?'

The reply that came was immediate, like fresh orchestration of the thunder overhead and a startling revelation of the numbers of 'Takwena gathered in the bush. At the end of a long roll of thunder it came in deep waves, from far, far down in resonant throats, far down from the well of the past, straight from the source wherein the vital being of a great people springs, came the response:

'Oh! How can you ask the way of our going,
How can you wonder at the measure of our feet,
When, look, the blood on our spears is warm
And the last of our enemies with the day is dead.
Aye, look! We go the way from victory,
Home in the evening:
We go to our cattle and our kraals and our women by the fire
In the blue of Umangoni.'

I've heard this chant on many occasions. I've joined in it myself more times than I care to remember at the end of a day's hunting . . .

[15]

Wherever the men of Umangoni gather, sooner or later it is sung. The words may vary, but the music is always the same and has not, I believe, varied by a single note since far back an unremembered 'Takwena heart first experienced it.

Flamingo Feather, Chapter 12

Even the way these ricksha-pullers were dressed seemed utterly unrelated to our brash, busy, colourless and European day. This man's head-dress, for instance, was made of tall feathers dyed green, blue, red, yellow and black in colour. From it protruded the horns of a great steer, so polished that they shone like warm Baltic amber in the sun. His broad shoulders and chest were covered with a canvas tunic, falling to his knees and worked over with beads of the same uncompromising colours arranged in precise geometric patterns. His arms were bare but the wrists flashing and jingling with bracelets of copper, steel and outsize brass curtain rings. His legs below the knee were painted white, but his ankles again were bright and shining with more circlets of metal and bone. As he blew his glittering whistle, his teeth would show a dazzle of white against his black skin, and whenever he came down from the peak of one of his great leaps, the glass and metal jewellery upon him resounded like some percussion of antique music. His jewellery did not sit upon him like decoration imposed from without, but seemed as natural as painted feathers are on a bird of paradise. Even the spokes of the wheels of his ricksha were hidden behind cardboard disks bright with harlequin colour, and the passenger seat was covered with leopard skins. He looked like some messenger from the court of time, and indeed his vehicle might have come straight from Bacchus to fetch us to some harvest festival of great summer. Instead it was the cheapest form of transport available in a modern city. Today I wonder at the iron limitations of our awareness that prevent us from seeing how great the heart, and how heroic the spirit, that can make carnival of so mean a trade.

The Hunter and the Whale, Chapter 12

The great contribution to the regeneration of Africa as I saw it would have to be a profoundly apolitical reassessment of values – a rediscovery of the overriding values of the dignity of man and the reverence for life of which politics could only be a servant and not the initiator and master.

First Catch Your Eland, 'Prelude'

In my part of Africa my indigenous countrymen, when they want to convey to another person that they recognize him fully, will say: 'Indeed, you throw a shadow,' implying that he is not one of those thousands of see-through strangers but real, because only real things throw shadows.

About Blady, Chapter 6

Black and White

I suppose black is the natural colour of what is strange and secret in the human spirit. It is the uniform of the unknown.

The Hunter and the Whale, Chapter 6

What is least and most despised in the life around us? The black man, of course . . . And who is the natural man in our unnatural society? The black man again . . . And who is growing great with revolt on behalf of the unrecognized future? The black man . . . If you ask yourself questions on those lines then surely you must see how truly and poignantly the image of a little black man, member of a natural instinctive people, expresses all that is natural and truly unfulfilled within us . . .

The Face Beside the Fire, Chapter 16

The black man in Africa does not feel himself to be black. He feels himself to be as filled with whiteness as we do. He too stains the white radiance of eternity like a dome of many-coloured glass until death tramples him to fragments. Black in this ancient language of the spirit has precisely the same meaning for him that it has for us, and the colour of a man's skin is not the colour of his being.

The Dark Eye in Africa, Part III, 'The Discussion'

This then is the great, the joyful and the tragic drama of the African's life: its glory and its humiliation. As far as the will takes him, he follows the body and its interests across the gulf of our split natures into that dark country on the other side. He puts all his trust and faith in the splendour of his body, he encourages it to shake and convulse with desires of flame, and appetites so violent and clear that their satisfaction alone may become purpose and end enough. He is strong, brave, enduring and patient in their service, but at heart there is still this 'Oh no! Oh no! Oh no!'

It is not enough, there is a hunger still that escapes, that will not be satisfied. There must be something else, something more to give it, but what and how and where? Perhaps there is magic. Ah, he has tried that, and goes on trying it, but in the end the circle rounds on itself, leads the old trail back to the devouring stomach, the beating heart, to the world below belt and navel.

He belongs to the night. He is a child of darkness, he has a certain wisdom, he knows the secret of the dark. He goes to the night as if to a friend, enters the darkness as if it were his home, as if the black curve of the night were the dome of his hut . . . He does not really care for the day. He finds his way through it with reluctant, perfunctory feet. But when the sun is down, a profound change comes over him.

He lights his fire, he is at once happy and almost content, sings and drums until far in the morning. And what should he do about it?

We could tell him – we who have too much of the light and not enough of the night and wisdom of the dark. We could, but we will not because we are split against ourselves, we are infinitely prejudiced against the night.

Half the love we give ourselves would do for him; half for our bright morning selves, and half for him. It is enough for both: two halves for a whole, and the whole for both.

Venture to the Interior, Chapter 23

In a profound sense every man has two halves to his being; he is not one person so much as two persons trying to act in unison. I believe that in the heart of each human being there is something which I can only describe as a 'child of darkness' who is equal and complementary to the more obvious 'child of light'. Whether we know it or not, we all have within us a natural instinctive man, a dark brother, to whom we are irrevocably joined as to our own shadow. However much our conscious reason may reject him, he is there for good or ill, clamouring for recognition and awareness and a fair share of life, just as the less conscious black man of Africa is struggling and clamouring for life, light and honour in our societies. I need not emphasize how the rational, calculating, acutely reasoning and determined human being that Western man has made of himself has increasingly considered this side of himself not as a brother but as an enemy, capable with his upsurges of rich emotion and colourful impulses of wrecking conscious man's carefully planned and closely reasoned way of existence.

The Dark Eye in Africa, Part II, 'The Basis for Discussion'

[Michael] Dowler was a bachelor. He was a man of about thirty-five. He was sensitive and loved civilized things – music, books, good food, and comfort. His house on the lake bore eloquent testimony to all this; but, if he wanted civilization, why come to Africa? He lived by the great lake with a certain royal abandon. He had four handsome, well-dressed African servants, who were obviously devoted to him and he to them. He watched over them with a solicitude remarkable in one so young. The more I got to know Michael, the clearer became my impression that he gave these children of African nature the consideration and affection he would have liked to give his own dark, unfulfilled self, only centuries of so-called European civilized values prevented him from doing this. We all have a dark figure within ourselves, a negro, a gipsy, an aboriginal with averted back, and, alas! the nearest many of us can get to making terms with him is to strike up these vicarious friendships with him through the black people of Africa.

Venture to the Interior, Chapter 19

We do not understand that we cannot do to others what we do not do to ourselves. We cannot murder and kill outside without murdering and killing within. We turn our hate on to the native, the dark people of the world, from Tokyo to Tierra del Fuego, because we have trampled on our own dark natures. We have added to our unreality, made ourselves less than human, so that that dark side of ourselves, our shadowy twin, has to murder or be murdered.

Already there is the smell of murder approaching far off in the sky over Africa. And this need not be, that is the pity of it. If we could but make friends with our inner selves, come to terms with our own darkness, then there would be no trouble from without.

But before we can close our split natures we must forgive ourselves. We must, we must forgive our European selves for what we have done to the African within us. All begins with forgiveness.

Venture to the Interior, Chapter 23

South Africa

Apartheid, to me, is a truly horrible political expedient because it is evolved by a people who know it to be unworthy, and who merely exemplify man's capacity for finding good reasons for doing bad things.

'Introduction' to William Plomer, *Turbott Wolfe*

[This is how, in 1929 at the age of twenty-three, Laurens van der Post viewed the South African situation.]

People in Europe seldom realize what powerful emotional forces complicate the coloured question in South Africa. In the detachment created by distance, and the feeling of not being personally involved, it is so easy to see it as an economic problem only, or to regard it as that formidable pamphleteer, Mr Wyndham Lewis, regards most coloured questions – as chiefly the result of the inferiority complex which certain romantic novelists, gushing pink sentimentality over the world's noble savages, are supposed to be thrusting on Western Europeans and Americans. But actually the native problem is not as simple as all that. It is as much, if not more, an emotional as an economic problem, because at the back of the white South African's attitude to the native is always fear of the bitterest kind; not the fear inspired by any feeling of inferiority, but fear derived from the smallness in number of his own kind. He has looked at the native so often along the barrel of his rifle that he never sees in him a potential co-operator, but always a dangerous enemy that at the first opportunity may rise and take by arms what is now denied him. Whenever the native agitates for reform, the white South African's first impulse is to reach for his rifle.

At the school I went to in South Africa the native problem came up for debate at least once a year. With only a few exceptions, in reply to the history master's question, 'What is the best solution of the Native Problem?' the whole class would howl back even before the debate could begin, 'Shoot the lot!' The history master, however, was inclined to be something of a liberal, so he suggested to the class that South Africans should model themselves on the old colonists, 'who treated the native like a useful dog, gave him food, clothing, shelter, doctored him when he was ill, and flogged him when he misbehaved'.

I do not pretend that this is the position in South Africa today. Flogging, much to the constantly voiced regret of South African farmers, is illegal, but I mention it as an illustration of an attitude which an innocent, blue-eyed, and comparatively well-educated South African thought natural and right. It is this mentality to which General Hertzog's policy is designed to appeal. General Hertzog has always possessed a keen sense of the value of racial feeling in politics – a fact to which the success of the Nationalist Party testifies. By far the greater number of South Africans would sooner support the politician who appeals to their racial sense, than the politician who presumes to appeal intelligently to their reason. The old conflict between the Englishman and the Afrikaner is more or less solved; its solution must have lessened considerably General Hertzog's pull over his own people, so he seems determined to strengthen his party by forcing South Africa into, or rather by intensifying, another racial struggle, which can be quite easily far more disastrous than anything South Africa has experienced . . .

If the old die-hard attitude, which will deny a native his rights as a man because of his colour, triumphs in South Africa, it is not improbable that the policy of the Union of South Africa may become the policy of the colossal area stretching from the Cape to Abyssinia. When that takes place the position of the white man as time goes on will become more and more precarious. Materially he will never prosper for any length of time: for to imagine, as South Africans imagine, that one section of the community can prosper by repressing the remaining four-fifths is merely ridiculous. The ranks of 'poor whites', already alarmingly great, will continue to grow, and on the mental and physical level on which most poor whites exist the taboos of his race lose much of their power. On that level, intermixture with the native becomes easy and for him even desirable, and those who, like General Hertzog, now talk so glibly of preserving white civilization will have greatly accelerated its end. To declare miscegenation illegal, as Mr Tielman Roos has done in South Africa, will not be much good. Sexually the white man has often enough recognized no colour bar, and the laws against miscegenation will only make criminals of people who otherwise had some chance of becoming respectable citizens.

To reinforce his decreasing numbers by immigration, while the native is being artificially restricted to his present standard of living, will be impossible, because no race has yet been able to colonize against a lower standard of living. That is the reason why South African immigration in the past has been insignificant in comparison with that of Canada and Australia. The only chance of survival the white race in South Africa is likely to have would be by entering into a competition of hardihood and efficiency with the native, in raising the native standard of living as near his own as possible. Otherwise, as a well-known native leader said to me once, 'We shall be putting on muscle, while you put on fat.'

What the colour bar and the white South African's prejudice, backed up by law, has done in South Africa is to give the white man endless opportunities to loaf. Like most societies who have created in their midst artificially privileged classes, white South Africa is beginning to pay dearly for its privilege to loaf. Out of the European population of $1^3/_4$ millions about 160,000 are poor whites. These people as a rule have enormous families, and as the native can live on about one-tenth of what they need, few employers in full possession of their senses are, in spite of their colour bias, inclined to give the poor whites work.

In addition to all this, South Africa has complicated matters by declaring that the white man alone must do skilled work. The spade work on the railways, digging mines – that is nigger's work; and most poor whites are sufficiently snobbish to consider such work ignominious. But the overseer, the man who stands with his hands in his pockets and sees that nigger gangs do not slack working, is a skilled labourer. In short, the type of European South Africa is encouraging was naïvely suggested in a local advertisement, which asked for a man 'who understands animals and can handle natives.'

Most South Africans, of course, claim that they have a perfectly rational ground for their attitude to the native. Theirs is not, they claim, a defence dictated by feeling masquerading as reason, but a defence justified by cultural and scientific evidence. To hear the average South African discussing native policies, one would imagine that the country was existing in the golden age of pure reason. A few months ago when a European farmer was sentenced to seven years' hard labour and a flogging for beating his native servant to death, petition after petition was sent to the Prime Minister to prevent the execution of the second part of the sentence. One of the leading Dutch newspapers argued that it was rationally inconceivable that a white man and a native should ever be punished in the same way. The white man, this paper claimed, had such a sensitive soul, as a result of two thousand years of culture, that to punish him in the same way as an ordinary uncivilized nigger was unjust, because he suffered by punishment much more than any insensitive black man ever could. For a country that accepts the principle of capital punishment, it would, perhaps, have been more logical to argue that when a man, in spite of two thousand years of civilization, is guilty of brutality rarely equalled by any ignorant nigger, he is such a hopeless case that the community ought to get rid of him at any price.

But this feeling, passionately held by thousands, that there ought to be different standards of justice for the white man and the native runs right through South African society. There is, the white man believes, some peculiar and innate intellectual drive about him which places him on the crest of one wave of evolution, leaving the native in a trough a thousand waves behind.

Some years ago a Dutch clergyman tried to convince me that the brain capacity of the native is only nine-tenths of that of the white man: he repeated this statement afterwards in an incredible book that he wrote on the superiority of the South African women. He happened to know several native languages, and he agreed with me that Zulu was one of the most highly organized languages he knew. The average Zulu, he said, was a better talker than the average white South African. Yet the argument boiled down to this, that the ability to use words clearly, with a remarkable freedom from platitudes, was not of the same value as the ability to drive a motor car, handle a rifle, or wear a top hat with dignity, something which the Zulu, fortunately, is incapable of doing. What constitutes civilization for him and for most South Africans does not postulate a single quality which cannot be acquired by imitation. It has all the attributes of the civilization which Japan acquired in a generation, without any great loss of stability. To pretend, therefore, that people who have created one of the most attractive languages in existence have not the brains to do what Japan has done, is certainly non-proven.

A tax-collector in Natal once, in trying to persuade an old native chief to consent to extra taxation, told him that he would get his money back in roads. 'Is not that', the old Zulu replied, 'like cutting off a dog's tail and giving it to him for food?' The native in the past has so often been in the position of the dog that he is vaguely determined to obtain a less exacting form of diet in the future. He cannot work for reform through parliament because he is for practical purposes not represented there, so he is coming more and more to organize into trade unions. An organization like the ICU (Industrial and Commercial Workers' Union), for example, shows clearly what he is doing in this direction. The ICU was founded less than ten years ago with a membership of twenty and a subscription fund of twenty shillings. It had come into existence obscurely, originating in that time-honoured South African pastime of pushing natives off pavements. Its founder, Clemens Kadalie, and another native, had one day been assaulted by a white policeman merely because he happened to lurch into them on a pavement. Kadalie and his friend sued the policeman, won their case, and afterwards decided to create an organization which would protect and promote the interests of the native. Inadequate as the law is in South Africa from the native point of view, it does protect them far more than they realize. Moreover, most natives believe that the law is always on the side of the white man – since natives on serious criminal charges have been given the right to choose between a trial by jury and trial by a judge and two assessors, they have decided nearly always against the juries . . .

It may be a pity that the white man did not stay in Europe instead of venturing abroad and forcing his civilization on people with whom he had no natural desire to mix. Today, at any rate, he cannot eat his vast colonial pudding and yet have it. He has twisted the native so firmly into his own life that there can be no going back. Every time General Hertzog's administration lays down a new railway, builds another road, opens another wireless station, sanctions a new industry, the black people of South Africa are unavoidably drawn more tightly into the life of the country. Every day the native is being grafted more and more into the organic structure of South African society. The process of levelling up and inter-mixture must accelerate continually, and it is difficult to see how General Hertzog or any die-hard politician can ever drive the native out of the life of the country without destroying its present social structure. Such a process will be against the deliberate trend of our age.

The annihilation of distance and time, the comparative destruction of geographical isolation which is taking place in South Africa, the general tendency towards standardization and uniformity must in the end have a profound influence on the country's racial prejudices. There are signs already that racial distinctions in the world, in spite of postwar resurrections of nationalism, may become more and more blurred. The world is tending, perhaps, towards economic rather than racial units. The feeling of a pedestrian against a motorist may one day be, if not more violent, as real as the antipathy of white for black – a conclusion which is not as fantastic as it seems when one considers the history of modern America.

Artificial privileges such as those possessed by white South Africans weaken the race they are designed to protect. It is in the interests, therefore, of the races which Hertzog champions that the standard of the native should approximate as closely and as unrestrictedly as possible with their own. I do not say this because I have any sentimental feelings about noble savages, but because I suspect that a country which, like South Africa, seeks for one-fifth of its members all the honeyed conveniences of civilization without any of its responsibilities, at the expense of paralysing the rest, is fundamentally self-destructive. Neither is it a question, as Mr Wyndham Lewis suggests, of preferring the culture of the savage to that of the European. European civilization, with all its faults, is probably superior to that of the coloured races, but its superiority does not diminish but increases our responsibility to them. If European civilization is to be preserved in South Africa, General Hertzog and his followers will have to concentrate with all their power on two things: on preparing the native as quickly as possible for the same position and opportunities now open to the white man and on making South African contact with Europe as easy as possible.

Personally I cannot see why European civilization should be incompatible with a coloured skin, although it is perhaps too much to expect of Hertzog's disciples. The future civilization of South Africa is, I believe, neither black nor white, but brown. Races do not spread out rigidly like the branches of trees. They are not parallel lines that do not meet this side of infinity. They have probably mixed and interbred since the beginning of the world and will continue to interbreed even in South Africa. But this need not distress any hundred per cent worshipper of colour, for by the time this process is completed all those feelings which make such a conclusion repugnant to him will have subtly disappeared.

Article in the British magazine, *The Realist*, 1929

I know it is useless to abstract people and events from the context of their own time. Perhaps one of the most prolific sources of error in contemporary thinking rises precisely from the popular habit of lifting history out of its proper context and bending it to the values of another age and day. In this way history is never allowed to be itself but is given such a vicarious and negative extension that whole nations, classes and groups of individuals never really live their immediate present but go on repeating a discredited pattern of the past. Nowhere is such a negative entanglement with history greater than in my own country. On one side, there are those of my countrymen who have made a determined effort to suppress and falsify the history of the Afrikaner people in order to show our forefathers establishing themselves as saviours in Africa. On the other side they are presented as a race of human monsters from which has sprung a monstrous generation in the present. Neither is right. But I am certain we shall never be free of the destructive aspects of our history until we can honestly look our past in the face and truly see ourselves for what we were: ordinary in our human fallibility, with much that was dishonourable and inadequate in our behaviour as well as a good deal that was brave, upright and lovable.

The Lost World of the Kalahari, Chapter 2

It was extraordinary how most people took for granted the terrible tensions in their lives and the violence gathering in and about them. They seemed to find it perfectly normal to sleep with loaded pistols under their pillows in Johannesburg, to have their houses elaborately wired with electric alarms to the nearest police stations, to have night watchmen armed with clubs patrolling their grounds until morning, and from fear of the blacks to go by closed car for dinner at night to a friend's house barely a hundred yards away. I felt safer alone with my African bush, or with the Bushmen in the heart of the desert, than I did by day in the main streets of the greatest city in South Africa. Nor did the average person appear conscious of the damage inflicted by the national attitude to black and coloured – how it must shatter his own honour and integrity as an individual human being. They behaved as if there were no risks out of the ordinary and they could keep up their negative attitude indefinitely.

It is true they hardly talked any more about anything except their national problems. They had become one of the most subjective peoples on earth. It was alarming how objective lines of communication between them and the world without had broken down. Within a few minutes of greeting one, even old friends seemed incapable of more than a perfunctory inquiry after one's well-being, so eager were they to discuss their public affairs. An elder statesman whom I had known since childhood, for instance, was sitting in the same chair at the same table where I had said goodbye to him five years before. He did not pause to ask me how I was, but beckoned to me urgently to sit beside him and forthwith put to me the same question he had put the last time I saw him. 'What do you think of our native policy now?' There might have been no years between the two occasions, and in a sense there were none: like the rest of the country he was still living in the same moment, only more so.

That is the hallmark of the obsessed: time, losing its true meaning as a process of fulfilment, stands still for them. They are locked out of the healing procession of the seasons. When he had discussed or rather talked at me about his ideas of native policy, this statesman discussed other tensions. They were not hard to come by. South Africa has a greater variety of human tensions than any other country in the world: there are tensions between white and Asians, black and Asians, white and Cape coloureds, Afrikaner and British, and between both Afrikaner and British and black. But he discussed them all entirely as events in a broad external social pattern. There was no hint that he thought the origin of these tensions might also be in himself, or that despite the diversity of the surface patterns they were all members of a single family. Such was the blackout within himself and most of our countrymen.

The Heart of the Hunter, Chapter 9

Many individuals are finding they have been so busy living history that they were not living their 'now' at all. With a sub-sonic tremor of new music and a reverberation of the feet of the new community in their ears, they then discover themselves becoming whole directly they refuse to remain identified with the sick and dying aspects of their societies. This process is going on also in Africa. I confess it is much more retarded there but it is in being. The desperate problem there is to reverse, before it is too late, the trend of the basic myth of my people. For, as I hope I have made clear, there is nothing wrong with the basic myth of my people. If instead of believing that they are the *only* chosen people they could believe that we are all chosen people charged in our unique and several ways to bring the journey to its contracted end, our differences honourable, equal in dignity and adding to the variety and wonder of life, then all could be well.

The Dark Eye in Africa, Part III, 'The Discussion'

On my way, I talked about it to one of the judges of the Supreme Court of Appeal. He is a man who behaved with great courage and integrity during the battle fought in the Law Courts over the removal from the South African Constitution of the entrenched clause which guaranteed the franchise of the Cape coloured people. I told him that what appeared particularly sinister to me was that psychologically we did not see the black and coloured people in

[28]

Africa at all. I said that vision was complete only if we saw reality with both the outer and the inner eye. Not doing so, we commit the error of the one-eyed vision of which Blake accused the scientist. Our trouble was that we saw the African only with the outer eye and not through the eye of the heart as well. I believed one did not know human beings really until one saw them that way as well – in other words, knew them also through a kind of wonder they provoked in one. Not knowing the African that way, was what I meant by being psychologically blind to him.

He thought about this for a moment before saying, with a note of humility that touched me deeply, that the remark had suddenly taught him something about himself. He said that every day at the end of hours of concentration on the bench he found relaxation in playing a childlike game with himself. He would walk back home from the Supreme Court, pretending he was a kind of Sherlock Holmes and deducing from the appearance of passers by what their occupations were. For instance, he would say, that young girl judging by her dress must be a typist, that boy an apprentice, that woman a midwife, and the fellow behind her obviously a solicitor. Until I made my remark about our one-eyed vision, he had never realized that he had not yet played the same game with a black or coloured person, though of course there were far more of them about than white people.

The Heart of the Hunter, Chapter 9

I find nothing about sanctions constructive, nothing whatsoever . . .

And I think that the idea of applying sanctions is morally obscene, irreligious in the extreme . . .

To single out one country which is by no means the worst, and to apply the worst form of punishment to it, is mad. There is something sick in people who want to make a sick society sicker still . . .

You do not treat the good and the bad all in the same way. And what sanctions would do is to harm not ten innocent but close on thirty million people who are politically innocent in South Africa. And why? To damage and show abhorrence of something that a government is doing to them all. For you must never forget it is not the people but a government, a government that polled less than three-quarters of a million votes in the last election, that is our common enemy; a government, moreover, opposed by thousands of white people as well, whose numbers are daily growing. You simply cannot inflict a vast, blanket punishment like that, not on moral, religious or even sensible practical grounds. You cannot achieve the right end with the wrong means.

A Walk with a White Bushman

Trying to live your goodness not in your own life but in somebody else's life is a classical projection ploy and evasion, and is played off on South Africa in an enormous way just now. People want to feel good by proxy, not their own, but at the expense of the South Africans. One of the most terrible consequences of this form of interference, which comes out of national projections, is that you prevent other people from living their own problems. Now the problems of life, the problems of the universe, the problems of man, are our most precious possessions because they are the raw materials of our redemption . . . no problem – no redemption. No problem – no meaning. They are the raw material of our increase. When you take another man's problem away from him, or another country's problem from it, you rob them of all opportunity of redeeming themselves, of getting to know themselves. This is one of the evil consequences of living other people's lives for them, telling people how to live a life of which you know nothing and of which you will not have to endure the consequences.

A Walk with a White Bushman

I think that Africa has a very, very hard, desperate road ahead because it needs an urgent, enormous and sustained act of education. I think we should admit that in a way Africa was given a form of political government for which it was not ready and for which it is not yet prepared. The democracy we gave it on the whole failed, since it did not possess the prerequisite of a spirit in which one cares as passionately for the rights of the person disagreed with as one's own . . .

I believe one of the greatest sources of error and disaster in our lives today is the assumption that all great social problems must have political solutions. All the solutions of our problems must also, sometime, have a political expression but in the first instance they are apolitical, and no instant ideas, ideology or new law can bring them about. They arise first as intimations in an area of spirit where our master values have their origin. They must be nursed, grown, lived and fertilized in the imagination of men everywhere before they can become decently political.

A Walk with a White Bushman

I know the potential heroic capacity of my countrymen as you could not be expected to know it, and I still have faith in the power of the myth which brought my countrymen to Africa and compelled them to set out on their great journey into the interior. Even to this day the imaginations and spirit of my countrymen revolve round the Great Trek with an obstinacy and intensity which is not capable of easy rational explanation. Their imaginations are still obsessed with this passage in their history as the spirit is obsessed only by visions that have not yet reached their end, and I am certain that the seed of suspicion is already planted in their hearts that the great journey of their forefathers must have another meaning beyond the surface values of their recorded histories.

The Dark Eye in Africa, Part III, 'The Discussion'

I am certain that no one will ever understand the complex and desperate situation in Africa unless he realizes first and at bottom it is an affair of honour. But besides the hunger for honour there are other great hungers as well: that for justice, for forgiveness, and the one that sums up all – the hunger for love.

The Heart of the Hunter, Chapter 3

Africa as a Mirror

Modern man . . . finds that life holds up Africa like a magic mirror miraculously preserved before his darkening eyes. In this glass of time the inmost reflection of his ancient, timeless spirit stares out at him and he can, could he but realize it, rediscover there his despised and rejected natural self, recognizing before it is too late the full horror of his stubborn rejection of it. Perhaps therein resides the miracle and meaning of Africa for all of us.

Introduction to William Plomer, *Turbott Wolfe*

One of the interesting things in the modern scene is that in practically every country and every society there is a sort of 'Afrikaner psychology'. By that I mean people who are trying to preserve an identity which they see imperilled and which is their greatest value. They are fanatic about it. There is no great distance in psychology between Afrikaner and Québécois, particularly if you remember their common French origin. And there are other enigmatic variations on the same theme: the Basques, the Bretons, the Irish, even the Welsh or Scots, all still have hankerings, a great nostalgia for their ancient identities, their ancient psychologies and their ancient ways. Once you think of life today along these lines, you think of it in terms of what used to be called the 'soul of a nation'. Then what the Afrikaners fear, and battle for as they see it, does not seem so unnatural. It only seems unnatural because they are small in number. But if you think of the intensity and the reality of what they try to defend, and also that these little diversities are enormously precious to life, one does not want to see them wiped out. One just wants to see them in proportion and one wants to see them defended in a decent way – and apartheid is certainly not a decent way, or even a way that could succeed. In fact it is a certain way of crushing the Afrikaner for ever. The only way any identity or spirit can survive is on its merit to life.

A Walk with a White Bushman

The situation which I believe we are all facing in the world today was one which the primitive world, the past life of Africa, knew only too well. It is a loss of first spirit, or to put it in the old-fashioned way, a loss of soul ... the Zulu prophet ... regarded this as the greatest calamity that could come to human beings. Other examples flooded my mind of how the keepers of man's first spirit in Africa constantly warned him against this peril. Indeed, the primitive world regarded the preservation of first spirit as the greatest, most urgent of all its tasks. It designed elaborate ritual, ceaselessly fashioned myths, legends, stories and music, to contain the meaning and feed the fire of the creative soul.

The Heart of the Hunter, Chapter 10

Africa was but the glass wherein darkly I learnt to find
Vision of your face and reflect of your mind

Last lines of a poem by Laurens van der Post

Chapter Two

Japan and the Power of Friendship

When I first went to Japan in 1926 I was really little more than a boy. I was tremendously changed at a very profound level, in my psyche, as it were, in my soul. That experience has been one of the great and most creative influences on my life, a meeting at a deep level of metamorphosis. And it has not come to an end yet. I notice changes are still going on. Today, I can see a lot of it consciously but I am not seeing anything that was not there unconsciously. So although this process of understanding started inevitably as an instinctive reaction, its conscious consequences were profound and have gone on all my life.

A Walk with a White Bushman

Two Cups of Coffee

It was a very cold, early winter's afternoon and I hurried to my favourite coffee house where I knew I could consume the kind of national delicacies which had been our special delight as children in the interior. I had hardly started my coffee, together with a generous helping of waffles, honey and cinnamon, and was at last beginning to feel warm, when suddenly I heard a shrill feminine voice crying out in Afrikaans: 'I won't have niggers in this place! Get out!'

I looked up, disturbed more by the note of hysteria in the voice than its loudness and offensiveness. The woman behind the long counter at the entrance, pale with emotion, was glaring down at two comparatively small men in belted macintoshes. They were standing, hats in hand, puzzled and surprised at so rough a reception. They looked at each other for enlightenment and, finding none, back to the woman again.

Their hesitation raised the pitch of her hysteria and she shouted again even more loudly: 'I told you I can't have you in here! So get out, will you?'

Automatically I rose from my table as fast as I could, went up to the woman and asked her, in her own language, what was the matter? The sound of her native tongue had a soothing effect and she explained more mildly, but still with an underlying passion: 'Well, it's obvious, isn't it? I can't have any coloured people in my place.'

'Why not?' I asked her. The question seemed to agitate her so much that I thought it would provoke another outburst. But controlling herself with difficulty, she said: 'Well, if I do I'll lose my customers.'

'If you don't,' I told her firmly, 'you'll lose my custom.'

Before she could recover, I turned to the two men and said in slow, deliberate English: 'Would you gentlemen join me and do me the honour of having some coffee with me?'

The café, fortunately, was not crowded or I think the woman may well have appealed to her other customers for support. But I had acted so quickly that she really had no time for reflection. As she saw myself and the two strangers in full possession of my discreet table, she had no option but to serve them.

I had from the start recognized the two men as Japanese and now found that they were, like me, newspaper men. One, Mr Shirakawa, was from the *Osaka-Ashi* and the other, Mr Hisatomi, from the *Osaka-Mainichi*, which were then perhaps the two greatest newspapers in Japan. They were not merely representing their own newspapers. They had been chosen by the Japanese as part of a far-reaching design to develop trade between Africa and Japan and to explore the possibilities of advancing the new policy of empire on which the country was about to embark. It was a policy that included visions of the creation of Japanese spheres of influence in Africa, with an ultimate dream wherein Abyssinia, the last of the non-colonial countries in Africa, would be turned into a colony of Japan. To give some idea of the professional stature of the two men, I should add that Mr Shirakawa was destined to become one of the most distinguished foreign correspondents in the history of journalism in his country, and was to be chosen to serve his newspaper in Washington during the critical years leading up to the war. Mr Hisatomi's development ultimately took a different line because, as a distinguished sportsman himself, he became a leading sports executive and controlling influence in the making of his country into the great sporting nation it is today. But of course at that particular moment they were only concerned with the new task of making their own people more aware of Africa and its economic and political potential for Japanese ambitions.

I took to both men immediately. It was astonishing how I seemed to have no difficulty in understanding not just the literal meaning of what they said to me in their very careful, calculated English, but also appreciating the idiom of meaning which predetermined their choice of words.

Consequently I gave them my address in Port Natal and for about a fortnight I entertained them and helped them all I could in their work. Yet, when they ultimately came to say goodbye and sailed for Japan (which to me seemed physically just about as remote as any country could be), I did not think I would ever see them again. However, some months later, a colleague, Gerhard Pauli, who had taken over my duties as shipping correspondent, came to me with the news that the Japanese had started a new monthly service between Port Natal and Osaka, and that the captain of the first ship to pioneer this service had arrived in harbour that morning. He had asked if he knew me and whether a meeting could be arranged.

Yet Being Someone Other, Chapter 4

The world of the *Canada Maru* was . . . a microcosm of the macrocosm of Japan, a sort of bonsai tree of the spirit transplanted into this miniature pot of its culture afloat on a foreign sea.

Yet Being Someone Other, Chapter 4

The Canada Maru and Captain Mori

And so, that evening I accompanied him to the docks and to the berth of a ship called the *Canada Maru*.

By that time, since it was still winter, it was too dark to have an adequate grasp of the vast, mixed concourse of shipping of which the *Canada Maru* was part. The ship, therefore, was in the best possible situation to make its own impact upon one's senses without interference from comparisons, which was probably just as well as she was in fact wedged between the Royal Mail ship *Walmer Castle* and the British India passenger liner *Khandala*. Though the stern of the *Walmer Castle* and the bow of the *Khandala* towered above the *Canada Maru*, the bulks of those imposing vessels were vague and indistinct, and they made a kind of frame within which this first vision of the *Canada Maru* has hung as a swift impressionist painting in my memory.

There seemed at first nothing at all remarkable about her. She was merely a cargo ship of commonplace design; funnel, bridge and officers' quarters amidships; two slender and tall masts in the centre of the deck between the bridge and the raised poop over the crew's quarters in the fo'c'sles, with the after-deck similarly raised over the berths for the rest of the ship's company in the stern. Both masts at the base were equipped with derricks to serve hatches on either side, which made it clear that the *Canada Maru* was accustomed to calling at ports where there were no cranes to load and unload. Those derricks at that moment were neatly folded back against the masts. Even her tonnage, as far as the usual run of cargo ships at Port Natal went, was unremarkable, if not insignificant. She registered, Pauli told me, six thousand and sixty-four tons gross. Moreover, within those limits, she was so designed that she looked even smaller, and one tended to overlook the fact that for a mere cargo ship she had rather an elegant line, which provided enough of an arch to her structure to strengthen her decks against the onslaught of storm and wind in her own typhoon waters.

The hull was painted a ceremonial black, but, just between the hull and upper decks, two clear bands of white conformed to the swerve of the line and ran the whole length of the ship. Her upper decks, even in that dim light, were a refreshed, stainless white . . . The funnel, upright like the masts, was tall as befitting a ship which still burned coal and trailed a long pennant of black smoke all over the blue of its beat around the world. It, too, was black except for two bands of white just underneath the rim. The davits and the lifeboats tucked into them were white likewise, as were the ventilators. The mouths through which they breathed, however, were a startling pillar-box red.

It is only by concentrating on physical details such as these that I can prevent my initial impression from being overwhelmed by the ship of legend that the *Canada Maru* was to become in the evolution of the story . . .

However, as Pauli and I went up the gangway in the flickering electric light, I had no inkling of what was to come. I only remember that I was struck by the neat and orderly appearance of the deck. This order and circumspection seemed personified by a young sailor who appeared at the head of the gangway, not dressed casually as were his counterparts in cargo ships but in a smart uniform and a sailor's hat with a pair of black satin ribbons on one side. He saluted and bowed politely. Then, as he came out of the bow, he revealed an expressive young face of regular features, with an uncharacteristic expression of fun, if not mischief, in his eyes. It was my first meeting with a young quartermaster whom I was to know well by his first name of Gengo. He led us across the deck and, although I did not know it, across a far frontier in my own mind.

Yet Being Someone Other, Chapter 4

As we entered, one officer separated himself from the group and approached us. I assumed he must be the purser but as I noticed on his sleeve four rings of gold braid, I realized that he had to be the captain. He was in fact Commander Katsue Mori.

He was barely thirty-six years of age. He was obviously young for the command even of a single ship, let alone for heading what I suspected was no ordinary commercial mission. The directors of the Osaka Shosen Kaisha, as well as the unseen makers of the long-distance policies of Japan, must have been fully satisfied that he possessed qualities which outweighed any claims of seniority. In a quick appraisal he appeared to establish himself as a man of un-usual quality and authority. Confidence and dignity appeared to sit easily upon him and to fit his spirit as if tailor-made for it, like the immaculate, navy-blue uniform that he wore. He was of more than average height for a Japanese of that period. I say 'period' because the Japanese today, thanks to their improved diet, are taller than they were when I was young. In addition, he was of a well-proportioned and almost athletic build. He had a face of regular Japanese features except perhaps that the forehead was broader and the eyes wider apart than usual. His eyes were full of spirit, intelligence and a suggestion of defiance. His hair was closely cropped in the new American style referred to as a 'Brutus' haircut. However my intuition told me that I was confronted with an unusually complex and paradoxical personality, resolute, experienced and stern, and yet underneath it there was perhaps a childlike innocence. With all this went a gift of laughter belied by the air of entrenched authority and predetermined dignity which presided over our welcome.

Yet Being Someone Other, Chapter 4

I now saw much of Mori and came to know him well. The more I knew him the more I liked him and appreciated the elements of greatness in him. He was by far the greatest sea captain I was ever to meet. For him sailing the seas was not just a physical and technical venture but the fulfilment of a mission to which he felt himself born by life itself. He knew his task as a ship's master by heart and performed it superbly; and with an authority that never lost touch with humanity. But ultimately there was far more than that in his conception of his vocation. Love of his country and people, love of duty and, above all, love of a life of meaning and a search for greater being were all united in it. This enabled him to contain extremes of paradox and tensions that daily tested him. As we talked at the heart of his special world, reflected once more in mirrors of his special sea and uplifted in temples of cloud, I often thought that Conrad would have loved Mori too and put him in a story where through the heightening of perception, which is the role of fiction, the essential quality and truth of the child-like man would shine out.

Yet Being Someone Other, Chapter 6

Japanese Ways

Japanese, as I now began to learn it, appeared firmly connected with its aboriginal beginnings and tended, to my delight, to express reality more in terms of feeling than in ideas and intellectual abstractions, at which the Chinese excel. For instance, in writing 'tree', divested of any phonetic obligations, one drew, in fact, a simplified picture of a tree, and in the process the imagination was enriched with all the associations it had with trees, in a way that is not possible by just saying the word. The 'sky', as something higher than the trees, was represented by another simplified picture of a tree and a line above it; 'heaven', as something beyond the sky, was yet another line above the line representing the sky. Tree, sky and heaven, therefore, were joined in a vision of organic unity from the earth wherein it was rooted, to the heaven at which all that grew from it was aimed. The East, for which we were bound, was not just a cardinal on a compass but was shown like an outline of one of those ancient stone lanterns that light the way to some shrine in Japan: as the lamp of the rising sun shining behind a tree from the direction along which light and life were renewed out of darkness and death. And so the process went on and on, to be orchestrated into a great symphony of more and more complex relations of forms as, for instance, in characters like that for 'rest', which is a picture of a man underneath a tree; or 'anxiety', which was an immediate favourite, i.e. a heart at an open window.

Yet Being Someone Other, Chapter 4

> On this ocean
> without season
> the moon writes
> in So-Sho
> the symbol
> for Autumn
> and declares
> it is full
> because it is
> about to die.

Moon-poem by the Japanese purser aboard the *Canada Maru*,
Yet Being Someone Other, Chapter 4

It must be added that in a country like my own, so firmly in the grip of racial and colour prejudices of all kinds, warnings like those of the Kaiser about the 'yellow peril' were still echoing from the walls of our little world which was so much closer to the heart of the matter. They rendered more plausible the protest of commerce and industry which saw another form of danger from the new Japan. They held that Japanese businessmen and manufacturers were not to be trusted; that they stole their industrial designs from the West, pointing to the common charge that Japanese pencils, which were apparently driving their own out of the market, had lead only at the ends and were hollow in between. It did not seem to strike anyone that all this could have been honest error due to the haste in making up the 'leeway of the centuries'. Only a few years previously the Japanese had been arrested in a feudal system so involved that only three per cent of the population were engaged in business, and the makers of money were almost a caste of untouchables. Considerations of money, indeed, had been matters of contempt to Japanese gentlemen and their followers for so long that a whole system of rituals of almost metaphysical complexity had to be evolved for bringing financial reality to their notice by these despised orders who were engaged in so indispensable a traffic.

Yet Being Someone Other, Chapter 4

He had always felt even when he was in Japan that the Japanese were a people in a profound, inverse, reverse, or if I preferred it, even perverse sense, more in love with death than living. As a nation they romanticized death and self-destruction as no other people. The romantic fulfilment of the national ideal, of the heroic thug of tradition, was often a noble and stylized self- destruction in a selfless cause. It was as if the individual at the start, at birth even, rejected the claims of his own individuality. Henceforth he was inspired not by individual human precept and example so much as by his inborn sense of the behaviour of the corpuscles in his own blood dying every split second in millions in defence of the corporate whole. As a result they were socially not unlike a more complex extension of the great insect societies in life. In fact in the days when he lived in Japan, much as he liked the people and country, his mind always returned involuntarily to this basic comparison: the just parallel was not an animal one, was not even the most tight and fanatical horde, but an insect one; collectively they were a sort of super-society of bees with the emperor as a male queen bee at the centre.

The Seed and the Sower, 'A Bar of Shadow'

All round this city, dedicated at its founding to 'Peace and Tranquillity', these two themes were continued more openly and enlarged and enriched not only in temples, monasteries and hermitages but gardens, villas, palaces and pavilions in numbers that were hardly credible and which made me aware of how bleak and impoverished in this dimension of life was the world of my own origin. I felt I was in Japan now almost as an orphan in a storm of riches. I have only to have a roll call of the names still waiting like actors in the wings to be called on to the full stage; as for instance those of the Temples of 'Enlightenment', 'The Blue Lotus', 'The Essence of Unlimited Light', 'The Three Treasures', 'The Great Science', 'Benevolent Harmony', 'The Dragon's Repose', 'The Calm Light', 'Serene Quietude', 'The Celestial Dragon', 'The Absolute', 'The Pure Fountains', 'Western Fragrance', 'Gratitude', 'The Miraculous Law' and the imperial villa of 'The Ascetic Doctrine', 'The Poets', and finally the 'Palace of Noble Fragrance'. Any one of these could have held one's attention for years.

Yet Being Someone Other, Chapter 5

The formal entry of Geisha and attendants demanded our immediate attention. It was, for me, an enchanted moment. All European preconceptions about the role of the Geisha in the social life of Japan, and the popular tendency to look on them as courtesans and prostitutes of a most select kind, had been erased by what Mori and my teacher had already told me. I cannot pretend that even then I knew and understood their profound and complex role. I do not understand it even today, in the way it should be understood, because understanding was not a matter for knowledge so much as experience. But knowledge such as that imparted in the ship, rooted as it was also in experience, helped. I knew that they were professional hostesses and entertainers of men on special occasions such as this. I knew that they were chosen carefully not merely for their appearance but their intelligence, quality of spirit, wit, culture, and gift for dance and music and much else beside. I knew that they had to go through a training and discipline derived from traditions grown over many centuries and of an exactitude not unworthy of our own more austere monastic orders. I knew that they did form liaisons with men but by no means automatically and, in general, for a balance of many considerations over which their sponsors, to whom they were bound for years by exceedingly exacting contracts, had little if any influence. I knew that those who became truly distinguished in their profession exercised great influence over remarkable men and in most important areas of society. I knew that the most illustrious of all had been sought out by politicians and powerful men because association with renowned Geisha would promote their careers and increase their power. I also knew that even in those early years their presence at these essentially male occasions was becoming too expensive for ordinary well-to-do people, and the process had already begun whereby today only those who can do so on expense accounts, and for reasons of state, can afford reputable Geisha parties. I knew that their arduous training and their magnificent clothes and upkeep were so costly that they had to mortgage years of their future to repay their patrons. But all this was elementary stuff, insufficient for an understanding of all, and inadequate even for my own after one glimpse I was to have before I left Japan, of a certain freedom not attainable any other way, which they found in bondage.

Our introductions, bows, responses, almost religiously ordered with an atmosphere of remote and enchanted symbolism, prompting all from the wings of a stage set for traditional theatre, were obedient to another sort of protocol in which I thought I discerned Mori's fine hand of command. He and William were allocated the senior Geisha and her attendants; Mr Tajima and myself the second in rank, and diplomat and agent the third. Number One was called Teruha, 'the Shining One'; number two Chiyono, 'Eternity'; and number three Tamako, 'Jewel'. I had been told there tended to be three types of faces in Japan: one of a more Mongolian strain, another tending towards a somewhat Polynesian cast, and the third and most prized, as the oldest and most authentic, the type of the original Japanese who conquered the Ainu aboriginals of the island, which was called Yamato with all the mystique implicit in the word. Tamako's face conformed to the Mongolian, almost Chinese type; Mr Tajima's and my Chiyono to the Polynesian. Polynesian-wise she was rather plump and, although of pleasant expression and features, podgy enough to deny her the look of eternity which her name was designed to uphold. William's and Mori's Teruha possessed the classical Yamato features and all their subliminal capacity of legendary evocation: fine-boned, eyes wide and their slant a slow but precise curve which allowed them to show a light as from afar and enveloped in her name, while her nose, delicately drawn, had a subdued yet clear suggestion of a Roman arch. All in all her face and bearing were of a natural aristocracy, making her one of the most attractive and interesting women I had yet seen, so that I was resentful of the middle-class estate that was my lot for the evening and imposed on me a position of compromise between outer-Mongolia on my right and the aboriginal order of the feminine in Japan on my left. My reaction was all the keener because it was unexpected and found me with no immunities against it . . .

The wide sleeves of her kimono, as she flicked them to compose herself, rustled like an air of darkness in the silence caused by anticipation of her performance. She sat there for a moment still, eyes looking inward, until her attendant brought her a samisen, whose strings she stroked tenderly as if to wake a delicate child from sleep. Then she played to us . . .

Much of the art, philosophy and imagination of the people of Japan is profoundly preoccupied with mood and states of mind at the expense, it would seem, of the external realities that we put first. Truth to mood and fidelity to state of mind, if there are priorities in the human regard for truth, often come first, and some subtle new mood was in command of Teruha. For she followed this Buddhist theme by more music in the same direction, with a delicate intimation of denial of the popular version of her kind, namely the life that the Japanese call the 'world of flowers and willows' and 'transient things', terms inspired by the Buddhist influence on the national character. Her music by evocation and suggestion, more than direct statement, indicated that she too had immortal longings. For she sang of her own world of Geisha as impossible of definition and capable of being understood only through experience. She sang of states of heart that had their seasons, and bloomed unrecognized by man to fall like petals of a flower of a beauty that made grace out of its own decay. She sang of the moment when memory of the beauty itself was enough and the pain of renunciation awoke a realization of things that had always been and would be, even though the 'floating world of appearances' vanished like mist before the sun. Her voice at times trembled as if in pain, and the samisen matched so truly that the decline of subtle flower and fall of petal into grace was so moving that the impact was as much a visual as a musical one . . .

That traditional goodbye of Japan, the sayonara, the 'if it must be', particularly from its women, the deep bows, whispers of the irrevocable word, a rustle as the last air of summer of the long wide sleeves of their kimonos, always from the beginning has had the power of upsetting me as no other form of 'adieu' that I know. It had, for me, a finality about it that made it not so much a human gesture demanded by custom as an act of human beings about to set out on a journey from which they would not return. A silence fell over us all. Outside in the street I heard clearly the urgent 'Kara-Koro, Kara-Koro', as the Japanese describe the sound of their wooden Geta on streets, of some inordinately retarded person hurrying home. Far away, beyond and yet above the 'Kara-Koro' there rose the sound of incomparable purity of a limpid shakuhachi.

Yet Being Someone Other, Chapter 5

The Power of Friendship

Going down the mountain one morning and walking along a spur towards the beautiful valley below, called Lebaksembada because, as the name states, it was indeed 'well made', I came to an area where the path widened and formed a small plateau. I had hardly reached it when trees, ridges, the footpath, and the wild, tasselled and tall buffalo grass along the edges shook, bubbled and erupted with Japanese, who charged on me with their bayonets fixed and looking even longer and more pointed than normal. I myself knew only that there was no escape, and that there was nothing I could do to stop them; I did not even have a pistol on me, and every pocket of my jungle-green bush-jacket was stuffed only with M & B tablets and pills of quinine for the wounded and sick. But something else in me knew different. It took over command and called out in a loud and clear voice as of a stranger with special and singular authority over the occasion. It called out moreover in a Japanese that I no longer knew I remembered, and whose nature should be explained in order to make its impact comprehensible. There are many degrees and nuances of polite speech in Japanese, ranging from what passes for good manners among peasants but would be rude if used on others, to the highest which is used only when one dares to utter in the presence of Japan's Emperor and Son-of-Heaven. The normal 'Dōzō, chotto mate, kudasai' ('Would you be good enough to wait a little') I remembered and would have used had I still possessed a mind of my own. But it did not seem adequate in the circumstances to this other person in me who rushed into command of my senses, and rounded off the address with the highest of all polite forms, taught to me one day not by my teacher but by Mori himself, as an example of how great and important these degrees of politeness were for the Japanese.

As from afar, this voice, in contrast to my naturally quiet tone, now rang out clearly and loudly, at the same time as my right arm shot up high into the air like a traffic policeman's signal to stop: 'Dōzō chotto mate, kudasai!' As the call caused confusion, I quickly followed it up with Mori's version: 'Makotoni osore – irimasu-ga shibaraku cmachi kudasai-ka?' I can only translate it idiomatically as 'Would you please excuse me and be so good as to condescend and wait an honourable moment?'

Nothing, it appeared instantly, could have had a greater effect on the Japanese. They had clearly expected all sorts of military responses: rifle and machine-gun fire, hand grenades, explosives and possibly even a mortar or two; but certainly not the highest degree of politeness. Immediately a solar-plexus shout of command broke out of a slight Japanese officer who was running at me sword in hand. His soldiers halted and stood their ground, bayonets at the ready. In a stillness which, in the acute sensitivity with which confrontation with death equips one, sounded loud above the surf of sunlight breaking over the lofty cathedral of trees high above us, the Japanese officer came up to me, fixed the point of his sword on my navel and asked, as if in a daze, whether it was truly Japanese that I had spoken to them. When I said 'Yes', he asked where I had learnt it, and when I answered 'Japan' his bewilderment gave way to a reassuring amazement. He hissed between his teeth before the inevitable 'Ah, so desu ka?' broke from him, to be followed by: 'You have been to Japan?'

Yet Being Someone Other, Chapter 7

In the midst of all those years so crowded that I often thought I could not manage, I was nagged at all sorts of moments by a voice, as of a kind of conscience, reminding me that I still had an account to settle with my experience of Japan. It insisted that I could not leave it with that unpalatable war and brutal imprisonment on my mind if I were to practise what I had preached, namely the significance of the role of the individual to the universe. So I still had to transcend the last instalment of my Japanese experience in a personal way. That way, the nagging process unfailingly suggested, led straight to Mori. I had to make a private and personal peace with him, as the world had already made peace with his country. I had to do it all the more because I believed that, in such a time of disintegration and retrogression, renewal could only come through a kind of recognition of the increased sanctity of friendship and a deepening of all personal relationships . . .

Significantly enough, although I was not without apprehensions about visiting Japan, I had none about Mori. My apprehensions seemed to focus on the fact that, although I had spoken Japanese daily in prison, and had continued reading and writing it so that I could then almost think or rather feel in it (since it is a feeling rather than the thinking empiric tongue which, for instance, Chinese is), all memory of it had been erased. That, I thought, suggested a profound area of unresolved hurt in me. And as I fear unconscious injury more than any conscious wounding of the spirit, I was nervous about what re-immersion in the life of Japan could bring back to the surface for me. But as for Mori, I was convinced I had only to tell him how the thought of him had helped me and several thousands of others under my direction and all would be well. Indeed, all was well from the moment we met. And because all was most movingly well between us, and our friendship re-proved and increased, all manner of things were well likewise.

Yet Being Someone Other, Chapter 7

From that moment on, my contacts with Mori by letter and exchange of friends were resumed and increased. Not a year has passed wherein someone special has not gone as an 'envoy extraordinary' of friendship from him to me, and me to him. Some of his children have used my home in England as their own; and apart from many letters, I have trunks full of photographs illustrating Mori's rise once again from hardship and the danger of social oblivion to a position of well-being and honour. Every event of meaning to him was photographed and then despatched with heartwarming urgency to me . . .

One of the last of the series shows Mori at the summit of his well-deserved recognition: namely, his reception by the Crown Prince and Emperor, as a principal performer in a modern Noh drama written to honour the ghosts of all sailors who had been drowned in peace and war at sea. At one point in the theatre, he had to 'roar like a lion', and I have various views in technicolour of him roaring accordingly, as well as a tape-recording to show how uninhibited and loud the roaring was, loud enough to be audible beyond those amber walls of mortal senses that define reality between the now and the undiscovered light in the night beyond.

All the while Mori tried to persuade me to persuade William [Plomer] to come back to Japan to see him and the host of his old pupils who remembered him with love. But William would not heed it. [Then William died of a heart attack.] . . .

As soon as immediate practicalities allowed, I arranged the despatch of three full-rate cables: the first to Mori, the second to a Japanese headmaster who had been a favourite pupil of William's, and a third to one of his closest friends in England.

Mori cabled at the most immediate priority: 'On receipt of cable went immediately to shrine of ancestors to report tragic news and light two candles to spirit of beloved departed. Writing.'

The favourite pupil cabled almost as soon: 'Moon rising when sad news arrived so took my shakuhachi and played to moon where souls of departed rest on their way beyond.'

The third, from the close friend, read: 'Regret cannot interrupt holiday in France but will attend memorial service.'

And people still wonder why I like the Japanese.

When Mori finally wrote, he blamed himself bitterly for not having come to England as he had intended the year before and chosen instead to 'roar like a lion' before his Emperor. We must all, he said work harder at our friendships. He proceeded to do so with characteristic energy. Within a few months, although over eighty, he attached himself to a package tour which took him to all sorts of places that he had no desire to see but which, at a price he could afford, gave him three days in England with me. On the very first day he insisted on going to Brighton to pay his respects to William's scattered ashes. I called for him at his hotel in Whitehall and found him in full dress uniform, complete with decorations, and his eldest son Hiroaki, reverently binding a wide length of black crêpe round his right arm. From there we went to visit St Martin-in-the-Fields, where the memorial service for William had been held, and Mori said a prayer. Then we made for Victoria Station by way of St James's and Buckingham Palace. At once, some extraordinary things began to happen. Both at St James's Palace and Buckingham Palace the guards behaved as I have never seen them behave before or since. The moment we went by, they came smartly to attention and presented arms to Mori. At Victoria we found just three first-class places left in a crowded first-class coach of an overcrowded train. Immediately an Englishman by the window stood up, bowed to Mori and in perfect Japanese and with the highest degree of politeness, insisted on his taking the seat by the window so that he could see the country. At the crematorium where William's ashes were scattered, Mori reduced the director to a condition of penitence and contrition bordering on tears because no plaque to commemorate William had yet been placed on the crematorium wall. Moreover he compelled the gardener to give him a cutting of the white lilac that was in a fire of flower under the spring sun where William's ashes lay, to take back and transplant in Japan. Alas, the cutting failed to take root and the failure weighed heavily on Mori, as if it were a direct consequence of 'not having worked harder at his friendships', and his letters contained more and more urgent pleas for another white lilac plant to take the failed cutting's place.

Although warned once again by the Japanese embassy in London that the import of plants with roots was still strictly forbidden in Japan, instinct insisted that I should take a white lilac with me. Accordingly I set out with a robust little tree, its roots washed of all traces of soil, wrapped in masses of wet cotton-wool and stuffed in a plastic Harrods shopping bag. I arrived at Narita airport outside Tokyo in due course and, as I presented my passport, saw on the walls beyond what I had never seen in any airport before: a large black arrow pointed at the ominous legend: 'Plant Quarantine'.

I made for this fearsome place before approaching Customs, and was met by two young officers in immaculate uniform, with discipline written all over their faces. I placed the plastic bag on their desk and explained carefully what it was and why it was there, without infection.

After reflection and grave consultation, they said with immense courtesy and real regret that it was against the law to admit such a plant into Japan. To my amazement that 'other voice', after so many corrosive seasons, was still alive and spoke up in me to ask:

'But do you realize this plant is above the law?'

At once a flicker of totally non-official interest appeared in their composed and formal expression. Above the law? they questioned politely. Would I be so good as to explain how that could be possible?

So I told them the story at length, and as I told it they listened more and more attentively until I believe none of us was, except technically, in a vast official establishment any more. When I finished, I noticed from their eyes and a slight quiver of lips how absorbed and moved they were. We stood in silence as one, perhaps for a minute, as people do before a cenotaph of remembrance. Then they looked at each other briefly before the senior of the two took his stamp, pressed it firmly over the 'Harrods' on the bag and bowed, before saying: 'We shall be honoured to receive this flower in Japan.'

As a result, it now flourishes in full bloom in the latest photographs of it, with all the Mori clan arranged in impeccable order of protocol of proliferating generations around it. It was preceded by a series of others recording its unimpeded growth, and I like to think of them all as witnesses of a transmigration which carries the parable that began with two cups of coffee as far as it can humanly be carried. I say this all the more because, all the while I was in Tokyo, the story of the white lilac had to be told and related wherever I went. It has become for great numbers of Japanese what it is for Mori and me, the most eloquent symbol of the transfigurative power of friendship available in our friendless age.

Yet Being Someone Other, Chapter 7

Dear Hiroaki,

You ask me for some words to be read at the memorial gathering for your father. This is difficult because he is almost everywhere in all my writing to do with Japan, particularly in *Yet Being Someone Other*. But to sum it up, I would say overall that he was a great man. One of the confusions of our times is the belief that only big things, 'muchness' and great positions make men great. The truth is, and the tragedy is, that very often the great offices in places of power in life are occupied by small men, and as a rule – and at the most – by men who just get by. The really great people of our time come from somewhere else. They are people who are great because within themselves they lived truthfully and did the thing for which their natures destined them to the best and fullest extent of their capacities. People who do this live a life full of meaning for themselves and for others with whom they come into contact. In this world of meaning the importance of the office, the physical extent and bulk of the work, are unimportant – only the truth and the meaning matters. It is from this that nations and periods of time derive their singular qualities – the undismayed numbers of anonymous human beings who do what is on their doorstep without complaint in a dimension of life where they keep company in which everyone is equal, from captains and kings to peasants and priests and streetsweepers.

Your father was great in that he lived to the full a life of meaning. In this sense he represented the best of the whole of a tremendously fateful era in the life of Japan and the world. There is a saying in England that those whom the gods love die young. That, in history, has often proved to be so. But I also believe that those whom the gods love most live longest of all, so that for me all that I say about your father is confirmed by the fact that the gods made him live to celebrate his hundredth birthday, still so conscious and alert that he could recognize men around him whom he had not seen for forty years.

We should look no further for signs of the fact that your father was 'not two'. We are blessed to have known him, and I perhaps most blessed of all because we started from such remote and far away places that all the odds were against our meeting, yet we met and we remained friends to the end, despite many things that divided other men and, in a sense, your father proved that deep down in all our natures there is a hunger everywhere in the world for an increase of bonds such as these. I feel myself singularly blessed not only to have known him but to be still alive to go on knowing him and speaking about him to one and all who knew him not, as my memorial of him.

Letter to Captain Mori's son Hiroaki on the death
of his father in 1989.

Chapter Three

From War to Forgiveness

War

Perhaps the main lesson for me was that war did not come to us by some form of spontaneous generation in the human spirit. . . It was monstrously born of the way we all lived what we called 'the peace' . . . Only by understanding how we were all a part of the same contemporary pattern could we defeat those dark forces with a true understanding of their nature and origin. This was vital if we were to be free to embark on a way of peace which would not lead to a repetition of the vengeful past.

Jung and the Story of Our Time, 'The Time and the Space'

History teaches that men as a rule do not break with specialized processes which apparently have served them well, without the help of disaster. The firmer and more intellectually plausible the grip, and the longer the habit of a specialized development, then the greater the disaster and catastrophe needed to free the human spirit from the drowning embrace of exclusive conditionings.

I had only to think of the war that was raging all round me to have overwhelming proof of this fact. Already I saw how Clausewitz's definition of 'war as a continuation of policy when all other means had failed it' could be rephrased in depth. It could be seen as a continuation of a profundity of spirit trying to be lived but hampered by sharply sided men who not only failed it but tried to pin it down to the one aspect of itself which they found desirable. This explained to me the strange relief 1 had observed in many beings at the outbreak of the war. It was not just relief that what had appeared for long to be a menace was about to be fought and overcome. It was also a relief that a way of life which had been apparently devoid of purpose had now, with the declaration of war, suddenly again acquired meaning.

Men could once more serve a cause greater than any egotistical pursuit of themselves. War, I concluded, was perhaps a terrible surgeon of life called in to cut away some atrophied limb of the human spirit. And this war in which I was engaged had been made inevitable, I suspected, by another one-sided extraverted process of evolution after the Renaissance. This process too had now served its purpose. Outworn, it had to make way for something greater. But since we had lacked both the vision and the vitality to clear the way of our own volition, once more war had come as the terrible healer to this tragic bedside of our spirit.

Jung and the Story of Our Time, 'The Time and the Space'

War, I knew from my own experience, had been a direct product of the nature of peace; that, and not armaments manufacturers and generals, was the villain of the whole piece which we all augmented with our own little villainies . . . The war that had to be won, if another cataclysm of the world was to be prevented, was the insidious war in the mind and spirit disguised in the ample folds of a cloak of peace.

Yet Being Someone Other, Chapter 7

We had only to study German mythology to see how the German spirit was fully mobilized for a mythological charade of the most shattering proportions that the world had ever seen.

I failed to convince even my closest friends, and in the end began a book to show how a mythological design obsessed the Hitler phenomenon. That was by far the most frightening part of it. German mythology was the only mythology that I knew in which the gods themselves were overthrown by the forces of darkness. In Hitler's Germany, surely we were watching precisely a massing of the forces of darkness for the overthrow of such forces of light as were still in the European spirit? We were witnessing, in fact, another horror instalment in the long serial of history similar to the 1914–18 war, on the eve of which a British Foreign Secretary pronounced the words, prophetic in more dimensions than he knew or consciously intended. 'One by one the lights are going out all over Europe.'

Jung and the Story of Our Time, 'The Time and the Space'

It is almost as if from childhood Churchill was preparing himself for a meeting with destiny. He could hardly pass through school, or into the army. But when, in India, with a hurt foot and being unable to play polo, he started to read Greek history, the penny dropped. From that moment on until the day of his death, Churchill was educating himself. He was reading, and re-reading, history. He also had an interest in the evolution of science and its applications, and in every way instinctively was preparing himself for something unique.

A Walk with a White Bushman

First man, as I knew him and his history, was a remarkable, gentle being, fierce only in defence of himself and the life of those in his keeping. He had no legends or stories of great wars among his own kind and regarded the killing of another human being except in self-defence as the ultimate depravity of his spirit. I was told a most moving story of how a skirmish between two clans, in which just one man was killed on a long-forgotten day of dust and heat and sulphur sun, caused them to renounce armed conflict for ever. He was living proof to me of how the pattern of the individual in service of a self that is the manifestation of the divine in man was built into life at the beginning and will not leave him and the earth alone until it is fulfilled. It is no mere intellectual or ideological concept, however much that, too, may be needed, but a primary condition written into the contract of life with the creator.

The Voice of Thunder, 'The Great Memory'

A Prisoner of War

I came into contact with the Japanese again in prison and confronted their dark, shadow side. We all have a shadow within but here I was meeting a specifically Japanese shadow, the aspect of their character aroused by the violence of their transition from the pre-Meiji empire of Japan, moving overnight, as it were, from a medieval culture and structure into the modern age; and making the mistake we continue to make, in spite of all the evidence and warnings, of thinking that you can make men and their societies contemporary by merely heaping our terrifying technology and its horrendous power on them. They did not realize what damage they were doing to their instinctive selves. And here in the war it was bursting out, presenting itself in the most brutal way. Yet it was never something which was totally inhuman to me. It seemed instinctively that I could understand it. Even in its most frightening forms, I could understand it in a way that I could not understand the Nazi phenomenon. It seemed important somehow that our salvation in prison depended upon enlarging this process of understanding.

A Walk with a White Bushman

The parade had been called in such a hurry that we stood in line in haphazard order without regard to rank or seniority. I came about twelfth in the front rank of officers . . .

Each officer in turn was beaten up, both with fists and a piece of the shattered chair, with Kasayama now joining in more and more with kicks to help the punishment along. This to me, still unbeaten, and trying to appraise the situation and its full potential of consequences for us, was one of the worst moments of the afternoon, because I knew, as no one else in the camp did, how this powerful collective sense of the Japanese and their converts, which I have already mentioned, tended to take over in such situations. For instance, even on lesser occasions when we had been slapped and beaten for minor offences, every other guard or soldier on duty had somehow felt compelled, as if by some instinctive sense of honour, to join the beating in their turn and show their solidarity of spirit as a Russian Marxist would have had it. I could visualize that before long the rest of the guard, already on the verge of flocking to Mori, might join in unbidden, but worse still, for the first time in years I saw a machine-gun being mounted at the gates. I began to wonder if my interpretation of the cause of the parade had not been too naïve and that this might not be just a pretext for the ultimate solution I had feared.

Still in a turmoil of doubt and wondering what I should do to resolve the crisis, my turn came to face Mori. I walked towards him suddenly feeling strangely calm. It was as if I had become another person and somewhere far down within me, someone far wiser and with the benefit of having had to face this kind of thing ever since the beginning of man on earth, took command of me. I faced Mori, and this other self gauged Mori's blows and anticipated his kicks so accurately that it was able to make me move my head and body at the last moment before the blows and kicks fell in a manner not perceptible to the enraged man and his satellites, yet sufficient to rob them of their severity – to such an extent that I hardly felt them.

Indeed the physical impact of what Mori was trying to do to me seemed so irrelevant that, during the whole time of his assault on me, this process within me of appraising the full meaning of the incident and searching my imagination for a way of putting an end to it all before it developed into something worse, even something which Mori himself might possibly not have intended, went on unimpeded, and if possible with greater clarity than before. The result was that, when Mori delivered his final kick and pushed me back to my place in the line and I once more caught a glimpse of the machine-gun at the gates, it was as if I heard from deep within myself very clearly a voice of command from this other self, ordering me as with the authority of life itself: 'Turn about! Go back and present yourself to Mori for another beating.'

Rationally, everything was against such a course of action. If there were normally anything which provoked the Japanese to extremes of punishment it was any action on our part that broke their rules and sense of order. Yet this voice that rang out almost like a bell within me was so clear and insistent that I turned about without hesitation, walked back and once more stood to attention in front of Mori before the next officer could take my place.

Mori was already in a position to beat up his next victim. He was on the point of attacking again when the realization came to him that he was being confronted with the very person whom he had beaten just a moment before. The shock of this slight variation in a process which he had taken for granted was great, and showed immediately in his eyes. He looked at me over his raised cudgel, arrested in its downward move, as a cliché would have it, like someone who was seeing a ghost in broad daylight. Indeed, so grave was the shock that it utterly broke up the accelerating rhythm of passion and anger in which he had been imprisoned. Slight as the irregularity was, it began drawing him out of the preconditioned processes of collective and instinctive reaction in which he had been involved and made him, I believe, suddenly aware of himself as an individual facing not an abstract and symbolic entity but another individual being. He stood there glaring at me, a strange inner bewilderment at this unexpected turn of events showing in the sombre glow of his dark eyes. Then, taking another sort of half-hearted swipe at my head, he grumbled with a kind of disgust that he thought the whole matter utterly incomprehensible and beneath contempt. He gave me a shove in the direction of our line, turned about, and still muttering tensely to himself walked away and out of sight.

The Night of the New Moon, 'Story'

It looked as if the pain could tear him apart and, in desperation, I would suggest to him that he should do what we did in the war at times when our wounded had nothing to still their agony; that he should groan as hard and as long as he could, because it could make a rough music of the pain and diminish it accordingly. And, strangely enough, there were moments when this was more effective than the drugs to which he had become habituated.

About Blady, Chapter 3

Great as was my admiration for the British officers in prison with us, it could not be compared with the respect I had for the ordinary soldiers, sailors and airmen who formed the majority of British prisoners. They seemed to me, even in the categories from which one might have least expected them, to possess qualities of the highest order as, for instance, men from the slums of the great cities of Britain like London, Birmingham, Glasgow and Liverpool, whose physical appearance often showed the consequences of severe malnutrition during the years of their neglect by the ruling classes before the war, like the rickets of childhood which gave them bowed legs and Rowlandson bodies and faces.

Yet their spirit was always high, cheerful and invincible. I had never yet known a crisis, however brutal, in which they had lost their nerve.

Appeals to their pride and honour had never been in vain. Always they had responded instinctively in a measure as great if not greater than officers born, bred, well nourished from childhood, schooled and trained for precisely this sort of trial. Their need of honour, of a life of self-respect too, was as important as their need of food. They were, as I said in the beginning, all slowly dying from lack of food at the time, but there was no hint of impending death in their conversation or sign of defeat in their emaciated faces. Instead there was only an extraordinary and intense kind of gaiety that to me was far more moving than any signs of depression, melancholy or defeat could possibly have been.

The Night of the New Moon, 'Story'

In many ways . . . we showed that an officer's condition was not created to give him special privileges. If anything, an officer in these circumstances should have less than his men. That is what being an officer meant: to lead by serving more than anyone else. That was why the British forces were for me so movingly called 'services' and why, contrary to their television image of today, they were not reflections of class and capitalistic systems but great brotherhoods; indeed monastic orders of sorts.

A Walk with a White Bushman

It is a law of life that you should fight for life truthfully and honourably as long as you can, and that you as the individual cannot decide to abandon life – that is a thing which is left to God and therefore we had to do everything we could to go on living. The only weapon we had – because we were completely helpless – was to live truthfully and not to allow the madness which surrounded us to distort our vision of the truth. I could have been wrong at any moment, but I felt that as long as we lived truthfully we had a chance for survival. And the proof is that we did survive.

A Walk with a White Bushman

For during those long, seasonless and tranced Indonesian years, I had been dogged by the thought of my friends and countrymen going out daily to battle, while I withered behind prison walls.

I had promised myself then that if I survived, which at that moment seemed most unlikely, I would never again return to a life of nothing but private profit and personal gain. I would try never again to say 'NO' to life in its full, complete sense, no matter in how humble or perplexed a guise it presented itself.

From where I was in the midst of it, the war seemed essentially a product of profound negation; the fearful problem child of 'NO' parents; of so many generations of such a planned, closely argued, well-reasoned and determined no-ness, that just saying 'NO' to living in its deep, instinctive aspects had become the dreary unconscious routine. By this wilful, persistent no-ness we had turned one half of life, potentially a rich and powerful ally, into the active and embittered enemy of the other.

Venture to the Interior, 'Preface'

Soon after dark, some thousands of men and hundreds of their fellows too weak to walk, many near dying and carried on stretchers, marched out of the prison for the last time, all of them on the first stage of their way to liberation and home; except me myself, who was now faced with another immediate mission, physically weak as I was, and with several more years of a new sort of war in south-east Asia ahead of me. But the feeling of gratitude to life and Providence that all these men were safe at last overwhelmed everything else in me at that moment. It was a feeling as of music everywhere within and about me.

As I watched the long slow procession of men march into the night, this feeling of music everywhere rose within my liberated senses like a chorale at the end of a great symphony, asserting a triumph of creation over death. All that was good and true in the dark experience behind me, combined with my memory of how those thousands of men, who had endured so much, never once had failed to respond to the worst with what was best in them, and all that had happened to me, in some mysterious fashion seemed to have found again the abiding rhythm of the universe, and to be making such a harmony of the moment as I have never experienced.

The Night of the New Moon, 'Story'

In the process, a kind of healing came to remove the hurt and negation of the day and to reinforce me for the next. Without this I know even now with a certainty greater than ever despite many waters that seek to quench the memory of long eventful years, we would not have survived. And more important even than survival, we could not have come out of prison so much a something *other* than we had been before: an *other* totally bereft of bitterness and of longing either for revenge or for an exercise of uncomprehending fundamentalist justice.

At the end Nichols and I could count on the fingers of two hands the numbers of multi-racial thousands we had served with in prison and who had re-emerged embittered and diminished. In fact, going back, as I did, straight from this to more years of war in Indonesia and extraordinary military duty, I was sustained by hundreds of letters that I received from fellow prisoners, saying how strange they had found it to be taken to rehabilitation camps in Britain where they thought the people in need of rehabilitation were not they themselves but the officers and officials in charge of the camps. Many of them went further and told me how one look at the world awaiting them frightened them more than the Japanese had done. They haunted London and other great cities in groups out of a fear that dispersal into the life that they saw would take away what they had earned and cherished together in prison.

Yet Being Someone Other, Chapter 7

War Trials

Like all condemned persons, Hara was alone in the cell. When the door opened to let Lawrence in, although there was a chair at hand Hara was standing by the window, his face close to the bars, looking at the moonlight, so vivid and intense by contrast to the darkness inside that it was like a sheet of silver silk nailed to the square window. He had obviously given up all idea of visitors and was expecting, at most, only a routine call from one of his gaolers. He made no effort to turn round or speak. But as the guard switched on the light he turned to make a gesture of protest and saw

Lawrence. He stiffened as if hit by a heavy blow in the back, came to attention and bowed silently and deeply to his visitor in a manner which told Lawrence that he was moved beyond words. As he bowed, Lawrence saw that his head had been freshly shaven and that the new scraped skin shone like satin in the electric light. Lawrence ordered the sentry to leave them for a while, and as the door once more closed he said to Hara who was coming out of his low bow:

'I'm very sorry I am so late. But I only got your message at nine o'clock. I expect you gave me up as a bad job long ago and thought I'd refused to come.'

'No, Rorensu-san,' Hara answered. 'No, not that. I never thought you would refuse to come, but I was afraid my message, for many reasons, might not be delivered to you. I am very grateful to you for coming and I apologize for troubling you. I would not have done so if it hadn't been so important. Forgive me, please, but there is something wrong in my thinking and I knew you would understand how hard it would be for me to die with wrong thoughts in my head.'

Hara spoke slowly and deliberately in a polite, even voice, but Lawrence could tell from its very evenness that his thought was flowing in a deep fast stream out to sea, flowing in a deeper chasm of himself than it had ever flowed before.

'Poor, poor devil, bloody poor devil,' he thought, 'even now the problem is "thinking", always his own or other people's "thinking" at fault.'

'There is nothing to forgive, Hara-san,' he said aloud. 'I came at once when I got your message and I came gladly. Please tell me what it is and I'll try and help you.'

From the way Hara's dark, slanted, child-of-a-sun-goddess's eyes lit up at the use of the polite 'san' to his name, Lawrence knew that Hara had not been spoken to in that manner for many months.

'Rorensu-san,' he answered eagerly, pleading more like a boy with his teacher than a war-scarred sergeant-major with an enemy and an officer, 'it is only this: you have always, I felt, always understood us Japanese. Even when I have had to punish you, I felt you understood it was not I, Hara, who wanted it, but that it had to be, and you never hated me for it. Please tell me now: you English I have always been told are fair and just people; whatever other faults we all think you have, we have always looked upon you as a just people. You know I am not afraid to die. You know that after what has happened to my country I shall be glad to die tomorrow. Look, I have shaved the hair off my head, I have taken a bath of purification, rinsed my mouth and throat, washed my hands and drunk the last cupful of water for the long journey. I have emptied the world from my head, washed it off my body, and I am ready for my body to die, as I have died in my mind long since. Truly you must know, I do not mind dying, only, only, only, why must I die for the reason you give? I don't know what I have done wrong that other soldiers who are not to die have not done. We have all killed one another and I know it is not good, but it is war. I have punished you and killed your people, but I punished you no more and killed no more than I would have done if you were Japanese in my charge who had behaved in the same way. I was kinder to you, in fact, than I would have been to my own people, kinder to you all than many others. I was more lenient, believe it or not, than army rules and rulers demanded. If I had not been so severe and strict you would all have collapsed in your spirit and died because your way of thinking was so wrong and your disgrace so great. If it were not for me, Hicksley-Ellis and all his men would have died on the island out of despair. It was not my fault that the ships with food and medicine did not come. I could only beat my prisoners alive and save those that had it in them to live by beating them to greater effort. And now I am being killed for it. I do not understand where I went wrong, except in the general wrong of us all. If I did another wrong please tell me how and why and I shall die happy.'

'I didn't know what to say.' Lawrence turned to me with a gesture of despair. 'He was only asking me what I had asked myself ever since these damned war trials began. I honestly did not understand myself. I never saw the good of them. It seemed to me just as wrong for us now to condemn Hara under a law which had never been his, of which he had never even heard, as he and his masters had been to punish and kill us for transgressions of the code of Japan that was not ours. It was not as if he had sinned against his own lights: if ever a person had been true to himself and the twilight glimmer in him, it was this terrible little man. He may have done wrong for the right reasons, but how could it be squared by us now doing right in the wrong way? No punishment I could think of could restore the past, could be more futile and more calculated even to give the discredited past a new lease of life in the present than this sort of uncomprehending and uncomprehended vengeance! I didn't know what the hell to say!'

The distress over his predicament became so poignant in this recollection that he broke off with a wave of his hand at the darkening sky.

'But you did say something, surely,' I said. 'You could not leave it at that.'

'Oh yes, I said something,' he said sadly, 'but it was most inadequate. All I could tell him was that I did not understand myself and that if it lay with me I would gladly let him out and send him straight back to his family.'

'And did that satisfy him?' I asked.

Lawrence shook his head. He didn't think so, for after bowing deeply again and thanking Lawrence, he looked up and asked: 'So what am I to do?'

Lawrence could only say: 'You can try to think only with all your heart, Hara-san, that unfair and unjust as this thing which my people are doing seems to you, that it is done only to try and stop the kind of things that happened between us in the war from ever happening again. You can say to yourself, as I used to say to my despairing men in prison under you: "There is a way of winning by losing, a way of victory in defeat which we are going to discover." Perhaps that too must be your way to understanding and victory now.'

'That, Rorensu-san,' he said, with the quick intake of breath of a Japanese when truly moved, 'is a very Japanese thought!'

They stood in silence for a long while looking each other straight in the eyes, the English officer and the Japanese NCO. The moonlight outside was tense, its silver strands trembling faintly with the reverberation of inaudible and far-off thunder and the crackle of the electricity of lightning along the invisible horizon.

Hara was the first to speak. In that unpredictable way of his, he suddenly smiled and said irrelevantly: 'I gave you a good Kurīsumasu once, didn't I?'

'Indeed you did,' Lawrence answered unhappily, adding instinctively, 'you gave me a very, very, good Christmas. Please take that thought with you tonight!'

'Can I take it with me all the way?' Hara asked, still smiling but with something almost gaily provocative in his voice. 'Is it good enough to go even where I am going?'

'Yes: much as circumstances seem to belie it,' Lawrence answered, 'it is good enough to take all the way and beyond . . .'

At that moment the guard announced himself and told Lawrence he had already overstayed his time.

'Sayonara, Hara-san!' Lawrence said, bowing deeply, using that ancient farewell of the Japanese 'If-so-it-must-be' which is so filled with the sense of their incalculable and inexorable fate. 'Sayonara, and God go with you.'

'If so it must be!' Hara said calmly, bowing as deeply. 'If so it must be, and thank you for your great kindness and your good coming, and above all your honourable words.'

Lawrence stood up quickly, not trusting his self-control enough to look at Hara again, and started to go, but as he came to the doorway, Hara called out: 'Rorensu!' just as he had once called it in the Commandant's office after Lawrence's weeks of torture. Lawrence turned, and there was Hara grinning widely, faded yellow teeth and gold rims plainly showing as if he had never enjoyed himself more. As Lawrence's eyes met his, he called out gaily: 'Merry Kurïsumasu, Rorensu-san.'

But the eyes, Lawrence said, were not laughing. There was a light in them of a moment which transcends lesser moments wherein all earthly and spiritual conflicts tend to be resolved and unimportant, all partiality and incompletion gone, and only a deep sombre between-night-and-morning glow left. It transformed Hara's strange, distorted features. The rather anthropoidal, prehistoric face of Hara's looked more beautiful than any Lawrence had ever seen. He was so moved by it and by the expression in those archaic eyes that he wanted to turn back into the cell. Indeed he tried to go back but something would not let him. Half of himself, a deep, instinctive, natural, impulsive half, wanted to go back, clasp Hara in his arms, kiss him goodbye on the forehead and say: 'We may not be able to stop and undo the hard old wrongs of the great world outside, but through you and me no evil shall come either in the unknown where you are going, or in this imperfect and haunted dimension of awareness through which I move. Thus, between us, we shall cancel

[65]

out all private and personal evil, thus arrest private and personal consequences to blind action and reaction, thus prevent specifically the general incomprehension and misunderstanding, hatred and revenge of our time from spreading further.' But the words would not be uttered and half of him, the conscious half of the officer at the door with a critical, alert sentry at his side, held him powerless on the threshold. So for the last time the door shut on Hara and his golden grin.

But all the way back to town that last expression on Hara's face travelled at Lawrence's side. He was filled with great regret that he had not gone back. What was this ignoble half that had stopped him? If only he had gone back he felt now he might have changed the whole course of history. For was not that how great things began in the tiny seed of the small change in the troubled individual heart? One single, lonely, inexperienced heart had to change first, and all the rest would follow? One true change in one humble, obedient and contrite individual heart humble enough to accept without intellectual question the first faint stirring of the natural spirit seeking flesh and blood to express it, humble enough to live the new meaning before thinking it, and all the rest would have followed as day the night, and one more archaic cycle of hurt, hurt avenged and vengeance revenged would have been cut for ever. He felt he had failed the future, and his heart went so dim and black on him that abruptly he pulled up the car by a palm grove on the edge of the sea.

Sadly he listened to the ancient sound of the water lapping at the sands, and the rustle of the wind of morning in the palms overhead travelling the spring world and night sky like the endless questing spirit of God tracking its brief and imperfect container in man. He saw some junks go out to sea and the full moon come sinking down, fulfilled and weary, on to their black corrugated sails. The moon was now even larger than when he had first seen it. Yes. Now Hara's last moon was not only full but also overflowing with a yellow, valedictory light. And as he was thinking, from a Malay village hidden in the jungle behind there suddenly rang out the crow of a cock, sounding the alarm of day. The sound was more than he could bear. It sounded like notice of the first betrayal joined to depravity of the latest and became a parody of Hara's call of 'Merry

Christmas'. And although it was not Christmas and the land behind was not a Christian land, he felt that he had betrayed the sum of all the Christmases.

Quickly he turned the car round. He would get back to the gaol, see Hara and atone for his hesitation. He drove recklessly fast and reached the gates as the dawn, in a great uprush of passionate flaming red light, hurled itself at the prison towers above him.

'But of course I was too late,' Lawrence told me, terribly distressed. 'Hara was already hanged.'

I took his arm and turned with him for home. I could not speak, and when he went on to ask, more of himself than of me or the darkening sky, 'Must we always be too late?' he asked the question, without knowing it, also for me. It hung like the shadow of a bar of a new prison between us and the emerging stars, and my heart filled with tears.

The Seed and the Sower, 'A Bar of Shadow'

I myself was utterly opposed to any form of war trials. I refused to collaborate with the officers of the various war crimes tribunals that were set up in the Far East. There seemed to me something unreal, if not utterly false, about a process that made men like the war crimes investigators from Europe, who had not suffered under the Japanese, more bitter and vengeful about our suffering than we were ourselves. There seemed in this to be the seeds of the great, classic and fateful evasions in the human spirit which, I believe, both in the collective and in the individual sense, have been responsible for most of the major tragedies of recorded life and time and are increasingly so in the tragedies that confront us in the world today. I refer to the tendencies in men to blame their own misfortunes and those of their cultures on others; to exercise judgement they need for themselves on the lives of others; to search for a villain to explain everything that goes wrong in their private and collective courses. It is easy to be high-minded about the lives of others and afterwards to feel one has been high-minded in one's own. The whole of history, it seemed, had been bedevilled by this unconscious and instant mechanism of duplicity in the mind of man. As I saw it, we had no moral surplus in our own lives for the lives of others. We needed all our moral energies for ourselves and our own societies.

The Night of the New Moon, 'Postscript'

Forgiveness

The conduct of thousands of men in war and in prison with me confirmed with an eloquence which is one of my most precious memories of war, that the spirit of man is naturally a forgiving spirit. I was convinced that if the cancellation of the negative past which is forgiveness could take its place, it would automatically be followed by the recognition that men could no longer change the pattern of life for the better by changing their frontiers, their systems and their laws of compulsion of judgement and justice, but only by changing themselves.

I had learnt to fear the Pharisee more than the sinner; judgement and justice had brought us far but that *far* was not far enough. Only the exercise of the law of forgiveness, the declaration for ever of an unconditional amnesty for all in the warring spirit of men, could carry us on beyond.

The Night of the New Moon, 'Postscript'

I have so often noticed that the suffering which is most difficult, if not impossible, to forgive is unreal, imagined suffering. There is no power on earth like imagination, and the worst, most obstinate grievances are imagined ones. Let us recognize that there are people and nations who create, with a submerged deliberation, a sense of suffering and of grievance, which enable them to evade those aspects of reality that do not minister to their self-importance, personal pride or convenience. These imagined ills enable them to avoid the proper burden that life lays on all of us.

Persons who have really suffered at the hands of others do not find it difficult to forgive, nor even to understand the people who caused their suffering. They do not find it difficult to forgive because out of suffering and sorrow truly endured comes an instinctive sense of privilege. Recognition of the creative truth comes in a flash:

[68]

forgiveness for others, as for ourselves, for we too know not what we do.

This perpetuation of so-called 'historic' and class grievances is an evil, dishonest and unreal thing. It is something which cannot be described adequately in the customary economic, political and historical clichés. The language that seems far more appropriate is the language of a pathologist describing cancer, the language of a psychologist describing a deep-seated complex and obsessional neurosis. For what is Nazism, or present-day nationalism in this southern Africa of my youth, but the destruction of the whole by an unnatural proliferation of the cells of a part, or a wilful autonomous system that would twist the whole being to a partial need?

Venture to the Interior, Chapter 2

One has said that there is 'no greater love than that a man should lay down his life for his friends'. Yet is it not, perhaps, as great a love that a man should live his life for his enemies, feeding their enmity of him without ever himself becoming an enemy until at last enmity has had surfeit and his enemies are free to discover the real meaning of their terrible hunger.

The Seed and the Sower, Chapter 2

We prayed so that all bitterness could be taken from us and we could start the life for our people again without hatred. We knew out of our own suffering that life cannot begin for the better except by us all forgiving one another. For if one does not forgive, one does not understand; and if one does not understand, one is afraid; and if one is afraid, one hates; and if one hates, one cannot love. And no new beginning on earth is possible without love, particularly in a world where men increasingly not only do not know how to love but cannot even recognize it when it comes searching for them. The first step towards this love then must be forgiveness.

A Far-Off Place, Chapter 15

Chapter Four
The First Man

Follow . . . the first man in ourselves, as well as the rainbow pattern of beasts, birds and fish that he weaves into the texture of the dreams of a dreaming self, and we shall recover a kind of being that will lead us to a self where we shall see, as in a glass, an image reflected of the God who has all along known and expected us.

The Voice of the Thunder, 'The Great Memory'

We have a Bushman in ourselves; we have a first man in ourselves, and it is by making what is first and oldest, new and contemporary, that we become creative. We work through this and once we are in touch with this area, as I find that Shakespeare continually was, then there is nothing ordinary left under the sun or the moon . . . It is not so much a conscious understanding as an act of man's living participation in his own being, of observing and recognizing that although a thing is outside, it also represents something inside oneself. So Shakespeare 'knew' in a way which is the greatest possible way of knowing. It is by using this consciousness that the artist creates.

A Walk with a White Bushman

He [the Bushman] was rich where we were poor.

The Heart of the Hunter, p. 139

A Childhood Pact

One day a man more picturesque than most appeared among the many colourful people who were always passing through our ample home. He was tall, lean, burnt almost black by the sun, and his skin of the texture of wild biltong. His grey eyes in a dark face glittered so that I could not take mine from his. He had just come from some far northern frontier and had been everywhere in Africa. Our rebel community frowned upon him because he was thought to be on his way to join the British in their Great War. Then one day I heard him volunteer casually that on a recent journey to an oasis in the Kalahari Desert he had found the authentic Bushman living there as he had once lived in the country around us. After that, I could think of nothing else. Later in the afternoon I locked myself in the study of my father, who had died some weeks before, and took out a diary in which, secretly, I had begun to write poetry and record my thoughts. The day was 13 October, 1914, and in High Dutch I wrote: 'I have decided today that when I am grown up I am going into the Kalahari Desert to seek out the Bushman.'

Many years went by, and the impact of remorse and resolution became obscured. I never lost my preoccupation with the Bushman and his fate, but my interest lost its simplicity and therefore much of its force. Part of the explanation, of course, is that, like all of us, I had to live not only my own life but also the life of my time . . .

Then the Second World War was upon us and all else was forgotten. Yet that is not altogether true. One of the most moving aspects of life is how long the deepest memories stay with us. It is as if individual memory is enclosed in a greater, which, even in the night of our forgetfulness, stands like an angel with folded wings ready, at the moment of acknowledged need, to guide us back to the lost spoor of our meanings . . .

Then suddenly one night round our first campfire on my first postwar expedition, I found myself and my companions talking about the Bushman with great animation. In a flash the grim inarticulate years between the confused soldier and the child ceased to exist. And the scene was repeated night after night in every camp as we went deeper and more widely into the Kalahari. Soon the newcomers to the land caught the fever, and I was struck by their spontaneous interest because it seemed to confirm that my interest was not purely subjective but valid also in the natural imagination of other men. Although none of my missions had anything to do with the Bushman, finding him became important to us all. Yet weeks passed before we saw any sign of him.

[71]

As we navigated our vehicles, like ships by the stars, across the sea of land, I felt deeply that it was not as empty of human beings as it looked. Our black servants and companions had the same feeling. Six weeks went by in which we covered some thousands of miles without meeting the Bushman. Then one evening at sundown, a hundred and fifty miles from the nearest known water, I came to a deep round pan in the central desert. It had obviously held water some weeks before, and there, clear-cut in the blue clay of the dried-up bottom, was a series of tiny human footprints leading up the steep sides and vanishing in the sand underneath a huge storm-tree. As I stood there in the violet light looking at the neat little casts in clay, I seemed to hear the voice of the old 'Sotho herder of my childhood saying again, close to my listening ear: 'His footprint, little master, is small and like no other man's, and when you see it you know it at once from those of other men' . . .

Increasingly, my own imagination became troubled with memories of the Bushman, and in particular with the vision of the set of footprints I had found in the pan in the central desert at the foot of a great storm-tree. It was almost as if those footprints were the spoor of my own lost self vanishing in the violet light of a desert in my own mind. I found myself compelled against my conscious will towards the conclusion that, ridiculous as it might seem, I myself ought perhaps to take up the spoor where it vanished in the sand. Then one morning I awoke to find that, in sleep, my mind had been decided for me.

'I will go and find the Bushman,' I told myself, suddenly amazed that so simple a statement had never presented itself to me before.

The difficulties were obvious. I was not qualified. I had no training. I was not a scientist. The demands on my time were many and exacting. And I could not possibly afford it.

But there was this pact I had made with myself in childhood. I could no longer ignore it, and somehow felt the difficulties would resolve themselves.

The Lost World of the Kalahari, Chapter 3

The Kalahari Desert

The sands of the Kalahari are fertile. They are part of the profound longing of the great African mother earth to produce and to nourish and to support an immense family of natural life no matter of what diversity and numbers.

About Blady, Chapter 1

The miraculous thing about the Kalahari is that it is a desert only in the sense that it contains no permanent surface water. Otherwise its deep fertile sands are covered with grass glistening in the wind like fields of gallant corn. It has luxuriant bush, clumps of trees and, in places, great strips of its own dense woods. It is filled too with its own varieties of game, buck of all kinds, birds and lion and leopard. When the rains come it grows sweet-tasting grasses and hangs its bushes with amber berries, glowing raisins and sugared plums. Even the spaces between the satin grass are filled with succulent melons and fragrant cucumbers, and in the earth itself bulbs, tubers, wild carrots, potatoes, turnips and sweet potatoes grow great with moisture and abundantly multiply. After the rains there is a great invasion of life from the outside world into a desert which produces such sweetness out of its winter travail of heat and thirst. Every bird, beast and indigenous being waits expectantly in its stony upland for the summer to come round. Then, as the first lightning begins to flare up and down below the horizon in the west, as if a god walked there swinging a storm lantern to light his great strides in the dark, they eagerly test the winds with their noses. As soon as the air goes dank with a whiff of far-off water they will wait no longer. The elephant is generally the first to move in because he not only possesses the most sensitive nose but also has the sweetest tooth. Close on his heels follow numbers of buck, wildebeest, zebra and the carnivorous beasts that live off them. Even the black buffalo emerges from the river beds and swamps shaking the tsetse fly like flakes of dried clay from his coat, and grazes in surly crescents far into the desert. When this animal movement is at its height and all the signs confirm that a fruitful summer is at last established, the human beings follow. What I feared was that this invasion into the normal life of the desert would make the genuine Bushman shyer and more than ever difficult to contact. I feared also that the return to the desert in summer of the so-called 'tame' Bushman who is reared in the service of the tribes and colonists impinging on the Kalahari might complicate my task. For the 'tame' Bushman, no matter how irrevocably wrenched from the pattern of his past, cannot entirely live without the way of his fathers. From time to time he refreshes his spirit by going back into the desert. Through the spring, as rain and electricity accumulate along the vibrant horizon, a strange tension mounts in his blood. He becomes moody and preoccupied until suddenly he can bear it no longer. Throwing away his clothes of service he commits himself, naked, to the desert and its ancient ways like a salmon from a remote river backwater coming to the open sea. Those who have inflicted a feudal vassalage on the Bushman wake up one morning to find him vanished. They do not see him again until the summer is over. I knew from others who had already been seduced by his plausible recapitulation of the aboriginal way that the 'tame' Bushman would only be distinguishable from the genuine Bushman by a protracted probe into both mind and history. I could not afford any confusion or delays of this kind. But I knew also that it was only the genuine Bushman who would stay deep in the desert through the worst time of the year. In those uncertain months between winter and the breaking of the rains all fair-weather life quickly withdraws from the desert, and only the desert's own carefully selected and well-tried children like the genuine Bushman remain to endure the grim diet of heat and thirst. It was their tiny feet that had been left in the pan, far from water and habitation, the set of footprints that now drew my thoughts as a magnet draws the dust of sawn steel.

The Lost World of the Kalahari, Chapter 4

The Bushman as Hunter, Lover and Storyteller

They said he was a little man, not a dwarf or pigmy, but just a little man about five feet in height. He was well, sturdily and truly made.

[74]

His shoulders were broad but his hands and feet were extraordinarily small and finely modelled . . . His ankles were slim like a racehorse, his legs supple, his muscles loose and he ran like the wind, fast and long. In fact when on the move he hardly ever walked but, like the springbok or wild dog, travelled at an easy trot. There had never been anyone who could run like him over the veld and boulders, and the bones of many a lone Basuto and Koranna were bleaching in the sun to prove how vainly they had tried to outdistance him. His skin was loose and very soon became creased and incredibly wrinkled. When he laughed, which he did easily, his face broke into innumerable little folds and pleats of a most subtle and endearing criss-cross pattern. My pious old grandfather explained that this loose plastic skin was 'a wise dispensation of Almighty Providence' to enable the Bushman to eat more food at one feasting than any man in the history of mankind had ever eaten before.

The Lost World of the Kalahari, Chapter 1

They started at once unloading the game, and went straight on to skinning and cutting up the animals with skill and dispatch. I watched them, absorbed in the grace of their movements. They worked with extraordinary reverence for the carcasses at their feet. There was no waste to mock the dead or start a conscience over the kill. The meat was neatly sorted out for specific uses and placed in separate piles on the skin of each animal. All the time the women stood around and watched. They greeted the unloading of each arrival with an outburst of praise, the ostrich receiving the greatest of all, and kept up a wonderful murmur of thanksgiving which swelled at moments in their emotion to break on a firm phrase of a song of sheer deliverance. How cold, inhuman, and barbarous a civilized butcher's shop appeared in comparison!

The Heart of the Hunter, Chapter 2

Yet with all this hunting, snaring and trapping the Bushman's relationship with the animals and birds of Africa was never merely one of hunter and hunted; his knowledge of the plants, trees and insects of the land never just the knowledge of a consumer of food. On the contrary, he knew the animal and vegetable life, the rocks and the stones of Africa as they have never been known since. Today we tend to know statistically and in the abstract. We classify, catalogue and sub-divide the flame-like variety of animal and plant according to species, sub-species, physical property and use. But in the Bushman's knowing, no matter how practical, there was a dimension that I miss in the life of my own time. He knew these things in the full context and commitment of his life. Like them, he was utterly committed to Africa. He and his needs were committed to the nature of Africa and the swing of its wide seasons as a fish to the sea. He and they all participated so deeply of one another's being that the experience could almost be called mystical. For instance, he seemed to *know* what it actually felt like to be an elephant, a lion, an antelope, a steenbok, a lizard, a striped mouse, mantis, baobab tree, yellow-crested cobra or starry-eyed amaryllis, to mention only a few of the brilliant multitudes through which he so nimbly moved. Even as a child it seemed to me that his world was one without secrets between one form of being and another. As I tried to form a picture of what he was really like it came to me that he was back in the moment which our European fairytale books described as the time when birds, beasts, plants, trees and men shared a common tongue, and the whole world, night and day, resounded like the surf of a coral sea with universal conversation.

The Lost World of the Kalahari, Chapter 1

I got Dabé to accompany me and walked slowly towards the furthest of the Bushman fires.

Out there between our camp and their shelters the desert was as dark and still as I have ever known it. The only other living things capable of uttering a sound were snakes, and no serpent would have been so foolish as to hiss while about his business on a night so profound. There was no fitful air of summer even, no heat eddy of the frightful day spinning about to rustle what was left of leaf and grass on the scorched earth. But there was this intense electric murmur of the stars at one's ears.

Then suddenly, ahead in a band of absolute black with no fire or reflection of fire to pale it down, I thought I heard the sound of a human voice. I stopped at once and listened carefully. The sound came again more distant, like the voice of a woman crooning over a cradle. I stood with my back to the horizon bright with portents of lightning, waiting for my eyes to recover from the glare of our great camp-fire. Slowly, against the water-light of the stars lapping briskly among the breakers of thorn and hardwood around us, emerged the outline of a woman holding out a child in both her hands, high above her head, and singing something with her own face lifted to the sky. Her attitude and the reverence trembling in her voice, moved me so that the hair at the back of my neck stood on end.

'What's she doing?' I whispered to Dabé, who had halted without a sound, like my own star-shadow beside me.

'She's asking the stars up there,' he whispered, like a man requested in the temple of his people to explain to a stranger a most solemn moment of their ritual, 'she's asking the stars to take the little heart of her child and to give him something of the heart of a star in return.'

'But why the stars?' I asked.

'Because, Moren,' he said in a matter-of-fact tone, 'the stars there have heart in plenty and are great hunters. She is asking them to take from her little child his little heart and to give him the heart of a hunter.'

The Heart of the Hunter, Chapter 2

Here at the sip-wells we found that the Bushman made also a special bow, a 'love-bow', as much an instrument of love between men and women as Cupid's bow was in the affairs of gods and ancient heroes. A Bushman, in love, carved a tiny little bow and arrow out of a sliver of the bone of a gemsbok, a great and noble animal with a lovely sweep of long crescent horn on its proud head. The bow was most beautifully made, about three inches long and matched with tiny arrows made out of stems of a sturdy grass that grew near water. The minute quiver was made from the quill of a giant bustard, the largest flying bird in the desert. The Bushman would stain the head of his arrows with a special potion and set out to stalk the lady of his choice. When he had done this successfully he would then shoot an arrow into her rump. If, on impact, she pulled out and destroyed the arrow, it was a sign that his courtship had failed. If she kept it intact then it was proof that he had succeeded.

The Lost World of the Kalahari, Chapter 10

Under the sun
The earth is dry
By the fire
Alone I cry
All day long
The earth cries
For the rain to come.
All night my heart cries
For my hunter to come.

Song of a Bushman woman

Oh! Listen to the wind,
You woman there;
The time is coming,
The rain is near.
Listen to your heart,
Your hunter is here.

The Bushman's reply

The Lost World of the Kalahari, Chapter 10

These people [the Bushmen] lived without ever losing their central conviction that a story truly told is a kind of religious experience without which life itself is diminished in colour and meaning. Their primitive capacity for recollection, which, in the absence of pens, paper, notebook and other civilized means of recording, was dedicated to precision and totality as a matter of survival, is still sustained by a passion to avoid error and serve truth to a degree undreamt of in our computer philosophies.

Yet Being Someone Other, Chapter 1

He [the Bushman] knew intuitively that without a story one had no clan or family; without a story of one's own, no individual life; without a story of stories, no life-giving continuity with the beginning, and therefore no future. Life for him was living a story.

The Heart of the Hunter, Chapter 13

'The story', the Bushman said, 'is like the wind. It comes from a far-off place and we feel it.'

A Story Like the Wind, 'Epigraph'

I had a feeling that all together these creations of Bushman imagination constituted an ancient, hieroglyphic code of great primary import and, if only I could find the key to the cipher used in the encoding, I would uncover a most immediate message of vital importance. I believed that in order to do so I would have to discover, as it were, the human and contemporary psychological equivalents of the role this long and crowded procession of animals, birds, reptiles and insects played in Bushman imagination and society.

A Mantis Carol, 'The Coming of Mantis'

[The praying mantis's] role in the imagination and life of the Bushman was producing an objective confirmation of what I already suspected; this particular pattern of the imagination of the despised, most cruelly persecuted and almost exterminated Bushman of southern Africa was not only of subjective importance to him and me but also mattered to an understanding of the nature of human imagination everywhere. His conscious mind corresponded in some sort to our dreaming selves and accordingly was one of the clearest mirrors accessible to us today for reflecting imponderables of meaning, that surfaced unbidden in unfamiliar images, as Martha Jaeger's mantis had done, from the unconscious of the most sophisticated mind of the desperate world of today, seeking apparently to inform it of an unknown and profoundly rejected self. Could it not be that, by rendering it in a contemporary idiom, the first and the last in life, which have become so brutally separated and pitted against each other in our spirit today, could be reconciled and joined again to give us back our feeling of continuity, the loss of which seemed to me the main cause of the profound sense of isolation and lack of purpose making a fragment of our own little day? Could it not perhaps also serve to mend and make whole the fracture of the spirit of our time . . .?

A Mantis Carol, 'The Coming of Mantis'

Whenever I tried to ask Nxou and his people about their beliefs I came up against a blank wall of resistance. They not only pretended to be unaware of what I was talking about, but refused resolutely to discuss my question, and became quickly so restless and uneasy that I desisted. Although Nxou, in my presence, had suggested to the little boy that he could bribe his grandmother with his tortoise into telling him a bedtime story, when I asked him or the others to tell me their stories they said they did not know what I meant by 'stories'. When I explained what I meant they said they knew no stories. One evening I surprised an old lady in the act of telling stories to the three children. But the moment she saw me she stopped. When I asked her to continue and to allow me to listen as well, she pretended to be too deaf to hear what I said.

'It's perfectly true! She's too deaf to hear,' the others cried, crowding around and instinctively supporting her.

'There!' the old lady told me, a look of relief on her wrinkled face. 'You see? It's as they say, I'm too deaf to hear.'

Of course, they, she and I all laughed loud and long at the manner in which she had given herself away.

The Lost World of the Kalahari, Chapter 9

I found nothing that was without meaning to these little people. They would look at the extraordinary shape of the baobab tree for instance – the baobab tree was said by Livingstone to resemble a carrot planted upside down. But the Bushmen are not so derogatory and prosaic about this tree as was this great man of God. They have a legend about it. They say that when the first spirit was handing out trees to be planted by all the first human beings and animals in the world, he had given away all the trees but one when the hyena appeared. The hyena turned to him and said: 'You complain that I behave badly, but are you surprised when you give every person and animal something to plant, but nothing to me?' Whereupon the first spirit relented and gave the hyena the only tree he had left to plant, which was the baobab. But, out of spite, the hyena planted it upside down and that is why the baobab tree looks as it does today.

'The Creative Pattern in Primitive Africa', Eranos Lectures

So close were the Bushmen to nature that they not only wondered at it and feared the appropriate aspects of it, but also could laugh with it. They noticed, for instance, that often in the Kalahari Desert the ostrich will leave one egg outside its nest. I myself have noticed this phenomenon and on this occasion I asked my Bushmen hunters the reason for it. They roared with laughter and said that a member of the early race and the people of the early race often did strange things; the ostrich was inclined to be absent-minded so he deliberately put an egg in front of his nest to remind him that he was hatching, otherwise he might forget what he was doing and get up and walk away! . . .

Then when the Bushmen noticed that the Kalahari hare had a split lip they had also to find the meaning of that. They recount that the moon once realized that the people of the early race were terrified of dying and decided to send them a message of reassurance. So the moon chose the hare as messenger because it was so fast and the matter was so urgent. It said to the hare: 'Go and tell the Bushmen that even as I die and am renewed again so too they in dying will be renewed again.' But the hare delivered the message wrongly and told the people on earth that the moon said that unlike the moon they would not be renewed in dying. As a result the moon in anger beat the hare upon the lip and that is how its lip comes to be split today.

'The Creative Pattern in Primitive Africa', Eranos Lectures

On the great swamp along the northern frontier of the Kalahari, the Bushman saw the hippopotamus daily emerge from the steaming waters and, unlike other animals, scatter his dung with a vigorous movement of his tail to fall spread out on the earth. He had a story about that as well. He said the hippopotamus in the beginning begged to be allowed to live in water, which it loved more than earth, sky, sun, moon, or stars. It was told no, because with such a big mouth and such teeth it would soon devour all the fish. It promised it would eat nothing while in the water, and would emerge at night to graze on the grass and plants of the earth. Still it was refused permission, until finally it contracted to come out daily from its beloved water and scatter its dung, so that all creatures could test its good faith by examining the dung for fish-bones.

The Heart of the Hunter, Chapter 13

The Bushman Inside Ourselves

Had I noticed, [Dabé, the Bushman] asked, how everything in life had a place of its own? For instance, the springbok had their pans; the eland and the hartebeest their great plains; the jackal, the hyena, the lynx, the mongoose and the leopard had each a hole of his own: the lion could come and go and eat and sleep where he liked. Even the locusts had their grass, the ants their mounds of earth – and had I ever seen a bird without a nest? The black man, the Herero, the Bastaards, had kraals and lands of their own, and the white man houses of stone. But could I tell him what and where was a Bushman's place? The echo of the New Testament cry about the birds having nests and the foxes holes but the Son of Man no place to lay his head, rang out so loudly in my head that I would have suspected Dabé of having heard it, did I not know otherwise.

Moreover, he went on, many of these animals were protected by the white man. If a Bushman killed a giraffe, an eland, a gemsbok or even a bird like the giant bustard for food because he was dying of hunger, and the police discovered it, he was taken away to prison and often never seen again. If the Bushman killed his own desert animals for food, he was punished. Yet no one punished the white man, the black man and the Herero when they killed their animals, their cattle and sheep for food. But if the Bushman killed the cattle and sheep that came into the Kalahari to eat the grass of his animals, again he was hunted down and punished. How could such things be? Did I know that, when the first white men came to the Kalahari, they would have died if it had not been for the Bushman? The same was true for the black man. The Bushman showed them where the water was, took their cattle to grass and helped them to live. Once the Bushman walked the desert like a lion from end to end with no one to trouble him, but today every man was against the Bushman. He alone had nowhere to go, no one to protect him, and no animal of his own. Again, was that how it was meant to be?

Finally, Dabé went sombrely on, there was another thing: if the black man at his cattle outposts in the Kalahari wanted a Bushman servant he just went out to hunt for one and took him. If he wanted Bushman

[82]

women, he just took them whether they had men of their own or not. If the men fought back, they were either killed or severely beaten up by the black man and his powerful friends. Should a Bushman kill his persecutors, the police were sent for to take him away. White men too would sometimes take their women, but above all they loved to steal their children. There in south-west Africa, working in European households, were many many Bushmen who had been taken away as children and were never seen again by their parents. Even he sitting there beside me – he beat his chest with a clenched hand – was afraid of what would happen to him in this white man's land to which I was taking him. What would the white man do to him when suddenly they saw his old Bushman face alone among them?

This last was an old fear of his. We had had to have it out right in the beginning before I could reassure him that I would protect him and so persuade him to come. But it all went far beyond fear.

More upset than I dared show, I asked, 'Would you like me to take you back to your people we have just left and leave you there?'

'Moren!' he exclaimed as if he had not heard. I repeated my question and added, 'I am willing to stop and turn right round here and now.' I braked and the labouring vehicle stopped.

'Oh, Moren! You know I can't do that.' He shook his head and looked at me reproachfully as if I had been unexpectedly cruel.

I might have remembered Ben telling me that Dabé, like other 'tame Bushmen', had frequently tried to go back. Every now and then they found life unendurable in the rags and tatters civilization sprawled around the few permanent waters on the vast fringe of the Kalahari. When the lightning called and the rains broke, they would vanish for a walk-about all over the desert in the way of their fathers; but after a while they would reappear like beggars at their former master's back door. Never had Ben heard of a single one who failed to return, and that, of course, was the agony of it. They could not go back and they could not go on. Looking in Dabé's eyes, I saw a soul in hell; for hell is the spirit prevented from going on, it is time arrested in the nothingness between two states of being.

The Heart of the Hunter, Chapter 3

[83]

Indeed I have lived with primitive people so much that I have an inkling now of the almost paralytic effect our mere presence can have on their natural spirit. It is as if, when they first encounter us, the independence of our minds from instinct and our immense power in the physical world, which to them is not composed of inanimate matter but is another manifestation of master spirits, trap them into the belief that we are gods of a sort. Either they feel it impossible to be themselves in our presence, or they find it so exhausting to maintain even a part of their selves that they are compelled to rid themselves of us by cunning, force, or running away. The longer contact is maintained, the more subtly does this process work in their spirit, and the more devastating its effects.

The Heart of the Hunter, Chapter 3

In comparison to the Bushman, the black African was a highly sophisticated man of property. He owned cattle, sheep, goats, hens, dogs and ducks, cultivated the soil and manufactured many things. The Bushman owned nothing, cultivated nothing and manufactured nothing except his hunter's and artist's kit. As a result, when they first met and the Bushman regarded the cattle of the white and black invaders of his land as he did the rest of the animal life of Africa, which he had a natural right to kill for food, a war to death began. Two utterly incomprehensible ways of life had man by the throat and in the end, just as Esau lost out to Jacob, the Bushman lost to black and white in southern Africa.

A Mantis Carol, 'The Great Divide'

As a reminder of how simple and clear his values were, how little he had asked of life and yet how much too much for us to give, there was a young woman in tears kneeling in the background. She was crying, soundless, with grief, feeling her honour impeached because, in pouring out some of their precious water from an ostrich-eggshell container, she had spilt a spoonful.

The Voice of the Thunder, 'The Little Memory'

As we were a very small group of just five, I had been tempted to make straight for Paradise Pan, because I knew nothing now could give my friends a truer rendering of what the Kalahari was like

[84]

when I first learnt to know it, but I had already had so many wounding lessons of the dangers of looking and going back over my tracks that I hesitated. I chose instead to camp at a place called Deception Pan, where some foretaste of that privileged world would inform us how wise it would be to press on, if at all, and kept the existence of Paradise Pan to myself.

It took only one night in Deception Pan to show me how impossible it was to go back to the reality I had known. I knew for certain now that the paradise we had recovered in the pan a generation before was lost. Even if it still held animals in the abundance and diversity which I had first encountered there, they would be animals who, like the world around this preparatory camp of ours, had lost their innocence and expelled man from their society as the wilderness around the pan was expelling him from its trust.

For instance, in all the years I had worked in the Kalahari I had never taken tents with me. I carried a light nylon tarpaulin which, in case of rain, I strung as a roof between my trucks and the trees. Otherwise we slept in the open every night, and although frequently we heard the lion roaring and other strange panting, snorting, snarling, hunting noises around us, followed very often by a leopard's cough, and occasionally the sound of a roving lone old elephant stripping the bark off a tree with a sound like gunshot, we trusted in our fire to keep a sufficient distance between them and us. But to my amazement, as we unloaded the trucks, which had been sent some days ahead of us to meet us at that point, we found that every one of us had been provided with a tent. Since the sky was clear and there was no prospect of rain whatsoever, I was just about to object to our camp organizer and tell him to put the tents away when he told me that it could not be done. I asked why not, and he answered emphatically that it was not safe. He said that the lion and the leopard had lost their fear of fire, as they had long lost their fear of man by night, and that many people nowadays in the desert had been killed because they were not in some shelter or zipped up in a plastic tent . . .

Not only had the lion changed but the milder antelopes, the gentlest of gazelles, even the little steenbuck with his concentration of purity shining like a lamp in the great pupils of his wide eyes, who would always find time to stand and stare, now on our first approach got up in alarm, and ran without looking back. The gemsbok would not pause in his shade under an umbrella of thorn to look and see who we were but was on his feet and instantly running. All in all, the change in the mood of animals and birds expressed a degree of the alienation of man even greater and more alarming than the total suppression of stone-age culture and rejection of the Bushman. I thought of the bitter truth in a remark put into the mouth of an old white hunter in another story of mine: 'Should the last man vanish from the earth tomorrow, there is not a plant, bird or animal who would not breathe a sigh of relief.'

The Lost World of the Kalahari, Epilogue,
'The Great and The Little Memory'

We must never forget that the greatest damage we are doing to the Bushman is to the Bushman inside ourselves – because what you do to another human being you do to yourself . . .

You cannot eliminate something precious in life without killing something in your own soul.

A Walk with a White Bushman

We need their spirit still. We who loom so large on the scene are not better than they, only more powerful with a power that corrupts us still. It is we who shall have lived in vain unless we follow on from where their footprints are covered over by the wind of the moving spirit that travels the ultimate borders of space and time from which they were redeemed by their story. Woven as it is into a pattern of timeless moments, their story may yet help the redeeming moon in us all on the way to a renewal of life that will make now for ever.

The Voice of the Thunder, 'The Great Memory'

Unless we recover our capacity for religious experience, we will not be able to become fully human and find the self that the first man instinctively sought to serve and possess.

The Voice of the Thunder, 'The Great Memory'

[86]

Although the Bushman has gone, what he personified, the patterns of the spirit made flesh and blood in him and all he evoked or provoked in us, lives on as a ghost within ourselves . . . Something like him, a first man, is dynamic in the underworld of the spirit of man, no matter of what race, creed or culture.

The Voice of the Thunder, 'The Great Memory'

Chapter Five

Our Mother Earth

═══════

. . . however indescribable, there was between man and his native earth an umbilical cord of life-giving imponderables that no circumstance could cut, not even long years of exile.

Yet Being Someone Other, Chapter 4

> Our Father which art in heaven
>   Thy will be done.
> Our Mother which art in earth
>   Thy love be fulfilled,
> And love and will made One.

A Far-Off Place, 'The Hunter's Prayer'

Wilderness – A Way of Truth

Wilderness is an instrument for enabling us to recover our lost capacity for religious experience. The religious area is far more than just the Church. If you look at the history of Europe since Christ, you will see that the Church has tended to be caught up in the social problems of its time, just as it is today, and to be less than the religion it serves. The churches and great cathedrals are really, in the time scale of human history, just tents on the journey somewhere else.

What wilderness does is present us with a blueprint, as it were, of what creation was about in the beginning, when all the plants and

[88]

trees and animals were magnetic, fresh from the hands of whatever created them. This blueprint is still there, and those of us who see it find an incredible nostalgia rising in us, an impulse to return and discover it again. It is as if we are obeying that one great voice which resounds and resounds through the *Upanishads* of India: 'Oh man, remember.' Through wilderness we remember, and are brought home again.

'Wilderness – A Way of Truth', Essay, p. 48

I think the two nations in the world who have been most influenced by nature are the English and the Japanese. English poetry is absolutely full of nature and a love of nature, a love of birds, grass, flowers, and even the common fly is 'gilded' as it 'lechers' in Shakespeare's sight. Wherever you go in London you see that everybody has a window-box with flowers in it; even if they cannot have a garden, they have a window-box at least.

A Walk with a White Bushman

For Jung they [animals] were 'priests of God' because they did not follow their own will but did only God's will. 'In the beginning was the Word –' Well, to me, every insect and animal somehow is part of the Word made life, made flesh, made real. It is the word in action. Everyone and everything carries this charge. It carries, as it were, a signature of creation. Nothing is unsigned in life; a great seal is stamped on great and small.

A Walk with a White Bushman

Nature is . . . the world of spirit made manifest.

A Story Like the Wind, Chapter 5

[Mopani Théron, the hunter turned ranger, speaks to François] 'Remember always, Little Cousin, that no matter how awful or insignificant, how ugly or beautiful, it might look to you, everything in the bush has its own right to be there. No one can challenge this right unless compelled by some necessity of life itself. Everything has its own dignity, however absurd it might seem to you, and we are all bound to recognize and respect it as we wish our own to be recognized and respected. Life in the bush is necessity, and it understands all forms of necessity. It will always forgive what is imposed upon it out of necessity, but it will never understand and accept anything less than necessity. And remember that, everywhere, it has its own watchers to see whether the law of necessity is being observed. You may often think that deep in the darkness and the density of the bush you are alone and unobserved, but that, Little Cousin, would be an illusion of the most dangerous kind. One is never alone in the bush. One is never unobserved. One is always known as people in the towns and cities of the world are no longer known. It is true there are many parts of the bush where no human eye might be able to penetrate but there is always, like some spy of God Himself, an eye upon you, even if it is only the eye of some animal, bird, reptile or little insect, recording in its own way in the book of life how you carry yourself.

'And beside the eyes – do not underrate them – there are the tendrils of the plants, the grasses, the leaves of the trees and the roots of all growing things, which lead the warmth of the sun deep down into the darkest and coldest recesses of the earth, to quicken them with new life. They too shake with the shock of our feet and vibrate to the measure of our tread and I am certain have their own ways of registering what we bring or take from the life for which they are a home. Often as I have seen how a blade of grass will suddenly shiver on a windless day at my approach or the leaves of the trees tremble, I have thought that they too must have a heart beating within them and that my coming has quickened their pulse with apprehension until I can note the alarm vibrating at their delicate wrists and their high, translucid temples. Often when I have heard a bird suddenly break off its song, some beetle or cricket cease its chanting, because of my presence, I have felt uninvited like an intruder in a concert in some inner chamber of our royal environment and stood reproved for being so rough and not more mindful of my manners.

'All of these animal, insect and vegetable senses put together add up to a magnitude of awareness, a watch so great, minute, many-sided and awesome that there is nothing small enough to escape its notice, and I have sometimes felt involuntarily exposed in the heart of the bush as I have only on some wide open plain of our blue highveld in the south when alone on a cloudless night of stars. It is difficult to express how small, vulnerable, confessed and revealed so immense and sharp-eyed a concourse of sentinels have made me feel, even in my innermost and most secret self. It is as if even the hidden frame of bone and sinew within me was apparent to their X-ray vision. You must be mindful, therefore, of the great company that you are compelled to keep, whether you like it or not, wherever you go. Remember that whatever you do will have its effect on them and influence them for good or ill.'

A Far-Off Place, Chapter 5

The natural vegetation of Africa, like vegetation everywhere else, contains as much poison as it does nourishment and we could obviously not have turned with impunity to what merely looked appetizing in that fertile and over-abundant bush. I have often thought that if we had access to a casualty list of all the men who have died in discovering what was poison and what was edible in the vegetable kingdom from the beginning of time, it might exceed the list of men who have perished in wars.

First Catch Your Eland, Chapter 1

Sanctified Moments

Suddenly [François] was full of memories of the beauty of all the sunsets and daybreaks he had ever seen in the bush; the rounded sound of the unimpeded song of the uninhibited bird, the lightning voice of the lion, the triumphal arch the impala imposed high on the columns of its flight, the look of morning in the eye of the kudu and the fall of night in those of the purple inyala; the victory roll of the peacock-blue winged and lilac breasted im-veve, the spitfire bird that their people knew as the pledge of truth; the lamp of the lynx; the fire of leopard and flame of the lion; the glitter of the red and mauve tsessebe moving exultant with the song of the wind of its own speed in its ears; the star-glitter of the voice of the crickets performing their devotions at night; the measure of the elephant; the hymn to the sun of the mopani beetles and the hallelujah of the massed choir of birds at nightfall and daybreak; the flake of snow of an ibis falling out of the high-noon blue and the plover's sea-whistle farewell to the star of morning. All these and many more which François could imagine for himself were with him just then, not just as visions of things of beauty but like a reveille on a trumpet calling his senses to awake and fulfil the abundance of life reflected in the mirror of the garden at their beginning. Yes, he had said beginning deliberately because, as he had implied, he now believed it was posed there not as a record of what had already been but as a kind of miraculous mirror to reflect the invisible in what is to come.

A Far-Off Place, Chapter 15

The sun was already drawing near to the top of the hill that we called Blue Cliffs, so named because the summit was a bare reef of cliffs composed of blueish compound stone. At the base it was covered with wild olives and lush bushes all glowing in the sun, and I knew that several small caves within the cliffs where families of red lynxes lived, members of one of the most star-like breeds of cat, would be shining like lamps just then. All in all this sort of blue summit seemed a proper foundation on which the temple of the deepening blue above it could rest securely . . .

I could not help pausing for a moment. In one of the clearest lights on earth, I could see the dust in four different places where other flocks were being taken to their kraals near permanent water points scattered over the farm. But, what was most exciting, I saw our own herds of springbok and blessbok moving gracefully in between. I always marvelled how at such distances and on such days the light made their bodies strangely insubstantial and almost transparent, so that they looked not so much flesh and blood, which we all share, as a flicker of flame and light thrown on to a screen of distance as if through a slide of some cosmic magic lantern.

And then there was something else which tended to sanctify the moment. There was the equivalent out of our earth as of Byzantine incense. As I felt the cool of evening moving around me where I sat above the bustle and the smell of dust and sheep, it brought that scent I have mentioned before, of the wild freesias that covered these ridges for miles on end. It is of course a scent which everyone finds appealing, but no one can know what it is really like until it has come to him on the air of evening or morning in the heart of Africa, where it is poignant and charged, as it were, with the quintessential quality of my native continent, which in nourishing so starlike a flower with so delicate and tentative a scent proves that in the sum of itself and all its incalculable passage of years and future to come, it would never allow its giant strength to be used like a giant.

About Blady, Chapter 4

For people so shackled with negative aspects of culture and civilization . . . there was in these sounds and sights something of the nature of a prayer for a way of life for sheer living's sake which is Africa's great gift to the modern world. They made the night a temple and I was always struck how, after the roar of one lion, in the pause before another answered it, all the other voices of darkness, like the crickets which raised their own Hallelujahs, would be silenced as if by divine command.

First Catch Your Eland, Chapter 1

. . . the wind in all times from the Stone Age to Greek and Roman has been the most evocative symbol of the spirit, urging man to a renewal and increase of the quality and nature of his being . . . The wind rises, the spirit moves, and one must try to live on into a new area of life.

Yet Being Someone Other, Chapter 2

I thought what an artist Africa is in the way it displays its great mountains. The greatest of them are never jumbled together as they are in Switzerland, the Himalayas or the Caucasus. They are set in great open spaces and around them are immense plains, rolling uplands and blue lakes like seas, so that they can see and be seen and take their proper place in the tremendous physical drama of Africa.

Venture to the Interior, Chapter 7

I myself know of no circumstances which make one feel more insignificant than finding oneself alone on a hot summer's day in the silence of the immense veld with the great clouds swimming above one in the blue like whales over a shrimp.

The Heart of the Hunter, Chapter 16

I knew that each of those stars, before their meaning was confined to what could be determined by telescope and spectrums, had had a personal significance for countless vanished peoples. I rejoiced, for instance, that the Pleiades of the Greeks could also be the Seven Kings to us, Seven White Heifers to the Amantakwena, and the Digging-for-Stars to the Zulus. It was the Southern Cross to the Portuguese, a Sword to me, and the Giraffe to the 'Sotho peoples of Africa. The great black hole on the edge of the Milky Way, the Coal-Sack to some Europeans, the Entrance to Hell for us, the Cave of the Night to the Abwatetsi, and in Sindakwena the Great Bull-Elephant's Killing Place. Sirius the Great Scorcher, the Dog Star to the Greeks, Eye of the Night to the Amantakwena and the Great Grandmother of Plenty to the Bushman – indeed Mother of Plenty seemed the most appropriate because Sirius does not shine like other stars but seems to contain light so abundantly that often, lying on the veld, I had had the illusion of hearing it overflow like crystal water and drip on the earth beside my head. I recognized them all, saluted them in my heart and felt acknowledged in return.

The Hunter and the Whale, Chapter 5

The rainbow [is] a natural testimony of the striving of the human spirit to raise consciousness on earth, since, as refraction of the white light of day into its constituent colours, it is vizualization of the discriminating, analytical element of the conscious spirit. That was its role in the Old Testament for Noah after the flood, the arc of man's first covenant with his highest meaning.

A Mantis Carol, 'The Place and the Season'

A Magic Bestiary

My old friend, the hunter . . . had told me that one of the reasons why nature, and animals in particular, were so important to us today was because they were a reminder that we could live life not according to our own will but to God's.

The Hunter and the Whale, Chapter 8

The animals from oysters to horses and pigs are epic and seminal material of the questing imagination of man when the abstract and cerebral world fails it.

The Voice of the Thunder, 'The Great Memory'

It was for her the final proof that the great innocent epoch of horses had for ever come to an end. Now, for good or ill, Luciana was at the frontier of the enigmatic age of man, where heart and mind have to dismount inwardly and go on foot, slowly, step by step, into the unknown future.

A Story like the Wind, Chapter 10

It was only by living with these horses that Gulliver could persuade himself to venture back into the world of men ...

About Blady, Chapter 1

I found myself left with the thought that it was the jockey's love of the horse and faith in the horse which gave him access to all the enormous energies which are in the province of man's immemorial associations with the horse, and the horse's with man.

About Blady, Chapter 3

It would seem ... that before the centaur in man could fulfil himself and establish how individual all points of departure were in the story of man, the horse had to find himself as something more than horse. This too is a special feature of Greek mythology: the horse has a crucial role in this unfolding of the drama of the universe and the painful evolution from a world of gods and titans towards one lone, individual, immortal half-horse, half-man, charged to save the gods themselves from their increasingly arrested selves by renouncing his own immortality to enable a renewal of life to take place both in heaven and on earth. At so many points when the progress of differentiated life on earth seemed arrested and in danger of faltering, the danger was overcome with the help of the horse – once even with the dreadful and spurious wooden horse of Troy – and life moved on again.

About Blady, Chapter 5

Marching at the head of the column too, as I now was, I was the first to encounter the insects both great and small, little hunting spiders, red, silver and gold like filigree Indian jewels in the sun, and red-bellied scorpions the size of lean, athletic young lobsters among the boulders, or again other spiders big as soup tureens, shaking like jellies on black, hairy legs, and blue-headed lizards with yellow throats and jade-bead eyes sparkling like powdered glass, drying off the cold dew on the sharp crest of loose iron-stone rock, and each reptile, as it stared unblinking into the sun, ceaselessly licking thin lips and lashing the stark light with the shadow of their flickering tongues.

Then there were the snakes, too. This morning, within an hour of sunrise, I saw their heads go up one after another as the first vibration of my feet reached them. At one moment there were so many glistening, swaying heads high above the grass in front of me on either side of the track that it looked almost as if I were about to be forced to run a ritualistic Maya gauntlet of lashing tongues playing like forked lightning over their poisoned mouths. Many of the trees, too, had one or two serpents either draped like a limp lash of an ox-whip across their branches, or else alert and active, hanging by their tails from the branches, hissing and making quick, threatening passes below. One large tree near a waterhole was festooned with them, and its dancing outline looked like the flaming silhouette of Medusa's hair.

Flamingo Feather, Chapter 9

For the hippo had a true ambivalence, and was a compound of two-way exaggeration, both negative and positive. His head was so big that he nearly toppled over with it, yet his ears were tiny and coral pink as a woman's. His jaw was like a lion trap and his tusks so powerful that he could have easily nipped the bottom out of a whaler, yet he was a mere vegetarian and so greedy of green and delicate things that I have known his kind walk ten miles from his water for a bite of lettuce. By day he would sleep with contentful ease in the water but by night he walked thus abroad. His chocolate skin was as thick and tough as any hide on earth, yet it carried a delicate goddess blush within. His legs were too small for his body and knock-kneed from his weight: his eyes were old from birth, being without lashes and lidded like a lizard's. He traded in many elements but was complete in none, and all day and night whether in water or on land he huffed, puffed and grunted with the effort of feeding enough air to the prehistoric current of such vast transitional being.

Flamingo Feather, Chapter 10

Tired, we all crept into our nets immediately after eating, and whenever I woke I heard the hippo-bull of the night before stamping and huffing and puffing with rising resentment around our beds. Once when he sounded almost on top of me I flashed my torch in his direction. The moon was rising. Though reeds and trees were too dense to reveal his shape, his eyes showed up long, slanted, and emerald green. Towards morning he seemed to accept us and withdrew to the moonlit waters with resignation. Thereafter, I believe, he learnt even to enjoy our company and the change in routine that our presence provided. He visited us nightly, announcing his arrival with a loud crash through the wing of reeds, a fat boy trying to make our flesh creep with fierce puffs of breath. For a while he would study us from all angles and then return, full of simple wonder, to his soft water, where he made solemn and reverential noises at the moon. Because he appeared alone, and celibate, and was full of devout utterance I called him Augustine, after one of my favourite saints, who I am certain would have been the first to understand since he, too, had been a bishop of Hippo.

The Lost World of the Kalahari, Chapter 7

Coming up carefully behind the first loose boulder, I saw a very old and very big baboon, sitting with his back to me in a toga of sunlight, his broad shoulders rounded, his head well tucked in and a long neurotic, oddly pedagogic finger, nervously scratching his head. He was obviously the look-out for some highland clan foraging for haggis of scorpions, stone-slugs, tubers and hillside tulip bulbs among the loose rock, but my mind, hungry for normal companionship, found his outline there in its cap and gown of sun so endearing that it made of him some natural professor of geology surveying material for an abstruse lecture on problematical stone.

'Hello! Adonis,' I whispered across the empty space, using the name my trekker countrymen first gave his kind a century or more ago.

He whipped round obviously not believing his ears. For a full second he stared at me paralysed with this unbelief but long enough for me to look into the wisest and most experienced pair of hazel eyes I've ever seen in a baboon's face. At the back of his twilight pupils a long reminiscence of life presented itself for comparison with this surprising situation, light and shadow racing across his face in quick succession. Then the last memory condemned, and his long experience drained, the darkness of fear came up like night in his ancient eyes. He blinked them several times quickly, his brow became incredibly wrinkled, and his lips began to tremble with hysterical pressure. Blinking thus, he came out of his trance, his hazel eyes went green with warning, and suddenly he turned a prodigious undignified somersault backwards, revealing an unacademic behind so bare and naked that it looked as if he'd torn the seat of his mauve, silk suit in panic on the rock, and vanished into space below.

Flamingo Feather, Chapter 4

Apes perhaps were intellectually the most adroit of all, but with this limitation – that their lives were short and their intelligence dominated by the most apprehensive imagination to be found among animals and one almost entirely devoted to survival. They had a pronounced sense of mischief, but no gaiety or sense of play. In Africa they were the supreme example of the animal living out of fear by their wits.

The Hunter and the Whale, Chapter 11

I could never look at meerkats without a feeling of the sheer fun of being alive reborn in me, and the reaffirmed gift of their affection for one another and joy in each other's company that sets their little kibbutzes apart from all other animal congregations, quickening an awareness of the love involved in the act and deed of nature, however disguised in the ruthless aspects enforced by its commitment to survival. They were constantly pausing to see if their friends were near, or turning about just to touch someone special with a tender and caring paw.

The Voice of the Thunder, 'The Little Memory'

The look of the elephant more than any other animal on earth is directed within – a strangely wise-old-man look, a profound human look – but no tears.

About Blady, Chapter 8

The elephant had a great natural intelligence, was totally without fear, possessed no instinct or need to kill except in self-defence, lived long and was able to match its thinking with its experience. A favourite African saying was 'He who travels much, doubts many things.' So with the elephant and as a result of all these qualities he had developed the most methodical and logical mind. He had evolved not just habits and customs, but . . . a tradition of life. The elephant when forced to kill, however violent and nimble his first charge might be, would complete the destruction of his enemies according to a well-thought-out plan. He was the one animal in Africa capable not merely of fighting a quick battle but of conducting a whole campaign.

The Hunter and the Whale, Chapter 11

I noticed that in Africa many animals, when they get really old, go away on their own.

So you sometimes see an elephant or a rhinoceros on its own miles from anyone. You might see a wildebeest or a buffalo, or a harte-beest or lion on his own. And lions do not grow quite as old as they could sometimes, because they have such problems in finding food in old age. For me, it's almost a religious pattern. It is as if when an animal has lived its life, has done his duty as a young animal and bull in protecting the herd, there comes a moment when he feels he must do something in nature that he has to seek, find and experi-ence on his own. They are what I call *Sanyassin*, after the name conferred in India on the men who renounce the world and all their possessions and take to the road on a great walkabout in search of resolution and holiness. As I come to the word *Sanyassin* I have a recollection, bright and electric as if it were lightning, of an old Kalahari lion I had once known over a period of days. There were, perhaps, somewhere over the horizon, other lions. It was lion country but I never saw any for days except this one, still great in his old age, a thick Titian red mane thrown almost nonchalantly over his tawny shoulder and every reason to walk in pride. And yet his bearing was without arrogance and his carriage of a certain dignity of profound meditation, and the last time I saw him was as he went over a yellow sand-dune and down behind it, and so into the heart of one of those deep mythological African sunsets we have talked about.

I can remember a rush of other examples, for the numbers of species in which this *Sanyassin* pattern applies is, I believe, great.

Take the elephant. I have seen elephant walking about on their own, and it is marvellous when you see a great lone elephant in wide open country which is not really elephant country, with the grass perhaps only up to his ankles. And, though walking slowly, with monumental dignity, it is amazing how fast he looms up because he takes such long strides. Black, vast basalt, he dominates the day and darkens the blue as he approaches with this deliberate tread, picking up and putting down his feet with an easy resilience as if to correspond to the drumbeat deep down in the heart of the earth. All about his movement is point and counterpoint of a vast orchestration of life with this drumbeat and pulse of the blood-red earth. He is almost upon one before one realizes how much his senses are not focused on the scene but on something inapprehensible ahead, almost as if he were a great somnambulist following a dream in his sleep. Trancelike he passes, leaving one with a keen sense of ritual, as if he were pledged at the head of a procession of pilgrims of life. And the mystery, the act following on below the burning horizon of faith and trust implicit in his going, is all the greater because one cannot remotely guess at any physical object of his search, there, some hundred miles from the nearest known water. One knows only that he comes in the world already armed with great instinctive foreknowledge, an unusual intelligence, formidable memory made more formidable by a long life. For myself, I can only vouch that I have never watched him and his kind come up, go by and down the blue horizons without being moved, knowing only that in their last long range they seek no ordinary food or water, but a round up of their ancient spirit.

A Walk with a White Bushman

I followed the line of his pointing finger and there in the sky between us and the mountain, wings stretched out to remote feather tip, wheeling and rising like a note of music in an organ peal of a morning psalm, was one of the great legendary eagles of Umangoni which . . . is 'eyes of the king and snatcher of sheep'. So high was the eagle that the raven-black wings, deep-sea foam breast, saffron beak, fawn riding breeches and purple talons, were all one dark colour, and that colour transformed by alchemy of the breaking day. For though we ourselves still stood in twilight, an effortless lift of the silver fountain of air whereon the bird soared now carried it out of the shadow of the night up into the light of the sun. For one moment it looked as if a fiery shaft had pierced the bird shattering it in a burst of flame, for the eagle seemed to vanish from our sight leaving behind only a gleaming fragmentary flicker, yet the flicker stayed; and then, with another wheel on seemingly motionless wings, it grew and re-established itself in the quick of the morning air as full eagle of flame in search of equal fire.

Flamingo Feather, Chapter 13

The honey-guide sat on a delicate, intricate ornate bough like a piece of third-Empire gilt in the morning sun, beating its wings and singing with a crystal clarity.

They heard its ancient refrain, 'Quick! Quick! Honey . . . quick!'

Xhabbo dropped his empty dixie, seized his spear and said, 'Person of wings and a heart of honey; look how hearing you, quickly I come!'

François immediately picked up his own rifle, haversack, water flask and ammunition pouches, calling on Nonnie, as Xhabbo called upon Nuin-Tara, to come after them with all their dixies as soon as they had scoured them out with sand.

The honey-guide, seeing that it was being followed, was in no hurry. It fluttered from tree to tree to perch where it was most visible in the full sun before it flew on to the next. As a result Xhabbo and François were joined by Nonnie and Nuin-Tara before they had gone very far, just in time to hear in the distance another strange, urgent whistling call followed by an almost chuckling sound, from far down the throat of some eager hurrying animal.

Xhabbo stopped, turned about and whispered that they must all be silent please; a most wonderful thing was about to happen.

Significantly, the honey-guide, perched on a branch a bare twenty feet away, was looking first to them and then in the direction of the new sound coming steadily nearer and sounding as if it were coming out of the earth a hundred or more yards away to their right. Suddenly the new sound ceased. At once the honey-guide became alarmed and resumed its call with a glittering, desperate intensity, beating its wings hysterically against its side, so that it could utter the maximum volume of command of which it was capable. Xhabbo's face was transfigured and transformed with wonder into an ancient Pan-like beauty as there came bursting into view a robust, grey-dark animal, trotting fast on sturdy, somewhat curved legs, with a distinct, business-like air that would not have been inappropriate on the face of someone who was something in a great city, determined to catch a bus.

'Good God, a ratel . . . a honey-badger,' François began in a whisper to Nonnie. But got no further because the moment the badger arrived under the tree to exchange passwords with the honey-guide, the honey-guide, paying no more attention to their little group, took off at full speed and they had to hasten after the ratel with his strange, flute-like whistle and odd Dionysian chuckle. This duet between ratel and honey-guide was transformed into a trio by Xhabbo, who now kept on informing their two guides ahead, in a crooning, soothing song: 'O person of wings, and a heart of honey; O bravest of the brave persons! Do not look behind but feel yourselves hastening and feeling it, know how hastening too, we come!'

François, in explaining all this to Nonnie, elaborated how there was no animal in, on or above the earth that was as brave as this animal and that even a lion, or the maddest of rogue elephants would leave it alone. Even for Mopani, who knew animals so well, it was the one animal who proved, as he put it, that in the world of nature as in the world of men, only courage made life free from fear. It was because of its utter freedom from fear, the Bushmen believed, that the ratel was given the ultimate reward of valour, that was honey.

Nonnie, watching the strange animal shape hurrying after the light, ethereal singing bird, entranced and excited by it, characteristically had an association uniquely her own which no sooner found than was revealed in the remark to François, 'How like Caliban he is, and how like Ariel the bird; and when you come to think of it, how like a magician, a sort of desert Prospero, your beloved Xhabbo looks just now!'

Before long they arrived at a vast termite hill, which in itself was a sign of how near to the end of desert sand they had come, since the hill was a temple of clay. The termites had long since gone, driven out by an ant-bear who had clawed a hole in its base and so made it a fitting home, full of vacant cells and cunning corridors for an immense concourse of bees, that were coming and going in long amber processions between the entrance and the distant waters and flowers of the swamps, which Xhabbo had declared were so near.

They watched the Ariel bird perch itself, silent upon the tip of the termite summit, still quivering like an electric bell just after the summons rung on it had ceased, looking highly pleased over the faultless way it had just performed a delicate duty, before it began sharpening and cleaning its beak between its wings and claws for the delight to come. But strangest of all was the behaviour of Caliban. No sooner had he arrived at the mound than he whisked about, went smartly backwards and thrust his sturdy behind firmly into the opening of the vast hive.

'He must be mad!' exclaimed Nonnie, mystified and aghast, 'to do a thing like that to bees.'

'Oh, Nonnie, this is the most wonderful part of all!' François announced, 'You see, he's gassing all the bees inside so that they can't sting anyone getting at the honey.'

Told this in a different setting at third-hand, Nonnie might have been inclined to laugh. But as a close witness, indeed a committed accessory before the fact, the wonder of the resourcefulness implicit in the whole arrangement into which she had been drawn, seemed miraculous and so beautiful that she watched it all with shining eyes. It was amazing. Almost at once there died away the steady reverberating murmur of bees chanting their devotions in that Gothic cathedral built by insect-priests. Soon the honey-badger could step aside, and for the first time turn his attention to them.

He looked steadily and fearlessly into their eyes as if to say, 'Now look, it's time you did something as well.'

Immediately Xhabbo, still crooning, went eurhythmically forward, knelt smoothly by the entrance and pushed his hands slowly and evenly through the dark cathedral door. After feeling delicately around within, he pulled out a long, broad comb of purple-black honey, and broke off a large segment. Held out towards the honey-guide it went translucent with morning sun and looked more like a dream of honey than any honey found on earth.

'O person of wings with the heart of honey,' he begged, 'take and eat.'

The honey-guide's precise shape vanished in a flutter of feathers and wings and emerged in a swift glide towards Xhabbo, who was carefully laying out honey in the shade of a bush like a feast. As he stepped back, the bird flew in and at once pecked away at the wax that encombed it.

Xhabbo went back at that same smooth ritualistic pace to the entrance, once more felt inside and pulled out another great comb, shedding large tears of glistening honey.

'O bravest of brave persons, who knows how to put the bees to sleep,' he called out, holding it like some magical substance towards the watchful badger. 'Take, oh please take, and eat!'

Moving smoothly forward, he laid the comb at his sturdy partner's feet, who strikingly enough made no move to eat but went on watching him keenly. And again Xhabbo went back, brought another comb and laid that too at the feet of the honey-badger and begged it to eat. This time the badger ate, and Xhabbo was free to extract two more great combs, bring them to Nuin-Tara so that she could break them up and store them in their dixies. François knew that in so great a hive he could have extracted many more combs but it was as if Xhabbo knew instinctively that never had it been more important to observe the proportions implicit in the claims of bee as well as man, bird and beast. With a movement of profound gratitude and his most respectful gesture of farewell at the honey-bird, the honey-badger and the hive, he turned about and in the same devout tone commanded, 'Now let us too take our honey before the bees wake from their sleep, and eat, my children eat!'

It was the first time Xhabbo had ever used a paternalistic expression. It was totally unlike him even now, and it sounded as if he were speaking on behalf of someone else. It could only have come, not because he was feeling fatherly, but out of a conviction that they all had been uniquely fathered just then.

It was one of the most beautiful events in which François and Nonnie had ever participated. Neither of them were capable of expressing what they felt. It was as if they had witnessed a manifestation of the sweetness that life could achieve if only man, bird, animal, insect and flower were allowed to enact fully the terms of the alliance to which they are in their deeps contracted by the act of their being. For this final taste of honey on their tongues which had long forgotten what sweetness was, seemed to erase all that had been bitter in their experience, to such an extent that even if this were to be their only reward, the travail to which they had been subjected would still have been worth it.

The camp they had just left, therefore, became the first camp to have its original name cancelled and to be renamed with a phrase which meant, 'The Annunciation of Honey.'

A Far-Off Place, Chapter 13

I was lucky enough to see the only occasion on which whales, other than sperm and killers, fed in our part of the ocean. It was when the sardines appeared.

This was an annual event. Once every year during the brief whaling season not shoals but a wide, deep, continuous river of billions of sardines came up the coast on the current from the south. The significant thing about this event was that it caused far greater excitement on land than it did among us at sea. Sardines or no sardines, our quarry was there. The whales, after all, were not there to feed but rather to graze in new sea-green pastures, to play, marry and give birth. We therefore had no overwhelming interest in the coming of the sardines. On land, however, the people of Port Natal seemed to go mad about the event.

The first glimpse of the head of this gulf stream of sequin fish life was flashed from far down the coast. Newspapers splashed it in large headlines on their front pages. Special correspondents were immediately despatched to keep visual contact with this flood of sardines pushing north.

As it came nearer the coast of southern Zululand and Port Natal, the excitement among people daily became greater. I do not know exactly why it was that in our part of the ocean sardines came so close to the land. Perhaps they found shallower waters there to escape the most voracious of their ocean enemies. Anyway the fact remains that here on the coast off Port Natal, and well within our whaling grounds, they came as near as possible to the shore, drawing their high-sea enemies after them. When that happened the population on land hastened to the south coast either to fish themselves for fish that would not otherwise come within hooking distance, or just to watch. Special trains were run to deal with this rush from town, village and hamlet. Thousands of men and women who never gave the sea a thought wanted to participate in this event, and eager landsmen spread along a hundred or more miles of the coast of Africa either frenziedly fishing or watching others do so.

A friend of mine told me years later that the impression from the shore was as paradoxical as it was astonishing. It was as if neither the fishermen playing the great fish, nor the great fish preying on the sardines, nor the crowds surging up and down to watch the struggles were in command of the situation. Rather it was as if fishermen, watchers and sea killers were being hooked and played by an invisible angler who was using the sardines as bait.

From the sea the sight was remarkable enough. It looked as if every enemy that could possibly be mobilized against the sardines was there. The ocean itself was a porridge of carnivorous fish, sharks, porpoises, the lot, all gorging sardines until from the foretop I saw them swimming slowly away as if in disgust from the scene.

Around the *Kurt Hansen* I had never seen so many whales. They had also come to do their bit in this war of nature and became so excited that they were blind to the fact that they themselves were being hunted. All we had to do was to steam among them and harpoon them at leisure. It was the only occasion when I saw the whole of our fleet simultaneously gathered in the same area. What was even more extraordinary to me was the excitement communicated by the fish, in their total abandonment to gorging and killing, to us. It was as if death and destruction were a powerful archaic wine whose taste had compelled these multitudinous diversities to unite in a common celebration.

Even the most gentle whales appeared drunk with the endless opportunity for killing provided by this miracle of abundance of minute fish in the sea. One whale in its excitement plunged so impetuously in among the sardines who were seeking safety ever closer and closer inshore, that it ran itself aground and perished there.

But even inshore the sardines could find no safety, for where the bigger fish had to break off pursuit, the birds took over. The sky was full of gulls of all kinds and gannets who, the moment they appeared over the scene, closed their wings and fell straight down exploding like mortar bombs on the blue water, gulped their sardine, then rose immediately to dive again for another. Where they went into action the sea was splashed with spray and foam as if with a regular bombardment from an army of gunners. I would watch one flight of gannets after the other quit so full of food that they could hardly fly; and as they left others appeared to take their place.

Yet, with all these forces mobilized against them, the sardines none the less survived. They lost their battles day after day, but they won the campaign, for we knew that the following year they would reappear undismayed in as great numbers as ever. I was to see this event four years running, and if anything it gained in importance and magnitude.

In this as in all else, Leif saw a lesson. Nature was all things, he said, a killer and creator, a builder and destroyer. He believed man's problem was to maintain the proportions, for life's deepest longing was to be rescued from these two terrible opposites. And surely at depth there was a point beyond which nature would take no more killing? Then its answer was to summon up its final and greatest weapon: the life of numbers. But this, of course, meant great sacrifices of complexity and quality in the system of life itself, for the bigger the number, the more inferior the quality. And the more the killer learnt to cope with the antidote of numbers, the quicker became the cycle of reproduction of the new inferior life mobilized against total destruction, until finally it would be so small that the most powerful electron microscope could not observe it nor any scientific filter hold it. Nature had an infinite abundance to draw on for its ultimate purpose of promoting life. If necessary, if indeed it were the only weapon left against the heretical life which was denying life, it would not hesitate to summon up an abundance of undetectable and unpredictable organisms to bring pest and plague back to discipline a world unaware of its own lust for killing.

The Hunter and the Whale, Chapter 8

Yet, fundamentally [the whale] remained true to all the best qualities of a land animal. For instance, he made love not like a fish but a mammal; he retained his warm blood; bore children the land way at sea, fed them on warm milk, loved them individually with the passion of the earth for a flower, and readapted, with an efficiency no laboratory could equal, so that his land organisms could function at sea. The udder of the whale was a marvellous example. An old Portuguese whaler from the Azores, a hand harpooner, had once seen a baby whale come to the surface of a flat sea, open its lips wide when the mother appeared, while she rolled on her side and from a distance of about ten feet squirted jet after jet of thick rich cream-yellow milk into the mouth of her beloved child!

How he wished he could have seen that! The same old whaler had told him there was no greater love between animals than that between whales. Their hearts matched their bulk. They were also believed to be monogamous, although they supposedly live to be a hundred and fifty years old. Yes, the great impersonal sea had changed the outward shape of the whale but at the same time it had confirmed and enlarged what was best in the spirit.

The Hunter and the Whale, Chapter 8

They are rather like lone animals . . . who can neither join nor leave the herd, but are forever moving around the far perimeters of their fellow creatures to lead a form of existence wherein they have to learn to make their peace with the fact that the most they can achieve is a satellite companionship. I can remember times without number when I have seen these satellite souls rebelling against isolation and the fate which compelled them to face alone the daily dangers of life in desert, veld and bush; dangers in which even the numbers of the herd were no certain protection.

It occurred to me that this kind of separation, even in the animal, was necessary to create a greater awareness which it was impossible to acquire in the context of sympathetic numbers of their own kind ... it was most striking how these lone phenomena developed senses so keen that the beasts who preyed on them and their kind would leave them alone, because they realized they were no match for the qualities of vigilance produced by loneliness and isolation. It was, in fact, easier to prey on animals who assumed that there was safety in numbers.

Yet Being Someone Other, Chapter 3

Man the Destroyer

Man was too estranged from nature and his natural self to react 'naturally' any more to most circumstances, and least of all to love.

A Mantis Carol, 'The Carol'

[The whaler Kaspersen] told me that no man, however great or important, had the right to tip the balance of fate either way in these conflicts of one species and another set up by nature both on land and sea. If man did so, he was certain that some terrible retribution of fate would follow.

Yet Being Someone Other, Chapter 3

On the horizons where the great empires, the Ninevehs, the Tyres, Thebeses and Babylons, have gone down into the dust and rubble which is all that is left of themselves and the abundant world of nature which nourished them, there is a terrifying statement of its danger to man, beast, and flower. There were, for instance, the great forests of central Asia which stretched from Isfahan eastwards to the Himalayas and the Hindu Kush, and north to the seas of the Caspian, and west to the wine-dark ocean of the Mediterranean. They have all gone. Humble woodcutters and charcoal burners feeding the needs and greeds of cities have left hardly a tree between Tehran and the Caspian. Where is the grass that Nebuchadnezzar ate? And where are the hanging gardens of Babylon? And what would not have been done sooner with the bulldozers and mechanical saws of today? North Africa from Nile to Atlas Mountains and the Pillars of Hercules, which was the granary of Europe, today is an impoverished fringe of earth on a man-made desert of the Sahara. The European shore of the Mediterranean, in spite of the vision of wealth and luxury it still holds for the weary industrial man, is a ghost of what it was in its Athenian day. Then, there was not a valley, a mountain, or a stream where men did not walk and commune with their gods, and dream in the company of satyrs, centaurs, nymphs, fauns, and the titanic forces of a world charged with magic and wonder. No one who has read his Homer, Thucydides and Virgil can be anything but terrified by what is left and in comparison looks like a scorched earth today.

Foreword to Dr Theo Abt, *Progress Without Loss of Soul*

One has only to look in the eyes of, for instance, the animals [man] has domesticated, to see that the compensations he offers in return for services rendered, are not enough. For those eyes, when they are not on their guard and focused in the service of his bidding, like those of the dogs that follow at his heels, the horses munching in his stables and the cows in his meadows, amaze and confound one with the sadness glowing at the far end of the long look that goes back to their remote beginning.

For human eyes that are still open to these things, it is a sadness that emanates from a nostalgia for a time when they were not enslaved but were free to be their immediate, instinctive selves. For ears that can hear, this nostalgia is there even in their voices, for what can be less joyful than the bleating of the sheep that is the ultimate in subjection to man? There is the pitiful nicker at night of horses haunted by dreams of their birthright of freedom exchanged for a mess of oats and straw and the security of luxurious stables. There is also the sound of cock-crow that has become part of the music of self-betrayal. In all these there is expression both of a persistent incurable sickness for the wilderness that was their garden in the beginning, and reproach to powerful men who have malformed a natural kinship and put an unnatural totalitarianism in its place.

A Far-Off Place, Chapter 8

Nature seldom inflicts on us anything for which it does not also provide the relevant immunities. It takes not nature but man, his slanted societies and savage intellectualism, to force us to bear the unbearable.

Jung and the Story of Our Time, 'The Vigil and the Summons'

The battle must be fought on every level . . . What life there is left on earth should be conserved. We need to worry not only about the pollution of the earth, but the pollution of the sea . . . It is no accident that we have this drug problem on our hands. Our own society is drugged. We use drugs in the earth, we are looking for short-cuts all the time, and the irony of it is that chemistry is no longer ours. You see its benefits in the works of the alchemists who are using it as a way to the ultimate wisdom, which is the mystical marriage of heaven and earth. We have forgotten this side of chemistry. We have got to bring the 'al' back to chemistry.

'Our Mother Which Art in Earth', Address.

Conserving nature is part of the conservation of the human spirit.

'Our Mother Which Art in Earth', Address.

Should the last man vanish from the earth tomorrow, there is not a plant, bird or animal who would not breathe a sigh of relief.

The Voice of the Thunder, 'The Little Memory'

Because numbers have replaced unique and human considerations in the faceless abstractions of our time, we feel lost in a world where nobody cares any more for what we are in ourselves. Inevitably we cease to care in return. One of the most awful consequences is that, as we lose touch with the natural man within, which demands a unique self of us, we lose respect for him. And as the natural man within loses honour, so too does nature without. We no longer feel reverence for nature, and defoliation of spirit and landscape are everywhere to be seen . . .

That is why what is left of the natural world matters more to life now than it has ever done before. It is the last temple on earth which is capable of restoring man to an objective self wherein his ego is transfigured and given life and meaning without end . . .

Follow the first man in ourselves, as well as the rainbow pattern of beasts, birds and fish that he weaves into the texture of the dreams of a dreaming self, and we shall recover a kind of being that will lead us to a self where we shall see, as in a glass, an image reflected of the God who has all along known and expected us.

The Voice of the Thunder, 'The Great Memory'

The new starlight walked the water, leaving a footpath of silver to run between me and the east like a life-line through the multitudinous creases in the palm of the sea's outstretched hand.

There is something most significant about the encounter of a human being in solitude with great abiding manifestations of nature. It is so intensely personal and specific that it demands some special recognition from one's imagination. That moment, indeed, grew great with natural divinity, and the vast uprush of light soaring after it with widespread wings became a miracle. I felt then as if I were witnessing the first day of Genesis.

The Hunter and the Whale, Chapter 5

Men are 'keepers of the trust of creation and the continuing task of creation'.

Our Mother Which Art in Earth, Address.

Chapter Six

At Home in the World

I (. . .) found myself thinking of a Sindakwena saying:
'The journey makes the stranger at dawn a neighbour beside the fire
at night'.

The Hunter and the Whale, Chapter 12

The Sea and Ships

Accordingly I look back on countless moments like those without
regret or even nostalgia, but only with unqualified gratitude to life
for giving me so privileged a chance of communion with the sea and
its meaning, both in the dimension of the here and now of daily life
as in the depths of the spirit where, through the symbolism of the
external world made manifest, we are in touch with all that has
been and all that is to come.

Yet Being Someone Other, Chapter 2

Both sea and ships are in themselves natural symbols of royal and
ancient standing in the mind of man.

Yet Being Someone Other, Chapter 6

Those who persevered to the true end, whatever their call to the sea,
would find it had the power, unequalled by any other natural
phenomenon, to transcend all and make mere man more than himself.

Yet Being Someone Other, Chapter 6

As the only so-called European among about a thousand people of the Far East, I might have been expected to feel more self-conscious of my Europeanism and so more of a foreigner. But, on the contrary, I felt at home to an extraordinary degree. And in so far as the obvious and real differences of race and culture were concerned, they seemed to me as valid and valuable or irrelevant as my own, and so a potential source of belonging rather than alienation. What was more, I surprised myself by finding, when comparing differences, that I tended to do so from a Japanese rather than a European point of departure. It was my first glimmering of an awareness that was to prevent me from ever feeling, I believe without arrogance and presumption, that I was a foreigner no matter where I went in the world. Indeed, only such an awareness, already a force in being from birth, could have made me as at home in the *Canada Maru* and Japan as I had been among the primitive peoples of Africa or indeed on my mother's farm. I could not foresee then how my life was to involve me deeply and even fatefully with a greater variety of races and cultures than perhaps anyone else of my generation. As a result of this seed of new awareness nourished in the *Canada Maru*, I was beginning to think of myself as a native of the world, and my love of Africa and the Britain to which I was increasingly committed became a universal provincialism destined to transcend and render archaic the imposing array of powerful nationalisms which still dominated the emotions of my time. It is true I would have to start out as a stranger, but the strangeness was relative and never greater or more exacting than the feeling of being a stranger in my own beloved province, and indeed alienated where I had taken belonging and understanding for granted. For all my unknowing, there was awakening then something which was about to make the world my home, a home of many mansions where my closest neighbours were not next door but in the far-off wings.

Yet Being Someone Other, Chapter 6

Our part of the South Atlantic ocean was in the beginning full of a unique life of its own. It was stocked with whales, walruses, seals, fish, penguins, dolphins and porpoises, just as the air was alive and vibrating with the wings of the most amazing variety of birds, from Mother Carey's chickens and stormy petrels, which were our own

Aeschylean portents of tragedy around our capes, to the albatross, gliding out of the remote Antarctic on the longest span of wings ever granted to a bird since the days of the vanished pterodactyl.

Yet Being Someone Other, Chapter 3

The August morning when I was driven by some friends from London to Southampton was warm, cloudless and full of a harvest-gold sunlight. The fields were ripe and high with corn, heavy heads of yellow seed already bowed for the sickle, and red poppies everywhere blazing in between as in some sort of remembrance of a vanished summer. They were proclaiming that the time had come for gathering a harvest not only of summer but also of history. England had never looked more English to me, nor the imagery more evocative, until we came to Southampton. There all memory of what it had been, was, and is still intended to become, seemed to have vanished. The great harbour which I had known so well for over fifty years, always crowded with purposeful shipping from the smallest to the greatest, was empty except for one or two outsize freighters and a lone passenger ship. Her black and red funnel, spotless white decks, lilac hull and grace of line were unmistakably and poignantly evident and revealed her as one of the Union Castle line, with a company of the prettiest and best-dressed ladies that ever sailed the incorruptible sea. But for good measure she flew a thirty-foot paying-off pennant from her main mast, to proclaim what was to come.

She was, of course, the *Windsor Castle*. However, except for the routine attention of local stringers of national newspapers and a perfunctory television camera, she was not at all receiving the courtesy to which good manners of history entitled her.

Yet her departure from the Cape, by contrast, had provoked a response to the significance of the meaning of the history that gave birth to it, and which had for so long nourished and contained it. The great harbour at the Cape had been packed with people, and the traditional mail-ship quay, long and wide as it was, was capable of holding only a fraction of the people who wanted to join in homage to this last episode of departure of the 'great mother' which the necessities of traffic and travail in her by sea had been to them. On the quay there was a military band to play the ship out to sea with a sort of music I had first heard in the company of my father when the shipping of the world glowed as in a fable devoted to increase of life and discovery without end. But the crowds on land, on the decks and at the rails of the ship dense with passengers and crew, were unashamedly overwhelmed with new emotions. Most were close to tears, and a great many wept without restraint. Cries that were more like despairing wails of pledges never to forget one another, echoed constantly between ship and quay, and diminished, for once, the dominance of voices of the squadrons of gulls, wheeling in preparatory patterns for their hereditary function as heraldic ushers of the mariner in man to his chosen sea. They were clearly audible, but only at intervals, and then in tones that were acute with alarm rather than the normal sadness of farewell. Coloured streamers were thrown from deck to quay and were held in such quantities that, when the great hawsers and cables that bound this last *Castle* of history to the land were cast off, it looked as if there were paper enough strung in between shore and ship to hold her in place for good.

Most significantly of all, as the last warning gongs, bells and siren blast sounded, there was a final rush of people from ship to shore and from quay to the overcrowded decks, and all sorts of varied estates of men and women embraced one another. The diversities which normally set us apart were erased for an instant by an eruption from this patient, brooding and ultimately irresistible urge gathering in the unconscious of the world, namely the power to assert one day, and for good, the values of the family of man on our journey ahead, however round about the route – just as our ship was bound for home. That sight of black, coloured, white, Indians, Pakistanis, Afrikaners and English, single and at one because the right occasion was there to reflect this concealed potential, still remains as a candle in the dark of what has followed on since. It remains, too, a reproach to the bankruptcy of a world that seems incapable of producing other and more positive evocations of the meaning of history, to make the manifestation of our latent human singleness not random and spasmodic but permanent.

Finally we broke the last of our paper streamers, and passed a lone Scottish piper in a Black Watch tartan standing on the tip of the last breakwater to grace our going with the kind of lament of which only the Highland soul is capable. We were followed out to sea by hundreds of little ships, and as they and a snow-storm of gulls escorted us out to the dark blue albatross-haunted roadstead of the South Atlantic, the land spontaneously sent us its own special message of hail and farewell. Wherever we looked from city to Lion's Head, Signal Hill to Sea Point, Devil's Peak to Fish Hoek and Simonstown, mirrors – of all shapes and sizes – reflected the levelling afternoon sunlight back at us, as if to say: whatever the rest of an indifferent and even hostile world may feel, we care still and can only reflect our care with light because, in so far as our history was an instrument of light, it was possible only because of the long line of ships of which you are so glittering an 'envoy extraordinary'. This may sound corny and banal. But I have long since learnt that all life is an orchestration of great and constantly recurring platitudes, and that our meaning is to be found in the way we re-orchestrate them from birth on to procreation, death and, through instinct of rebirth, beyond.

Long after the last of the little ships had given up, the gulls had turned about, and our escort of albatross on wings that for me, at least, always have something of heaven about them, had assumed the final office of Admiralty, I remained on deck. I remained there until the Cape itself sank into the sea, because I knew I would never again see it do so in that way. Moreover, I did so not in order to indulge in my emotions, because in a sense I had already had enough of them. I did it as someone who felt bound to bear some sort of objective witness to the last positioning of the future in the vacant place left by our farewell. I felt bound to bear witness to neglected meanings only accessible at such a time and on such an irrevocable course on an ocean stretching without impediment from Antarctic to Land's End, and add my final testimony to an evolution of meaning of which the process we call history is the instrument. We are contracted by life to live out this meaning as a great question before we can become aware of the one answer that can serve to transcend our private and collective conflicts. I seemed to know and to hear it, almost as a voice, in the rising murmur of sea and note of wind, comes to us first as the smallest and most improbable of intuitions. Indeed, such an intuition invariably strikes the established and institutional world either as some absurdity, clamouring clown-like for undeserved attention, or as a criminally subversive impulse. But to the individual who has the courage to let it into the shelter of his awareness, it assumes a clarity and certainty that makes end and beginning one.

Yet Being Someone Other, Chapter 7

I first came to Zanzibar and the coast of East Africa the way history came to it – from the east. My ship, a Japanese tramp, came upon the island at dawn . . .

All round us were the dhows that are still built, wooden nails and all, as they were a thousand years ago. The scene looked very much as it might have done when Vasco da Gama first broke so brutally into those waters, four hundred years before. As we rounded the headland, the sun rose, the sky flashed like a mirror and there was a little Arab city going down, tidy and compact, to the rim of the harbour front. We dropped anchor and when the rattle of the chains ceased I suddenly realized two things: that it was my lucky day, 13 December, and that a subtle perfume, strangely familiar and provocative although I could not name it, was coming from the coral shore and the gleaming white warehouses. It took me a good minute to realize it was the scent of cloves. The realization, slight as it was, evoked an immense vista of history because it was the hunger for spice in Europe that had led to the discovery of the New World, the establishment of my own ancestors at the Cape of Good Hope and the first appearance of the Portuguese in these tranquil coral waters.

Zanzibar and Pemba made their history out of trading in slaves and spice. The slavery had gone but the spice remained. Shortly after breakfast, I walked with the captain of the ship to the market-place; the air was so charged with the scent of cloves, it was stifling. The streets beyond the warehouses were constricted and teemed with a new kind of man: part Arab, part African, yet still so identified with his Asiatic origins that he wore a kaffia on his head and a curved golden dagger, like a crescent moon, at his waist.

First Catch Your Eland, Chapter 4

Great Britain

These associations which I have with London began for me when I first came to it in the 1920s. As I looked at its skyline from the highest vantage point on its northern boundaries, there was not a single thing in that gentle view to contradict its history. From where I first saw it, the composition of the town was the most organic compound I had seen of man, his home and social building, and his love of grass, trees and gardens. All was there, laid out as if in a blueprint of the human spirit which thought of a city as its fortress and light on a hill of the soul. As a result the skyline was for me the most beautiful I had ever seen in a city, and it was not so much broken as uplifted and sent soaring by the spires of its many churches like arrows bearing messages to heaven. There are smaller cities in the world which may have a greater number of churches, but I know of no city anywhere going about gigantic contemporary business that showed such aspiration to heaven as London when I saw it first.

About Blady, Chapter 3

There is not another people in the history of the world which has been less corrupted by great power than the British, in spite of the poor view they themselves take of their own imperial past. They possess a capacity for self-criticism unequalled in any other nation, and a sense of decency so imaginative and searching that less scrupulous opponents in the modern world have frequently used it as a weapon against them.

The Heart of the Hunter, Chapter 8

Capital [cities], I believe, should be the end and not the beginning of a visitor's schedule. They should be reserved to gather together and sum up all the ravelled ends of one's experience as they do the life of their nations, otherwise they tend to turn all that follows into a kind of protracted anti-climax.

Journey Into Russia, Chapter 2

France

I feel the reason why French culture and French civilization is so important to us is because at its highest point it was complete, it honoured two poles – it had its Descartes and it had its Pascal – two poles and infinite variations in between, and for a nation to be really complete it needs both these approaches to life.

A Walk with a White Bushman

I had a great longing to go back to the Mediterranean again. I had spent two long winters on an island in the Mediterranean. I had written my first book on this island, and the longer I lived there the more I felt that there was somewhere a Mediterranean person in my line of life between the past and the present. It may have been something that I owed to my love of Greece and its mythological manifestation. I do not know, but I remember feeling with a great and acute nostalgia, like a physical pain, that after so much war and fragmentation between exploration in desert and forest, and working in London, I should go back to my island again . . .

When the day came to arrange my journey to the island, I very nearly walked out of my travel agent's office, and thought I would change my mind. I knew that the Germans had occupied the island throughout the war and done some damage to it, and in general I had become afraid of going back on my physical tracks. I had discovered that one could not go back in time, as it were, in a wilful way as if there were always a straight line of approach between oneself and any places that one remembered. I had found that lethal to my memories, because when I had tried it, although the physical change in the places of return was not change in any particular, something had gone from the scene. The life that had been within it had been withdrawn, and one was presented with a kind of mummy, an embalmed and well-preserved something which once was as vibrant with life as it was in the memory but now found itself denied by the reality of the present. There was perhaps only one way of a true return, and that was a return that happened out of an immense circle of one's life: a final round up of all that one has experienced, bringing one back to the point of departure, so that it presented itself in a way so fresh and meaningful that it was as if one was seeing it for the first time.

The changes in the Mediterranean world since I first knew it at the end of the 1920s have been as immense as they are horrendous. I have already hinted at how far the world of Greece today was removed from the world of Greece I had entered through my reading and yet was being evoked continually so that it was more alive in my imagination than ever. Greece had become scorched earth and the physical scene such a terrifying metaphor of the deprivation of life brought about by the withdrawal of the gods and the heroes from the scene, that I could not leave it soon enough, and I never wanted to see it again.

But this island of my first book had been different. It was still an island in the Homeric mode. There was a small harbour for fishermen, and perhaps a score of fishermen's houses, all arranged in a square with a church presiding over it. The footpaths that led from the village to the extremes of the island were all made of earth, and there were perhaps half a dozen farms with modest little Mediterranean houses, surrounded by figs and olives and, of course, sizeable vineyards. Pine trees and the odd ilex or two covered the rest of the island from end to end, from the surf of the sea and its stretch of curved beaches to the hilltops and the cliffs on the stormy side of the island. In between, the trees were dense with undergrowth, with the smell of herbs of all kinds dominating and purveying the scent as of preparation somewhere for a banquet of ambrose and nectar. There was everywhere asphodel and myrrh, and a miraculous bush called *arbouse*, which grew the flower, the bud, the unripened fruit and the mature red-gold berry all at one and the same time, and seemed to be for ever in a state of production, decay and reproduction.

On the stormy side of the island there were some caves, and in one cave, which was still known as the Cave of Pirates, when the mistral was too much I slept with the fishermen and ate bouillabaisse laced with absinthe for breakfast in the cold dawn of their winter.

Happily, the island was privately owned, and the owner married into an English family I knew well. They loved the island and would not in any way allow it to be developed, but merely looked after it without violating its natural classical shape. I had a room of my own in a little hotel called L'Hôtel les Palmiers, wherein I could begin my writing work at last. I had eight months there finishing my first book and found that the island, through the nature of its earth, evoked so much of the climate of man's Mediterranean beginnings that it felt as if designed to fit my own need of rebeginning.

I do not think I have ever had happier or more meaningful months, writing from dawn to noon, and then walking all over the island in the afternoons, making friends with the fishermen and the few people around, and in the evenings reading in French as I had never read before, because the whole new flavour of life and civilization was like having the savour of a precious salt that had been lost, back on my tongue.

Sometimes, because I needed the money, I would work for some days with the fishermen, and even some nights, which I preferred, because fishing the way they did in a moonless dark brought strange excitement to my senses. They fished, I am certain, in the way that fishermen in classical Greece fished. I say this with certainty because they fished with tridents shaped exactly like the tridents I knew from visual representations of Poseidon. Every boat that went out at night had its expert 'tridenteer' – that is the nearest I could get to a name for him in English, rather than something like 'harpooner', which would diminish the image of a fisherman silhouetted against the starlight with the glow of the lamp focused on the sea beyond the prow, like a black silhouette from a Greek memorial vase. He would stand there as the boat moved silently and all was so still that one could almost hear the sound of the stars mingling with the lap, lap, lap of the crystal waters of the sea. Sometimes there would be a swirl on the waters, and giant eels would lash at the surface like the ends of wagoners' whips, but they would always be ignored, because what he was waiting for was the most cherished fish in the islands: the beautiful, the swift and the bejewelled *loup de mer*. And when at last he speared one of those 'wolves of the sea' with his trident, and leaned far backwards as he heaved it from the water and for a moment held the body in the glow of the lamp before it was lifted into the dark starlight, there was not a cheer so much as a musical vibration in the throats of the crew.

There were many moments such as these which maintained my connection with mythological beginnings, as for instance the wine harvest in the autumn, with all the women of the island washing their legs scrupulously and then treading the grapes with their bare feet until their white legs were purple with the juice of Bacchus; then the tide of history seemed to be rising in the great mould wherein they trod.

There were the things we talked about, too. I can remember a conversation that occupied nearly a week of the long intervals between dark and dawn at sea, when I thought that the crew were going to fight one another, and was certain they would not speak to each other again, because the arguments raised had been so long and violent and rough. Yet the subject would sound almost derisory when one thinks of the great world issues passionately debated by the Foreign Secretary one finds in every family, café or club in the world, because it happened to be the season of mushrooms, and the islanders cared passionately about which mushrooms were the best, where they grew, how they had to be picked and, above all, when picked, how they were to be cooked, and that really was the rub. That was fighting talk and, trivial as it may sound, was a warning sign to me of how near to nature we were.

I was somewhat appalled, then, at how I had agonized over returning to the island and how nearly I had not gone, for I realized that it had not suffered all the horror of change elsewhere and still possessed something recognizably of its beginnings. It gave me too, short as it was, a respite from myself, from a self that was rarely still but inclined always to travel, as if it were dangerous to sit still and to become a husbandman, rather than be a hunter and a searcher.

About Blady, Chapter 6

Ethiopia

In the shock of our meeting, the men of Ethiopia seemed far more surprised by the camels than the sight of foreigners. Indeed the leader of one group came to me and asked, as if pleading a cause of life and death, whether I would allow him to dart underneath the camel from one side to the other.

'But why?' I asked him, amazed.

'Surely', he answered me gravely, 'that would be a most remarkable thing to do.'

I still see him balancing himself on his toes, like a runner, at the side of the camel for at least a minute, eyeing the haughty profile of the animal with great suspicion. Then, summoning all his courage, he launched himself at the camel and ducked quickly between its legs. He might have just killed a lion single-handed, so proud was his stance afterwards and so respectful the praise of his followers.

First Catch Your Eland, Chapter 2

I have [a] memory that is a private symbol for me of all that Ethiopia has represented. This was a banquet at the Imperial Palace. I was one of some thousand guests summoned for a dinner which was part of the ceremony celebrating the twenty-fifth anniversary of the Emperor's return from exile. The dinner was preceded by a frightening display of fireworks in the palace gardens. There is a belief far back in the Ethiopian spirit, as there still is in the minds of men as far apart as the Chinese and the Spaniards, that loud noise and fire will turn evil away. This particular firework display was on such a scale and conducted with such violence that it shattered windows and blew the fuses of the lights in the palace.

When the dinner came, it was as moving as it was impressive because it was like a sacrament of the history of all that the kings and their captains, who are so fast departing from the scene, have represented in the life of man.

Casting around in my mind for adequate parallels at the time, I could think only of Versailles under *Le Roi Soleil*. There was a footman for every two guests at the table. They stood behind their allotted chairs in tail-coats of bright green velvet, faced with gold brocade, lined with gold braid at the hems and glittering with gold buttons. They wore waistcoats, satin knee breeches and silk stockings, all in white, and black patent leather pumps with silver buckles. They served the food with hands covered by white gloves. In between the sophisticated courses, young men and women, each group in the traditional dress of its province, danced the dances and sang the songs of Ethiopia with an energy that at times was Dionysian. The menu was not long but had been superbly chosen. For every European course there was an Ethiopian course to match it. For every European dish, there was a vintage French wine and the European wine list ended appropriately, in the French manner, with the best of dry champagnes served last of all and not spoilt as it is invariably in the English-speaking world by appearing at the beginning.

I did not touch a single European dish or even sip the European wine throughout the whole of the long evening. I drank instead the ancient mead, the tedj which had welcomed me at the beginning of my wartime journey. It was a refined and highly civilized liquid with the sparkle of a golden Hock. Instead of French bread I had injera at its subtle best. Instead of *hors d'oeuvres* and roast turkey I had chicken wat and a very special kind of alecha called minchet abesh. This differs from other alechas only in that the meat is more finely ground, and that instead of the usual ginger it is spiced with all the spices of Ethiopia. I could not imagine an occasion on which a comparison between Ethiopian and European, particularly French, cooking could have been more invidious. Yet as far as I was concerned, the national food and drink, culminating in coffee from the Emperor's own native province of Harrar, more than held its own. If I had any fears that modernization would remove from the life of Ethiopia what is good in the Ethiopian concept of cooking they vanished that night at the banquet given by an Emperor who had done so much to unite old and new into a greater whole in his paradoxical and tumultuous land.

The fact that he remained seated at the head of the main table while all his guests rose and departed, as has been the custom in Ethiopia for 3,000 years, took on a new meaning for me. From the steps leading down from the vast banquet hall I looked out into a deep, black sky, brilliant with stars. The Southern Cross was slanted low, the Milky Way was like the foam of midnight sea away on a reef of star-coral. A great red meteorite was falling briefly but with a blaze like a Roman candle towards a night profound as only Africa, great smith of darkness, can forge. And above the chatter of guests and the noise of cars, I heard the howling of the hyenas as they massed in the hills to begin their scavenging in the city.

How soon these lights were to be extinguished, and how near the darkness between twilight and dawn were, in a symbolic sense, I believe only the Emperor, sitting there with a calm as uncompromised as it was impressive, and I had an inkling. It made both that moment and the memory of it today unbearably poignant. I owed this intuition of the profound unease in his spirit and those closest to him, to a long audience I had with him. I had to leave before the rest of our diminishing band of old English officers, and asked for a moment to apologize and to say goodbye. Despite the pressure of the most exacting ceremonial duties, we talked for some two hours.

As always he spoke in that slow, tentative, shorthand French he had learned from a Jesuit tutor when young. Towards the end he reminded me of a night when the two of us had shared a tent in heavy rain, deep within enemy territory in the remote Gojjam province. Did I remember, he asked me, the outline of the principles of future policy he had given me? For example, no policy of revenge against the Italians who had conquered his country, only a new beginning, reconciliation and co-operation. Also, though the League of Nations had failed him and the world, he was convinced that the future could not be faced without an improved model of a world assembly. He would work with all his faith and devotion for some such new instrument of world order and an overall institution for serving the brotherhood of all men. Lastly, he would invest as much as the resources of a poor country allowed him for the education of the youth of Ethiopia. Education would be his main, his own freely chosen instrument for bringing Ethiopia out of its Richard II state, and transforming it into a truly twentieth-century country. Did I remember? Of course, how could I have forgotten so privileged a glimpse into the mind of someone truly great, who had suffered much and suffered unfairly far beyond the normal allotment of mere flesh and blood, and achieved the only triumph worth achieving in life: that of not being soured by his suffering or even tempted to the ultimate surrender of dignity of spirit into sullen desire for revenge? Yes, of course, I remembered. But did I remember too how, on the rim of the pass leading down to his capital and his restoration, he kept the imposing array of British and South African staff officers waiting and got off his mule to enter a little wayside Coptic chapel? And did I remember how he threw himself flat on the floor at the foot of the Cross and prayed silently, first out of gratitude and then for help to conduct his life and policies on those principles defined on the night of the plunging rain in the tumbled land, hard by the great Blue Nile gorges? Yes, I remembered all that and more, and especially the tears streaming down his cheeks as he stood up again and walked out of the chapel towards the dusty, winding road he now had to take and said, 'Excusez-nous. Pour le moment nous étions trop émus.'

Well, for twenty-five years, for a whole generation, he had kept faith with that moment and those principles, as well as one ruler could in a world even less principled than the one that had overthrown him. And the result? He paused, and those dark eyes of his were darker still with their unflinching perception of a new turn of the screw of reality, before he observed that the United Nations had failed in a far subtler way than the League of Nations. It had become the main instrument for defeating the purpose and spirit for which it was created. The education of the young was recoiling against him and undermining all he had tried to do, and could well be the undoing of his country. Only the policy towards the Italians had succeeded beyond his expectations, and that perhaps contained the most important lesson of all. So please, he begged would I come and see him whenever I could, for he was an increasingly lonely old man and needed the affection and the contact of those who knew and loved him, if he were not to lose, lion heart and all, and fail.

Accordingly I went to see him three times more and each time the mood was more sombre, but the resolution intact and the spirit still unembittered, as I am certain it was even when the men who are now in power and whom he raised in estate, strangled him, shot all his male relations and imprisoned their wives and daughters. Ill, half-famished, stricken in heart as they are, they have to take turns standing in their cells so that others can lie down and sleep while the men who did all this continue to sit in judgement on others, unchallenged at the United Nations in New York. But all this and more too I know will be rediscovered and remembered when the darkness, of which that last moment at the end of a great banquet was symbolic, is lifted and the new morning comes. He will be there, borne along in some chair of time itself, when those who killed him and so much else are blown away in the red dust of Africa.

First Catch Your Eland, Chapter 2

Russia

The Russian genius more than any other flourished most when it was free to move on and expand in its native land.

Journey Into Russia, Chapter 3

I thought . . . how Russia is fundamentally a 'marathon' country. It is not the short-distance sprints, the egg-and-spoon and three-legged races of life that catch the national imagination, but the impossible long-distance obstacle race with hope of victory against impossible odds.

Journey Into Russia, Chapter 14

The German, like the earlier Prussian model, had its origin in the thrust of a teeming people outwards. The Russian has its origin in a pull inward towards the interior of this vast, empty country . . . This too explains why Russia has always been so formidable in defence of itself. Hitler said he went 'the way fate had pointed him like a man walking in his sleep'. From what I had seen of the Soviet Union its rulers went their way like people who never slept at all.

Journey Into Russia, Chapter 13

'The East is to us what the West was to the Americans,' a Russian writer had told me in Moscow. 'They used to say, "Go West." We say, "Go East." '

Journey Into Russia, Chapter 13

Russians, I found, were at their best when travelling. Physically and mentally they are people still on a journey and so journeys release them from complex reserves and fears of all kinds and set them talking naturally and openly.

Journey Into Russia, Chapter 3

In the Soviet Union the train is not only a vital element in the country's communications but also a thing of wonder in the popular imagination and closely linked to the national faith in the machine and the immaculate conception of the railway.

Journey Into Russia, Chapter 13

It was my first encounter with what I believe is one of the most typical characteristics of the Russians. They are not a smiling people. With them the smile is generally only a preliminary to laughter and this perhaps more than anything else gives them their reputation for melancholy. The nuances of feeling for which the Western world uses the smile are either unknown to them or provided for in other ways. Indeed later I gathered from my Russian friends that they find our frequent use of the smile rather tiresome and meaningless.

Journey Into Russia, Chapter 1

I had been long enough in the Soviet Union to accept the discipline of prolonged states of unknowing. It is hard for Europeans and Americans to accept that there occasions when one just cannot know. We are so accustomed to our condition of all-knowingness that the moment we find ourselves cut off from our normal sources of supply we rush to fill in the blank spaces with our hopes, fears, suspicions and desires.

Journey Into Russia, Chapter 13

One of the most depressing aspects of Russian history is the total absence of the peaceful processes of evolution.

Journey Into Russia, Chapter 3

Lenin was God and the Party his one and only Church.

Journey Into Russia, Chapter 4

The Soviet state may build no churches but it does build many kinds of 'temples'. Factories, railway stations, Party and administrative buildings, offices of economics and state planning organizations, and other institutions of the system . . . have all suffered an inflation of form in no way concerned with their functions but derived purely from the unemployed religious energies of a people who are naturally deeply religious and yet denied any legitimate religious expression.

Journey Into Russia, Chapter 7

The picture the Italian writer Ignazio Silone painted was by no means an unfamiliar one. It was a rendering by an artist of great integrity and experience of the essential landscape of the intellectual idealism of my own youth which turned to communism and Russia as pilot schemes for the establishment of a new heaven on earth. It was the most poignant of reminders for me of the time when I had first come to London from Africa as a young writer and found myself spiritually completely isolated from contemporaries I loved by the fact that I could take no comfort whatsoever from their revolutionary approach to the problems of life and society of which Russia was the outstanding contemporary example, nor indeed see any cause for confidence in communism anywhere else as an instrument for the redemption of man and his societies. I remember how deeply I had felt this division between myself and my friends. Indeed there was a moment when I was the only one among the wide circle of young artists and writers who were my friends, who was not a communist, in spite of the fact that I marched in protest as they did with the unemployed miners in London. In this kind of isolation I was inspired to write my first book, *In a Province*. It was my first attempt at a testament of a faith which I hold to this day and which had to reject communism and revolution, no matter how great my own abhorrence of the obvious inadequacies and injustice of the life of this desperate time, and to turn groping towards some concept of wholeness of the human spirit as the only way of preventing men from forever being mere prisoners of an endless chain of action and reaction – a wholeness which would deny as scrupulously those who made revolutions as those who gave cause to them.

Journey Into Russia, 'Introduction'

The Russians are naturally a communal people because they are basically a primitive people: and primitive man is naturally collective.

Journey Into Russia, Chapter 15

I realized as never before that what loosely we call 'communism' is a state of mind long before it emerges into the world as dialectical materialism. Moreover it is a state of mind which obsesses people who have never even heard of Marx, Engels or Lenin and it can obsess many people who are fanatically opposed to the political communism of either Russia or China. As the French say, 'All men tend to become the thing they oppose.' Until we have all recognized this state of mind and its causes we shall never know properly how to deal with its secondary manifestations in our societies or in international politics. It is the existence of this state of mind which makes Russia dangerous, not Russia herself. What Russia is does not imperil us. But what does imperil us is what the world through the predispositions induced by this state imagines Russia to be. This fantasy can go so deep that it makes irrelevant all the contradictions, paradoxes, inconsistencies of its ideological application in society. All these can be freely exposed. Man can lie and deceive quite openly as the expediency of the moment demands because deeply there is the one predominant purpose of a highly charged and polarized mind which remains unchanged. For this reason communism as a social or political philosophy makes no sense to me. But conceived as abnormal psychology it is full of a sombre meaning.

Journey Into Russia, Chapter 7

Although the Bolshevik ideal of human society presupposed, for instance, a very advanced form of industrialization, Russia was the least industrialized great nation of the West. It was psychologically in a sense naked and unarmed to resist the ideology to which it was subjected and which increasingly made it material for one of the grimmest processes of experimentation in human history amounting to this day to a form of sociological vivisection.

Journey Into Russia, 'Introduction'

In general the state has abolished private property as evil and claims that since all belongs to the people through the state, by doing this it has dealt evil itself a mortal blow. But I have never been in a country where embezzlement, black-marketeering, bribery, corruption and stealing from the state were such a feature of the daily news.

Journey Into Russia, Chapter 15

It is the internal battle in Russia which seems to me to be most significant and likely to increase in scale and intensity as in the emergent Africa. It is essentially a struggle of men who want to live individually and specifically rather than collectively and generally. This for me is the underlying meaning of the conflict raging in Russia between the intellectual and artistic worlds and the state. It is the meaning, too, of the battle in Africa between tribal authority and the new educated Africans and explains the hatred of the new generation of Africans for their chiefs and tribal traditions who, together, claim to be able to rule over and think for the tribe. It is a battle which once joined has to be fought to the end for there can never be any return to a state of collective innocence. It is a battle, moreover, which only can be legitimately fought from within by those whose lives are committed to the consequences. I have no doubt that we have seen truly launched in the Soviet Union the struggle of Russian man, as distinct from the Russian people, to make the spirit of his nation contemporary as his country already is, technologically. Meanwhile it would be the most tragic of all ironies if we, under pressure from the extraordinary illusions and obsessions of our own fellow-travellers, assumed the shackles of mind and system which the young in Russia and Africa are struggling so hard to cast off. It would be, too, a betrayal of the Europeanism so desperately at bay in Russia. We can only prove an effective ally of this not by external interference but by giving full recognition of the difficulties of the task and by evolving what is best in our common European and Western selves.

Journey Into Russia, Chapter 15

'Incidentally,' I asked the teachers who assembled to see me off, 'what do you do about teaching your left-handed children?'

They looked dumbfounded until one of the Russians said brusquely: 'We have no left-handed children here.'

Journey Into Russia, Chapter 4

At a large experimental farm I visited I had an even greater success story told to me. The farm was lavishly equipped. The director himself showed us round and soon proved himself to be a dogged doctrinaire untroubled by saving doubts of any kind. His great speciality was artificial insemination. Even though he had the bulls (whose seed he disseminated by helicopter and plane far and wide all over Siberia), standing in sheds next door to his cows, he insisted on the cows being artificially inseminated too. The suggestion that his cows and bulls might be happier if allowed to procreate the natural way made the grey eyes behind his brass-rimmed glasses glitter. What had happiness to do with it? he asked. Hammering the desk with his fist he reiterated 'artificial insemination was best for both bulls and cows'. Clearly 'cows and bulls' were merely pawns in a master image of his philosophy of life. He had the typical revolutionary's mistrust of what was natural. Nature, for them, is a source of power but so savage that it has to be dominated without concession by man and his ideas.

Did I realize, he asked, that by artificial insemination they even got more twins than the 'other way'?

As a farmer myself I have a great respect for the value of artificial insemination but the value is relative and nothing we know of its consequences justifies us in making it the universal absolute.

'But do you think it is good for cows to have twins?' I asked because many experienced breeders in my world believe it is not.

'A good thing?' he exclaimed as if his senses were failing him. 'Of course it is a good thing! Anything that makes an animal produce more is a good thing.'

And there we were back in Soviet fundamentals: production and more production from the earth, the animal and the peasant. My imagination boggled at what the chairman's reaction would have been to the Zen proposition of 'Action through inaction'.

Journey Into Russia, Chapter 14

The circus has a permanent home in all the major cities of the Soviet Union and in the blue-prints of the new towns springing up all over the country a circus building too is included. To a person like myself who knew circuses only in their itinerant forms of great bell tents and marquees piled in painted caravans drawn creakingly along country roads and lanes by the placid and wrinkled pachyderms of India and Burma, some of these buildings seemed almost too good to be true. At Rostov-on-Don, for instance, the circus building with its front of soaring Corinthian columns and classical gable all patiently reconstructed after the destruction of the town by Hitler's hordes, has really to be seen to be believed. Inside it has more glittering tiers than a Hollywood wedding cake. Tier upon dazzling tier rise to a vast domed top, and boxes each lined with rich red velvet and finished off in curved cream and gold balconies festooned in plaster of Paris flowers, fruit and figurines *à la troisième empire*, mount above them. The circus itself, the symbolism of tight-rope and flying trapeze, the pantomime of harlequin and clown, the dogs, horses and wild animals finding meaning in submission to the will and spirit of man, were all presented with a lavish abandon, a zest for danger and a reckless disregard of the norms of chance and safety that seemed to come straight out of antiquity. Over and over again I was to feel that I was witnessing the continuation of a tradition that had been founded by gladiators and tempered in the hungry arenas and implacable amphitheatres of Byzantium and Rome. The response of the toil-worn crowds in their shabby clothes added to that impression. Sealed off by their system for some generations from the outside world as was the ancient world by its ignorance, they would look, their faces naked with wonder, at the appearance in the ring of the lions, apes, leopards, hippopotamuses and pythons. So living a bond existed between spectators and performers that the latter seemed spurred to ever more exacting and dangerous demands on their nerve and skill. I saw a beautiful young Armenian girl after taking what seemed to me far more than legitimate liberties with a trapeze, so fired by the response of the crowd, that she went further still. Her attendants produced an enormous black eagle which might have been the model of the bird one sees in Renaissance pictures feeding on the liver of Prometheus bound to his rock on Elbruz. Dark as one of Macbeth's midnight hags this giant bird was unhooded and placed on the top of two bars of a trapeze without being tied or secured to it in any way. It sat there swaying, balancing itself with its wings outstretched and its eyes green and hard as rhinestones with angry apprehension above a beak sharp as a Saracen's scimitar, staring through the limelight at the tiers of gaping human faces around and above it. Its talons were so long that they seemed to go twice round the bar of the trapeze and were great enough to have carried off many a lamb to its native cliff top in the mountains of Armenia. However this slender young girl seizing the lower bar of the trapeze in one hand then had herself hoisted about a hundred feet above the ring. There she began to swing high and fast from one side of the dome to the other. By this time all lights were out except a solitary spotlight kept directed on the eagle and the girl, see-sawing violently through what now looked like empty and unsupported space. The eagle's wings were stretched wider, trembling like a tuning fork. It looked as if at any moment it might fly off and attack the slight, sequined figure of the girl who was provoking it from below. From time to time in fact the two of them swung up and down so fast that it looked as if the eagle had her in its talons and was carrying her off into the night. But she herself seemed totally impervious to any sense of danger. At the climax she went through a terrifying series of turns and aerobatics on the trapeze until finally she was left hanging by the toes of one foot from the lowest bar, zooming like a swallow through space, her arms stretched out and smiling with a strange ecstatic expression on her young face. Meanwhile the eagle looked down on her, growing ever blacker, angrier and more frenzied as if he were the earthbound one and she had the freedom of gravity and wings. There before our eyes, so high up above the sawdust of the ring with not a net spread out below to break the impact should she fall, it all turned into a strange and moving kind of heraldry.

Journey Into Russia, Chapter 2

I believe the French Revolution is not over yet and that events in France since the Encyclopaedists only make sense when seen as a process of change in the French spirit with which they have not yet come to terms. Lincoln, Sherman, Lee, Stonewall Jackson are all dead and the fighting ended yet I do not think the Civil War in America is by any means over. But the very remarkable thing about the revolution in Russia is that to me it does seem to be over and to such an extent that the imaginations and emotions of the young now are rather bored by it.

Journey Into Russia, Chapter 15

Tikhomirov wrote in 1888: 'The Greater Russian cannot imagine life outside his society, to betray his peasant or village commune is for him the unpardonable sin, to go against it is wrong.' The Ukrainian on the other hand says: 'What belongs to all belongs to the devil.' The Greater Russian deduces his idea of his rights from the idea of public welfare whereas the Ukrainian takes as his starting point the exigencies of his individual rights. No wonder Stalin's attempt to impose collective farming was so desperately resisted in the Ukraine . . . Stalin himself lifted a corner of the tragic curtain one night to Churchill in Moscow during the war.

'Tell me,' Churchill had asked, 'have the stresses of this war been as bad to you personally as carrying through the policy of the collective farms?'

'Oh no!' Stalin answered. 'That was a terrible struggle. It was fearful. It lasted four years. But it was absolutely necessary for Russia if we were to avoid periodic famines.'

He continued his description until Churchill 'sustained a strong impression of millions of men and women having been blotted out or displaced for ever'.

Journey Into Russia, Chapter 12

Conversation was one of the things I enjoyed most in Russia and I enjoyed it as I enjoy conversation with my African countrymen. No flights of fancy were barred. It was with them as with many primitive people I know: the word is still newborn and glistening, full of wonder and capacity for increase. The Russians, like the Africans, seemed to have a natural 'aristocracy' of the word.

Journey Into Russia, Chapter 14

One of the paradoxes that gave me much trouble on my journey was the contrast between the delicacy, tenderness and sensitivity that I was aware of in conversation with the Russians I came to know best; and the total absence of these qualities in the world they were making for themselves.

Journey Into Russia, Chapter 11

'Women and men', my Russian friends had told me time and again, 'are truly equal only in Russia. Only here do they get equal opportunity of work and equal pay for equal work.' But I remembered Blake's 'one law for the lion and the ox is oppression'. In practice it seemed to me that the women, whose nature also commits them to child-bearing, worked far harder than the men in Russia.

Journey Into Russia, Chapter 13

The peasant in Russia has never been honoured by the state nor given the share to which his courage, endurance and labour has entitled him. Even those who understood him best and were designed to love him most, like Peter the Great, found it convenient to exploit and betray him . . . The irony is all the greater when one considered that the peasants made the revolution. The revolution was already accomplished by the peasants and their soldier offspring when Lenin and his small band of professionals took it over. Yet their first priority was to reject the peasant. Lenin may have been a kindly person but he had no faith in or love of humanity . . . This is one of the great difference between China and Russia. One of the first principles of Mao-Tse-tung's revolution was to base it on the peasant and for this, among other reasons, I believe the revolution in China could prove ultimately more creative than the Russian one.

Journey Into Russia, Chapter 13

Georgians and Irish were the only people who ever fully realized the positive creative uses of irresponsibility. They refused to take their conquest and conquerors seriously. They would fight their invaders savagely not for any principle but out of sheer love of life.

Journey Into Russia, Chapter 6

I was to find that all the minority peoples who have been bound to Russia either as an integral part of the Soviet Union, or as satellites, had evolved techniques of their own for denying their conquerors. What seemed to me most important was that within the limits of their own temperament and national character all these peoples, Bulgars, Romanians, Czechs, Hungarians, Poles, Latvians, Moldavians, Estonians and even the Ukrainians of little Russia, have in all the years of invasion and persecution acquired techniques for preventing conquest and political domination from penetrating their own spirit or, as it were, reaching their individual souls.

Journey Into Russia, Chapter 6

I read articles written by military 'experts' who all gave the impression that Russia, save for gallant Czech, Romanian and Yugoslav communist partisans, fought and won the war alone. We were scarcely mentioned. It is striking how a society which is continually exhorting the objective force and inevitability of history can show no concern whatsoever for the need of an objective presentation and interpretation of that history.

Journey Into Russia, Chapter 12

On my journey I was amazed continually how quickly persons in authority would go into committee with subordinates when an unfamiliar problem confronted them ... I think it is this which mainly distinguishes Russian totalitarianism from that of the Fascist dictators, even from that of Stalin. Contemporary Russian totalitarianism is not dictatorial. Somewhere deeply ingrained in the people there is an imperious pattern and belief in consultation which the totalitarian cannot ignore.

Journey Into Russia, Chapter 5

It seemed to me that in Russia the values of the individual (not of course of the state) are those of the ancient Christian and primitive European Russia which Lenin and Stalin thought to have destroyed for ever. I do not mean to imply that the Russians are 'pro-European', and that this is a political phenomenon. Rather it is a reawakening of an instinctive feeling of kinship, and a sharpening of the awareness of belonging, by right of birth, to the great complex of the European spirit.

Journey Into Russia, Chapter 15

Pasternak was the first to break through the sound barrier between Russia and the outside world ... His achievement was all the greater, too, because it was a reluctant achievement. If he were the first Soviet saint and martyr (as the new Russian writers regard him), his saintliness was made pure and capable of true increase by its reluctance. This element of reluctance is of the very quintessence of the matter, for the saint or martyr who seeks his fate with eagerness as a deliberate policy of his spirit never rings true. There is an abnormality in it which reduces the power of the example to influence and heal. Only those who grow into their role and reluctantly bear their bitter fruit (as, for instance, Thomas More) can change the destiny of the human spirit. This I believe Pasternak did and because of him Russia will never be the same again.

Journey Into Russia, Chapter 15

Spain

At a distance the capital had a clear centre which had a castle-like form and proved to have been the heart of what local legend told was the first Phoenician-Iberian settlement. Of course there were traces of all sorts of Mediterranean cultures, with the Roman era dominant, but there was evidence of the Moorish epoch in buildings and streets, a flash of garden here and a fountain there, but most of all in the genes of its inhabitants. We encountered faces that might have come out of *A Thousand and One Nights*, as well as of the dunes of the Sahara and the Atlas Mountains, striking, vivid faces, eyes full of Moorish lamplight, and noses of the men who brought mathematics, gardens, tapestries and carpets and all manner of things harsh and ruthless as the Bedouin blood of their origin demanded, but also refinements and a central Asian, knightly and heraldic state of mind, in the mould of the myth grown around Saladin.

About Blady, Chapter 7

I was so refreshed by morning that I dressed early, and as I was shaving I became aware of strange kinds of swishing sounds coming from the corridor. The sounds were fairly irregular and of a kind that I had never heard before but felt appropriate and singularly domestic. I could not place it until I opened the door of my room and, as I looked up and down the corridor, to the left and right of me there were silks of the most unusual and beautiful colours spread out on the carpets of the corridor and, leaning over them, almost in the attitude of Muslims in prayer, with expressions of singular reverence were the four bullfighters I had briefly seen the day before.

[139]

They took no notice of the opening of my door and me standing beside it, and I soon realized that they were not at prayer but bent over the biggest domestic irons I had ever seen, and obviously pressing the cloaks they were going to wear in battle with the bulls that day. The impression of men engaged in something special, if not sacred and close to prayer, remained.

About Blady, Chapter 7

I had never been to a bullfight before, though like everyone else in the Western world I had read and talked and thought about them a great deal, and I had come to this bullfight reluctantly because, for all its significance in what it tells one about the human being's need for some abiding ritual in transforming the dark and monstrous patterns of forces he has still unresolved within himself, I had no taste for it and on my own I would not have gone. But I felt that all the things in my life which had brought me to that place, at that time, demanded that I should see it whole and not just savour the bits that I thought I would like of the experience.

Once in the ring itself, without the sort of shoving and jostling one is accustomed to in the theatre world of the West, let alone so-called sporting occasions, the compound of impressions that I have described was instantly dissolved in the glitter of dress and colours and sounds and excitements of all sorts that came from what was the largest theatre I have ever entered. I say 'theatre' because I knew instantly that it was theatre of the most ancient kind we had come to see, a vastly orchestrated form of a classical first night of a play by a great dramatist . . .

It was, of course, a perfect ring, covered with the yellowest of sand, and everywhere one looked there were human faces staring at the gates where the uniformed servants of the theatre stood to open the doors and gateways, and guard the dark passages that led to the place where the men and the horses and, above all, the bull were being prepared for their entrance.

I thought of those passages between that place and us all sitting there in the early afternoon light of the Mediterranean sun, as a labyrinthine way, and the bull as the monster which Theseus had set out from Athens to Crete to kill, so that he could free Ariadne from the tyranny of the night of life. This connection with the myth was suddenly made, but of course it must have undergone a long preparation in my journey through the world of Greek mythology and legend, which started on that morning when I opened a gift from my father and found a book, especially composed for children, on the myths and legends of Greece.

In this way many of the reservations I had about participating in the bullfight were abolished, and it became part of a process of progression. That it was a ring in itself helped, because all rings possess instant qualities of whatever it was that originally made the circle magic. The greatest example of this was already in my mind because it came from Provence, whose earth was like Spanish earth and had that mysterious mix of Mediterranean Europe and Mediterranean Africa that made me feel so much at home in it. Provence, too, had its own way of acting out this drama of man's inborn role of providing male armour for feminine love, defending and rescuing the feminine from the monster in itself.

There were at least two schools of thought in the Mediterranean Latin world of how the man and the bull theme had to be orchestrated. For one school it was obviously connected, as I had just made my own connection, with the labyrinth in Crete, with Ariadne of the golden thread and Theseus and the great rescue of the youth of Athens from being annually sacrificed to the monster. The other, and the more prominent perhaps, was the Mithraic school that went back to the Roman legions whose god was Mithras who had to sacrifice to the sun, to the god of reason, the bull that was really loved . . .

Suddenly the doors were opened and, although these doors had uniformed footmen it happened so fast that I do not remember seeing any sign of movement from the attendants to tell us what was coming and that was, of course, the bull – moving so fast that the opening and coming seemed almost to be one and the same process.

The change of light and atmosphere and tier upon tier of human faces and strange horses all around him brought him to a standstill. His legs stiffened, the yellow dust spurted around him, and like an animal in a mist he shook his head from side to side and tested his horns and his muscles as if to see whether they were ready to thrust and to throw and to gore, rather as Olympic athletes do when they are trying out their muscles before the pistol shot launches them on their races. He did this and then looked around baffled, which was perhaps one of the most poignant moments of all, because one could not help wondering what horror had put him in such a rage to send him charging into a place, certain that he was called upon to fight and made him so determined to kill. And then he found this vacant tent of the blue of the sky above him, and thousands of human faces directed at him, knowing too well what they expected to be done to him.

Through other doors and openings in the balustrades around him other horses and men, above all the picadors whose task it was to dart him, were insinuated into the ring. Each dart had a pennant in proportion to its size and a bright colour of its own, perhaps not to decorate but to redeem the place of injury in some reminder that, ultimately, all was heraldic.

The course the bullfight followed has so often been seen and described that I have no intention of elaborating on it. Besides, I have not the power or the taste for it.

All that I should say, perhaps, is that as I watched I had no taste for the various ways in which the outraged and inflamed bull was goaded and the padded horses hurled against the wall supporting the crowded circles of spectators and one horse so gored and bleeding that it had to be rushed through a side door in the ring.

The faster and more dangerous the confrontation with the bull became and the more blood there was on the sand and splashed on the walls, and the more violent the movement of picadors and their horses and wilder their charges to inflame the bull, the more I expected at any moment to see whatever shape the drama had, shattered, and chaos take over. But all was so perfectly contained that, although there was a great deal that was ugly and, out of context, would have been inconceivably repulsive, the whole never touched on what one could call un-beauty and even at moments rose to a great beauty as all conformed to the rhythm and measure that came from the lone fighter at the centre of the storm. He was strangely still; his movements hardly ever displaced him, and even when the danger of him being thrown and gored was at its greatest I do not remember him ever being forced into the slightest sidestep. He did it all by distracting the bull's aim with the colour and movement of his cape and just a slight movement of his hips and angle of his body so that the horns missed him by a fraction of the millimetre that was as good as a mile. At that still centre he seemed, if he had to move at all, to do as a ballet dancer might, so that, whatever else the spectacle might have been elsewhere in the ring, there at the centre, at the place where the point had to find the right position for the kill, he did not for a second falter or blur the overriding magnificence if not miraculousness of it all.

All in all it was done, it seemed, not for indulgence of a Roman sensationalism but as an image of how futile it is to deal with the forces that assail us in terms of mere action and reaction, and how, no matter how much more powerful than the original action the reaction becomes, the action beyond it is raised to greater powers and the whole design of conduct and spirit becomes almost a clash of great irresistibles and immovables until they stand locked and bankrupt and in need of something else to take them beyond.

That 'beyond' was in the bullfighter's keeping, and I do not recollect precisely when the moment came, but suddenly he and the bull were alone in the centre of the ring. He had clearly decided that he had – perhaps far more than the call of his duty and gifts demanded of his role in that particular theatre – given the bull an honourable opportunity to prove itself better than he was, within himself; that he had done all that he personally could, short of destroying himself, to honour the power and the dark glory of the monster. For a moment he turned his back on the bull and raised his sword, I should imagine not so much to the crowd as to the lady who had his hat in her keeping. He turned about – but not before I had recognized the face of one of the bullfighters who shared our hostelry. Seated in privilege as we were, I could see his singular face very clearly and at once understood the pre-concentration of spirit which had already begun in that winding medieval corridor of our hostelry. But it had been raised now to something which I found almost unearthly and which passed my own comprehension. It was what the bullfighters call their 'moment of truth'. They have called it this ever since bullfighting began, way back in a very early Cretan moment of Mediterranean history. But one recognized it even in our own day, which blurs so much of reality with its superabundance of unnecessary things and trivialities. It was a moment in which there was to be nothing that was false or spurious or contrived, not for the spectators, for the bull or the man. It had come to what Euclid had called 'the point of it all', or, with mathematical precision, 'that which has no size or magnitude but position'. And that position was to be found in a moment of the greatest possible tensions and, above all, at speed somewhere small and narrow behind the head of the bull as it charged. If he did not find that place the bull would not be killed and the fighter could be dead.

I do not know how many thousands of us were there to witness what followed almost with the speed of lightning but with a grace and rhythm which lightning, however wonderful, never achieves. But since it is true, as everybody knows, that the numbers of people present at any particular event add to the intensity of everyone observing the event and make it a highly personal affair, I do not think I have ever had a moment of brighter and more dazzling attention, without any form of expectation. It was a moment when all the considerations which govern in the here and the now seemed to have become irrelevant and suspended. The bullfighter, slim, broad-shouldered, black below and green-gold above, suddenly stood on tiptoe, elegant and alert and arched like a bow and, just as the bull seemed on the verge of throwing him, his sword vanished into the neck of the bull and the bull fell, and died as it fell.

The bull lay still on his side, his head almost touching the silk of the matador's cape. The thrust had made the point of it all so well that the whole of the sword had gone into the neck of the bull and only the hilt showed above the skin. At that moment the matador was standing with his back to us, so that one could not see his face, but instantly it seemed he had withdrawn the sword, raised his right arm and extended it, sword and all, to the full. It was the antique world's greatest salute of honour with the most moving implication that neither the vanquished nor the victor had any share in whatever there was of praise or blame in the situation; that what had just been accomplished had been accomplished for the god of which they had been merely the instruments and the actors, the priest and the sacrifice, and had reached the point when the sacrament was fulfilled.

About Blady, Chapter 7

The golden fleece, the jewel at the bottom of the distant well, reunion in Ithaca, the promised land on the other side of the great desert, are one and all symbols of the brave new being with which the journeyman who has travelled the whole way with his myth is rewarded.

The Dark Eye in Africa, Part III, 'The Discussion'

Chapter Seven

Human Beings and
their Societies

The questions that have to be answered before the imagination is allowed through are not new but have to be redefined because of their long neglect and the need for answers to be provided in the idiom of our day. For instance, in what does man now find his greatest meaning? Indeed, what is meaning itself for him and where its source? What are the incentives and motivations of his life when they clearly have nothing to do with his struggle for physical survival? What is it in him that compels him, against all reason and all the prescriptions of the law, order and morality, still to do repeatedly what he does not consciously want to do? What is this dark need in the life of the individual and society for tragedy and disaster? Since the two World Wars that have occurred in my own lifetime, disorder and violence have become increasingly common on the world scene. Surely these things are rooted in some undiscovered breach of cosmic law or they would be eminently resistible and would not be allowed to occur? Where indeed does one propose to find an explanation for the long history of human failure? How can one hope to understand this aspect of man and his societies, and comprehend a scene littered with ruins and piled high with dunes of time which mark the places where countless cultures have vanished because men would not look honestly, wholly and steadily into the face of their inadequacies? The answers to none of these questions are available unless one is prepared through profound self-knowledge to relearn the grammar of a forgotten language of self-betrayal, and in so doing the meaning of tragedy and disaster. It is the ineluctable preliminary to our emancipation, especially for those priests and artists who have been subverting themselves and the societies which they are dedicated to preserve. Unless one is honestly prepared to do so, one is warned at this crepuscular immigration post that one had better not cross the frontier.

The Voice of the Thunder, 'The Great Memory'

The Crisis of Meaning

I marvelled more and more how throughout history these inadequacies and fallibilities of spirit, and the inflexibility of both individual and collective awareness towards the calls for renewal of life and not a narrowing but an enlarging of consciousness, would sooner or later draw attention to themselves: their impatience to be expressed in flesh and blood would show itself more and more, not only in distortions of our ways of looking at reality but through afflictions of the human body and in the end, if they were not heeded, a breakdown in the order and coherence of society.

Indeed, in the years between my departure from school and the war, this little experience, coupled with the old interest from childhood in the great plagues and sicknesses of the past, seemed to have become a basic assumption or hypothesis of my attitude to life, so much so that it figured prominently in my first book, written in 1930. I was still in my early twenties and not aware of any outside influence to bring me to the writing of this book. I was only aware that I seemed suddenly presented in my mind with a pattern which I had to obey. The book I am referring to is *In a Province*, and the title came from a quotation in the Bible (Ecclesiastes v.8): 'If thou seest the oppression of the poor, and violent perverting of judgement and justice in a province, marvel not at the matter.'

Significantly, and perhaps with a feeling of being vulnerable and alone in my endeavour, I turned also for support to a French writer who I came across on the French island where I was writing the book, just as I was finishing the story, and I quoted him: 'For the first time in ten thousand years,' he wrote, 'man is to himself totally, and without any semblance of knowledge, a problem. For he no longer knows what he is, and he knows at the same time that he knows not.'

About Blady, Chapter 2

It sometimes would seem that the brightness of our age is an illusion, and that we are living not in the vast cities and palaces of the mind which St Augustine knew so well, but in some lonely outposts at sundown on the fringes of what had once been a certain and forward-moving world. Out there in the darkness there is a horrendous tread and a reverberating thumping on the gate. There is something trying to enter but we are afraid to open the gate because of all the horror we have witnessed in our time. It does not seem to occur to us that all this emptiness, all this evidence of breakdown, all this decline in values, this diminishing awareness and sharpened sense of insecurity despite the obvious proliferation of material security in our lives – that all this might be the messenger or the forerunner of something new, and what is knocking at the door should be invited in.

A Walk with a White Bushman

One would have thought by now that the grave labour unrest everywhere could have testified irrefutably to the fact that its causes are not to be found in what are called inadequate living standards and social insecurity because this unrest and a new, subtler and more lethal kind of feeling of insecurity has grown with geometric progression as living standards have risen and social security increased. I would have thought it obvious by now that what makes not only labour, but societies, churches, doctors, historians and even the least specialized or ordinary human hearts alone with themselves in the silence of night full of a fearful unease, is the fact that there is no discernible meaning for man in what he is asked to do, and no overall and honourable value in the evolution of the society or culture to which he belongs to compensate him for the meaninglessness which affects him in his personal work and condition of being.

The crisis, I believe, is plainly one caused by an almost total loss of meaning, both individually and collectively. The human heart, as history proves, I believe, can endure anything except a state of meaninglessness.

Jung and the Story of Our time, 'Epilogue'

On the morning that Albert Michaeljohn raised his stick twenty-three times to beat David [his young son, accused of stealing a sovereign], by so doing he lengthened the axis of the earth which runs through him as, indeed, it runs through all of us. And by lengthening the axis he slowed down the motion of the earth and so produced such a realignment of cosmic forces that the aboriginal darknesses had been encouraged dangerously to close in on the uttermost outpost of starlight.

The Face Beside the Fire, Chapter 2

For we are none of us right; we do not know ourselves sufficiently. We have not faced up to the fact that we ourselves, not our institutions or stars, are the source of the error, and that until we have dealt with the error in ourselves we cannot deal properly with what is wrong in the world. It is the ineluctable preliminary to our emancipation.

A Walk with a White Bushman

I remember when . . . I sat at dinner beside a man who was said to control one of the great financial empires of the world, and heard him tell how important it was for his organization to keep expanding because the moment it ceased to expand it would lose its dynamic. I wanted to protest and say that this for me was a dynamic of death. This was so great a defiance of the laws of proportion that it could only lead to disaster. There must be a point at which enough was enough. Nothing in the dialogue which followed between us could remove the fact that, at heart, there was a confusion between 'expansion' and 'growth'. They are not the same. They are not even substitutes for each other, because this process of expansion out of control, which the skyline and the sprawl of London suggested that man was caught up in, was death to growth. Indeed, I had no doubt that expansion could only end in the death of growth in terms of a life of increase and wholeness.

About Blady, Chapter 3

Already the numbers are so great that the world scene regarded purely in terms of human survival reveals how fast the earth is losing its capacity to feed the proliferating millions, how fast the atmosphere is running out of air for the millions to breathe and stay alive. Even the life of the sea can no longer multiply at a rate to satisfy this hunger and, far from increasing or even standing still, sees its own forms of life diminishing and about to vanish altogether. It is as if procreation is become anti-creation and constitutes the most formidable attack that has ever been mounted on the totality of nature and the wholeness of man.

More profound and subtle – and far more dangerous – is the peril of men in such numbers that each man is induced to become a number himself and is steadily losing the vital differences on which his integrity as an individual depends, and substituting a kind of common denominatorism of the spirit in areas which were once his own and highly differentiated, enabling him to exorcise conformity and make a contribution uniquely his own to the life of his time.

About Blady, Chapter 3

He remembered his uncle telling him when he was little how the old Boer farmers used to sit all day, calmly and happily, on their stoeps, drinking coffee and smoking their pipes, never a word of bitterness about themselves, content both in their past and their future. And he could not imagine one of that pretentious crowd which filled the eating houses and cinemas of Port Benjamin to suffocation sitting still alone for even half an hour. Their thoughts, the moment they were alone with themselves, would follow a slant just like his own, turning inevitably to the secret sources of their common misery, and thoughts of this kind were just what all wanted to avoid. They clamoured daily for more time, more leisure. Yet the moment they got what they wanted they enslaved themselves to a new precipitation. The rush, the stampede for soporifics began. They fled from themselves, from the reality of their lives, to games, to cinemas and books which lifted them into a world where human beings were miraculously free from the natural consequences of their actions. The gaiety, the cheerfulness of everyone, except perhaps children, seemed to him but a disguised and painted joylessness.

In a Province, Book II, Chapter I

Above all in Xhabbo he had perhaps the greatest expert alive in this radar of meaning, built into every living being, navigating on courses of fire through the life of the dark bush around him, achieving its most comprehensive telegraphic intelligence in what Xhabbo called 'tapping'.

A Far-Off Place, Chapter I

. . . what is most important in human beings and their societies: not their activity, and not ultimately their 'being' alone, but the climate in which both these aspects of living are included.

About Blady, Chapter I

The time had come . . . to change the group approach, to make the collective individual and the universal specific, and to avoid mass solutions and the abstractions of numbers like the plague. Men and their meaning were in danger of drowning in a flood of the collectivism of numbers greater than the world had ever experienced, and all creation depended now on the speed with which men could be detached from it, breaking it up by being their own unique selves. Something along these lines, he thought, would make one a modern man. Did François and Lammie [his mother] realize that so far there had only been one truly modern man, and he had been crucified two thousand years ago?

A Far-Off Place, Chapter 6

I am frequently struck by the numbers of individuals who no longer feel contained in their national and social context. Already there seems to me to be in existence a new kind of human being who is living ahead of the meaning of our time, knowing only that meaning has to be lived before it can be known, and that every step of the exacting journey has to be accomplished before new being can be discovered. Already in the world there are many individuals who are so strongly attacked by this need of contemporary reality that they experience the inadequacies of their communities as a sickness of their own physical being. I know Germans who have died purely of the sickness of the pre-war German spirit. I know Frenchmen today who are sick to death of the plague of rational materialism of France. I knew many Japanese who lost the will to live because of the refusal of their nation to acknowledge the urge to new individual being in its midst. I know many of my own countrymen too who are gravely ill in the same way. They ail and die because the spirit of man is everlastingly aboriginal and, like the Australian blackamoor, cannot do without its 'walk-abouts' from the arrested moments of its conscious self into the greater meanings which surround it. The spirit of man is Bedouin, and only death possesses the right to bring to an end the journey to which his myth provokes him.

The Dark Eye in Africa, Part III, 'The Discussion'

In most lives, and particularly in a life such as mine, points of departure inevitably are arbitrary, so are ends, indeed, only of other beginnings. This end, too, which comes down like a curtain upon us is the end only of that search which brings a man to the threshold of his private and personal task, the task that life demands of him day and night in his blood: to live with love out of love; to live the vision beyond reason or time which draws him from the centre of his being . . . To serve this vision, to protect it against all plausible substitutes, reasonable approximations and coward compromises is still, I believe, the knightly duty of contemporary man. If he shirks it I believe he shall never know inner peace. If a man accepts the challenge, however, even if his vision is never confirmed . . . in flesh and blood, but forever beckons him in a quicksilver reflection of a cause beyond himself, then he has only to remain steadfast in pursuit of it and his life will achieve . . . something which is greater than happiness and unhappiness: and that is meaning.

Flamingo Feather, Chapter 18

History

One of the most deceptive of popular half-truths is the saying that history repeats itself. Only unredeemed, unrecognized, misunderstood history, I believe, repeats itself, and remains a dark, negative and dangerous dominant on the scene of human affairs.

The Voice of the Thunder, 'The Great Memory'

All men are inclined to see history only in part and in terms of their own brief and brittle measure of life. Only the truly inspired among them know how its processes are unbroken; how it maintains a continuity that stretches inviolate from the first living cell of creation to link our own butterfly ration of reality with all the infinite immensity of what is still to come.

First Catch Your Eland, Chapter 5

One of the most destructive characteristics of the emerging societies of the contemporary world is their deliberate conscious falsification and invention of histories to suit immediate political purpose. No man is free to commit himself to an honest future until he has first been honest about the past. Only the truth can make men free of their own history.

Journey Into Russia, Chapter 12

History is not just a progression of ascertainable cause and effect. It is not a result of what actually happens in life or what is true in demonstrable fact, but rather of what men imagine to have been true or to have happened. It moves without rhythm or logic, and after long periods of apparent stagnation leaps suddenly, melo-dramatically and often disastrously into great unknown areas of life.

The Hunter and the Whale, Chapter 13

History has its own metabolism. At its deepest levels it is inde-pendent of the denials and manipulations to which nations seek, periodically, to subject it to temporary ends and I feared that without access to this submerged idiom I would be unable to interpret the meaning of the contemporary scene.

Journey Into Russia, Chapter 1

There seemed to be an underworld of history filled with forces far more powerful than the superficial ones that history professed to serve. Until this world was brought out into the light of day and recognized and understood, I believed that an amply discredited pattern of self-inflicted death and disaster would continue to reiterate itself and dominate the human scene. I had even coined a name for it and called it the 'mythological dominant of history'.

Jung and the Story of Our Time, 'The Time and the Space'

Jung had a great sense of history. He believed profoundly in teaching history, but again, as with everything that Jung conceived, he felt it had to be done in a contemporary way. For him history was transformed from the school level to the story of the soul of man. That was the only history that ultimately mattered to him, yet today this important dimension of history seems to matter less and less. He was trying to bring the human spirit back into contact with history before it was too late. He was dismayed by the loss of soul and meaning already caused by this loss of history. All around him in Europe he saw this loss of soul and meaning orchestrating, and he wanted to stop it because he saw it as the way to catastrophe.

A Walk with a White Bushman

History, it appears to me, even when it seems to be exclusively a matter of crude warfare over physical frontiers, ultimately is shown to have been a confused question of extending the marches of life into new, and inadequately understood, meaning. It is a record of an unending battle to make man obedient to his own greater awareness. History shows that, no matter how obstinate and adroit man's resistance, ultimately all are forced to obey this new meaning or to be submerged.

Introduction to William Plomer, *Turbott Wolfe*

History is always, individually or collectively, a confrontation of the spirit of man with a choice.

Journey Into Russia, Chapter 15

The Great and Little Memory

Memory is a ripple that continues to radiate over the surface of a pond long after the stone which caused it has come to rest on the bottom. Does it resemble the reality as little as the ripples do the stone? Ah, there you have it. Memory is not an historian. It is a poet, a poet with many prejudices. It serves its prejudices better than the verity.

In a Province, Book II, Chapter 5

Young as I was, and although knowing that I had never been in that world before, I was increasingly convinced from thereon that it was my kind of world. It was my first encounter with a dimension of memory which has haunted me all my life – a phenomenon which one knows perhaps best as a child, loses in the process of being educated into the here and now which is our brief, provisional home, and only tends to recover as one enters the last of our allotment of seasons. It is an overarching memory which does not belong to man so much as to life itself, and no matter how much one may forget and ignore it, it never forgets or ignores whatever form of being is invested with life. It is a memory of all the life that has ever been; it is imparted to one through natural instinct and feeling, and yet it is also full of premonition of the future, and more. For my part, I can only say that to the extent to which I had become aware of it through the play of instinct and feeling in myself and intimations of dreams and images coming to me unsolicited and of their own accord – strong, real and often contradictory to all that the world and time surrounding me demanded – it remained some-where and somehow in supreme command of all that I possessed of meaning. I came to call it to myself the Great Memory.

When one took the span of the four score and ten years which the psalmist prescribes as our maximum allotment and compared it with this vast input of true and proved experience recorded in this long history of life even before the Word, it shrank to the littlest of a little. I was, of course, totally incapable of putting any of this in words at the time, but am certain I am expressing some of the impact of my first experience of the desert, and the sense of the innermost awakening, clear and imperative as a call of reveille on a trumpet at first light summoning its cavalry out of a dream of sleep.

The Voice of the Thunder, 'The Little Memory'

I spoke to a distinguished geologist who had worked for many years in the Kalahari and who had even, briefly, known my mother when she herself had been drawn to the Kalahari and found water where people said no water could ever be found, and had established herself at the very Stilton [the strangely named plot of land purchased by his father on the South-Western fringe of the Kalahari] where my own physical experience of the desert began. I asked this geologist in what sort of timescale people like myself who love the Kalahari had to think of it. From what the rocks, the sands and all those deep and dry watercourses told him, he said, it could be no less than one thousand million years, which I am certain is barely a step in the march of creation. So, somewhere, waiting to be unlocked in that memory, I am certain, is a pattern of life that will transcend and transfigure this arid and desperate moment of time wherein we live, and the first move towards that unlocking, I believe, is to absorb the horror of the story of what we have all done to the first man of Africa and the horror of what we are doing now to the plants and the animals that for one thousand million years at least were safe and multiplying in his and the desert's keeping. Never has it been so important and urgent, if human life on earth is not to fail the purpose which created it and gives it meaning, to begin again its ancient quest of seeking to remember what remembers us. It is because of my own brief experience of the power and the glory of this memory made manifest in the desert that I am certain, in its own time and after its own fashion, it will not allow us to fail, even if that means inflicting on us, as it has so often had to do in the past, the disaster we need to heed.

The Voice of the Thunder, 'The Little Memory'

I have learned from the natural peoples of Africa that there is in fact a positive aspect to 'forgetting'. A memory cultivated out of honour for the quality rather than the quality of human experience will

retain all that necessary to make it a compass for man in his search
for truth on his zig-zag passage through life.

Yet Being Someone Other, Chapter 3

Knowledge and Theories

We know so much intellectually that we are in danger of becoming
prisoners of our own knowledge.

The Creative Pattern in Primitive Africa, Eranos Lectures

Mopani realized more and more how a major source of corruption
in men was their excessive love of the power of ideas – a love so
excessive that they did not hesitate to kill and murder one another
for them.

A Far-Off Place, Chapter 15

It's the system, always the system, and yet again the system, for
you. You are always beating your wings against the system. I'm sick
of hearing about the system. The system is only an approximation,
a reflection of the rules that govern the little acts of each one of us.
Only it's an approximation so big that if you place all the emphasis
on it, the individual loses the sense of the responsibility for his little
share in it. It seems to me fatal. The starting and finishing-point is
in the heart of each man. At one time the responsibility for action
was placed on the individual, and I think the world was relatively a
good deal happier. But today if a man is a thief or a murderer, we
no longer blame the man, we blame his environment. If a man is
poor and hasn't enough to eat, we don't say that he has been lazy
or has made no consistent effort to better himself, we blame the
system. If a man rapes a woman or walks down the street and opens
his fly to a crowd, we don't blame his lack of self-control; we say,
'What can you expect of a system which forces such terrible sex
taboos on us?' It's always the system. Even scientists and philosophers have rushed in to help people like you. Man, they tell you, is
only a machine; put him in a certain environment and he must react
in a definite and calculable way. He cannot help himself, only his

conditioned reflexes can. And what conditions these reflexes? Environment. Oh, yes! The ground has been well ploughed! You have all the rationalization for your attacks on the system that you can want. Only man is losing the sense of his integrity, the sense of his responsibility to himself. He is already, for you, someone who can be improved merely by increasing his income. Everyone wants to improve the system under which he lives and not himself, and as he, or a collection of people like him, makes the system, it all ends in no improvement, no responsibility.

In a Province, Book III, Chapter 6

There is no hatred as great as that which springs from the love of perfection. The cunning with which hatred of the muddled, incalcitrant human being is concealed in an abstract love of humanity, seemed to me . . . so inventive that it defied general detection.

Yet Being Someone Other, Chapter 4

His claim to be in love with the future . . . did not convince me. Loving the future can be a way of hating the present. True love is love of the difficult and unlovable, both here and now. There are two main sources of corruption in life: the corruption caused by power and the corruption caused by suffering. We all recognize and condemn the corruption caused by power, but we tend to excuse the corruption caused by suffering which is so clearly condemned by the full implication of the New Testament admonition to 'turn the other cheek'. The whole meaning of life seems to dwell in the evolution of a man proof against these two corruptions.

Journey Into Russia, Chapter 8

The world I grew up in believed that change and development in life are part of a continuous process of cause and effect, minutely and patiently sustained throughout the millenniums. With the exception of the initial act of creation (which as every good Afrikaner boy knew was accomplished with such vigour that it took only six days to pass from chaos to fig leaves and Adam), the evolution of life on earth was considered to be a slow, steady and ultimately demonstrable process. No sooner did I begin to read history, however, than I began to have my doubts. Human society and living beings, it seemed to me, ought to be excluded from so calm and rational a view. The whole of human development, far from having been a product of steady evolution, seemed subject to only partially explicable and almost invariably violent mutations. Entire cultures and groups of individuals appeared imprisoned for centuries in a static shape which they endured with long-suffering indifference, and then suddenly, for no demonstrable cause, became susceptible to drastic changes and wild surges of development. It was as if the movement of life throughout the ages was not a Darwinian caterpillar but a startled kangaroo, going out towards the future in a series of unpredictable hops, stops, skips and bounds.

The Lost World of the Kalahari, Chapter 4

Democracy

Where will we find a government in the modern world, or even a committee, however select, capable of dealing with events in their beginnings? I would say, for instance, that the gravest threat to democracy is precisely the incapacity to deal with incipient events: this is unfortunate, because at its point of origin the gravest event has a certain plastic quality which makes it relatively amenable. Soon, however, events acquire through neglect a twisted character and a vengeful will of their own, as if they have discovered that the world will take them seriously only when they become considerable pressures. So they become explosive. In my own short life in Europe, the Far East, and Africa, I had seen some wonderful, innocent possibilities abandoned on the doorstep of life and allowed to grow into ugly, delinquent children of history, through our sheer inability to perceive their existence, let alone their significance, at the beginning. The point has long been passed where the answer could be found collectively. Today there is no answer and no safety in numbers, only a deadly proliferation of the same peril. The answer must be sought first by the individual alone, as it were in the desert of each of us. We have to accept this sense of something missing, however improbable or insignificant it may seem, as our guide towards distant life-giving waters.

The Heart of the Hunter, Chapter 9

Ballot boxes are, in a sense, the least part of a democracy, for they do not create it by themselves. We ought to realize how since the war, in country after country, we have allowed the ballot box to be used as an instrument for the destruction of democracy. In fact a far less sophisticated form of government with people using it well would probably work better than democracy used badly.

A Walk with a White Bushman

Work

'You have more doubts than are good for you. If they were doubts arrived at objectively I wouldn't worry, but they all seem to me only the measure of your failure to reconcile your thoughts, your interests, with what you are doing. Listen! When one has nothing but your sort of uncertainty, it's a sure sign that there's something wrong not with life as a whole, as one persuades oneself, but with one's own life. You seem to me nowadays terribly trapped between disgust and the need of making your living . . .'

'It's your duty to yourself to work for something you respect. If there's nothing in this life you love, there must be something it lacks that you love, and you must work to give it one day the thing you love. If you haven't got the courage of your love, God help you, for no one else can.'

In a Province, Book II, Chapter 4

Time

To hell with time and all watches who think they know what it's about.

A Mantis Carol, 'The Carol'

Until one acknowledge one's whole past, how painful and humiliating the process might be, and dignifies it with an honest, frank and full admission of its nature into one's daylight self, one is not free for a future of one's own.

A Far-Off Place, Chapter 12

It was wrong to judge things out of the context of the time which gave them birth.

A Far-Off Place, Chapter 15

The past stretched endlessly before him, the future long behind, and only this world of natural beauty, vivid and immediate with instinctive life that he was leaving, possessing intimation of ultimate reality.

A Far-Off Place, Chapter 15

We cannot follow the pattern of our own experience of the truth chronologically, since so much of the truth does not belong to the world of the clock and the calendar but, almost immeasurably, is a 'before' and an 'after' and at our own beginning is already part of an infinite compound which, as our own time becomes more specific, makes us feel as if we were looking into another universe within ourselves, spread out there as the night sky packed with stars presents itself in the southern hemisphere to the senses.

About Blady, Chapter 1

There was no short cut to a better life on earth. Impatience and short cuts were evil and destructive. There were no short cuts to the creative, there was no magic in creation except the magic of growth. Creation was growth and growth was profoundly subservient to time laws of its own, which could not be broken without destroying the process . . .

Obedience to one's greater awareness, and living it out accordingly to the rhythm of the law of time implicit in it, was the only way. Unlived awareness was another characteristic evil of our time, so full of thinkers who did not do and doers who did not think.

A Far-Off Place, Chapter 6

Not a day goes by without my hearing someone say somewhere, 'I am just killing time' – time of which we have so little and which in any case kills all in the end . . .

The rebellion against time shows itself perhaps most in the compulsion to make life faster. There is not so much a love as a lust for speed, for doing things quickly, which totally ignores the fact that time is nothing if not measured, and that every plant, animal, organization, stone, star and cosmic system has its own unique measure of time and this measure demands obedience to the rhythm of seasons and renewal. We, however, improve on the 'killing time' mentality with the slogan that 'time is money', speeding up all the processes not merely of traffic and travel, which is perhaps the least harmful of all, but processes of growth in plants, in flesh and blood, in reaching deep into the mystery of the ultimate genetic units and beginning to manipulate life for our own busy ends so that in systems everywhere 'being' has been taken out of life and a compulsive and frantic 'doing' and busyness put into its place.

About Blady, Chapter 3

As he said it, there was a glimmer at the back of his mind of one of the basic realizations of the imagination brave enough to look into the mysterious role of time in the life of man: the fact that the very time which passes so slowly and reluctantly because of separation or unhappiness, seems, on looking back, to have vanished in a flash almost as if it had never been. Yet time which is charged with meaning and joy goes so swiftly that one longs to stop it. Once over, it has this paradoxical compensation that, in recollection, it seems to have lasted longer.

A Story Like the Wind, Chapter 11

Time flows subtly, paradoxically. From day to day it seems to drag with an extreme reluctance, seems almost, if we submit ourselves entirely to its movement, not to move at all. And yet if the mind is withdrawn consciously and fixed on time's cumulative effect, the impression received is one of unbearable swiftness, of a terrible uniformity of speed. One feels that one is passing from the day into the night, clutching only the reality of a twilight transition. Nothing, it would seem, could be swifter; yet if this inexorable movement is married to an absolute uniformity of existence, one is bowed down with terror before the speed with which even time accelerates, until the years seem to be darkening around the world like a tropical evening. The shortest life, one knows then, is the most uniform life, and one prays to be preserved from uniformity.

In a Province, Book I, Chapter 12

Time, if only we could feel it again, as it sang within our blood, was not just a lineal measure but the beat of the heart of love, the rhythm of its growth and increase in life, the rate of its advance and its patience in the conversion of error and redemption of imperfection, so that when all error has been corrected, all imperfection redeemed and life made precise with love, there will be no need of time, and time will pass away and another dimension will come to take its place. But love will stay.

A Mantis Carol, 'The Carol'

He saw me and went still with shock. His dark eyes looked into my blue ones and I saw their light was still imprisoned in a moment far back in time. How well I knew it and how clearly I understood it now that I was free. Had I not learnt lately that death is not something that happens at the end of our life? It is imprisonment in one moment of time, confinement in one sharp uncompromising deed or aspect of ourselves. Death is exclusion from renewal of our present-day selves. Neither heaven nor hell are hereafter. Hell is time arrested within and refusing to join in the movement of wind and stars. Heaven is the boulder rock unrolled to let new life out: it is man restored to all four of his seasons rounding for eternity.

The Seed and the Sower, Chapter 5

This was my point of departure, and was part of something that had no substance or magnitude but possessed only position. Once one had position, the retreat of chaos began and meaning was born. The sense of meaning that I was finding on this trail in and out of time, and with a seemingly absurd and random chronology of its own, made no sense of the chronology of watches that tick and clocks that sound the alarm.

About Blady, Chapter 5

Time is the dream in between when time was not, and when time will cease to be.

A Walk with a White Bushman

Heart and Mind

[*You always jump over walls and escape definition: journalist, writer, soldier, farmer, conservationist, explorer, wise man, political adviser.*] This is the 'yet being someone other' . . . It was not my intention to be, but it happens that I have become that. To me the Zen exhortation to do instantly with all your heart and mind what life presents you with, however enigmatic, is the beginning of the way.

A Walk with a White Bushman

We suffer from a hubris of the mind. We have abolished superstition of the heart only to install a superstition of the intellect in its place. We behave as if there were some magic in mere thought, and we use thinking for purposes for which it was never designed. As a result we are no longer sufficiently aware of the importance of what we cannot know intellectually, what we must know in other ways, of the living experience before and beyond our transitory knowledge. The passion of the spirit, which would inspire man to live his finest hour dangerously on the exposed frontier of his knowledge, seemed to me to have declined into a vague and arid restlessness hiding behind an arrogant intellectualism, like a child of arrested development behind the skirts of its mother.

The Heart of the Hunter, Chapter 10

He had reached the point when the human being realizes that no amount of knowing diminishes the amount of the unknown. Knowledge moves and searches for meaning.

Yet Being Someone Other, Chapter 3

One of the most striking features of the desperate age in which we live is its genius for finding good reasons for doing bad things.

Venture to the Interior, Preface

The gloomy Dean Swift once remarked that you could tell a man of genius by the number of dunces gathered against him. If the dim-witted, ignoble and ill-informed were the only impediments in these matters, the bearer of new truths would find his work far easier. Unfortunately it is the opposition of the intelligent, honourable and public-spirited men who should be the first to welcome the pioneer who usually make his task so difficult.

Jung and the Story of Our Time, 'The Vigil and the Summons'

How little mere thinking helps a soul in trouble. What a wayside mongrel it can be, running the length of the threatened kingdom of our being, barking at one master instinct after another, sniffing at the trees of our natural selves for the scent of a bitch it can tumble, or whining at the back door of our first warm-lit emotion

The Face Beside the Fire, Chapter 7

The secret knowledge of where thirty years of high-principled living had led her sounded its own submerged warning in her blood. She came as near as she had ever been to the realization that flesh and blood need a loving and understanding heart far more than a just and knowledgeable mind.

The Face Beside the Fire, Chapter 2

'Mopani [Mopani Théron, the ranger] said that the smaller and the stiller the voice is within oneself, the more one should listen to them.'

A Story Like the Wind, Chapter 10

Murder

[Murder] is not [only] done by bright and flashing steel, nor even an honest stab in the back, but by the slow and subtle poison of enticement from our true individual destinies. For it is not destiny that is fated or doomed, but our evasion and betrayal of it.

The Face Beside the Fire, Chapter 16

We had all been beaten up for no apparent reason. As always when this happened, I had noticed a strange, unseeing look in the eyes of the Japanese. It was focused not at us but at something beyond us. Were they afraid that, should their eyes focus on us, they would recognize our common humanity, and so the cruelties they were inflicting would not only be challenged but extinguished?

Yet there was again something extraordinarily familiar to me about this look. Where had I seen it before? In the eyes of my men and fellow officers there was an expression of utter bewilderment. Yet that, too, seemed just as familiar to me as the look on the Japanese faces. Then suddenly I had it! I had seen that look of bewilderment so often in the law courts of my native South Africa when some black native countryman was being tried in a language he could not understand, and for a breach of laws that often he did not even know existed. And even when he did know of their existence he certainly had no understanding of the assumptions that served as their justification. The judges too, in passing sentence, rarely looked at the uncomprehending accused. Their eyes too were generally focused on some abstract of vision beyond the ragged and tattered creature in the dock, as if afraid that one glance would deprive him of his capacity for passing judgement.

The implication followed the recognition. We too treated the black man in Africa as we did because we had abstracted him from his human reality and allowed him to become a symbol of our own unawareness. We were projecting upon him an unknown part of ourselves; punishing him and at the same time punishing a dark, rejected aspect of ourselves. It was another intimation of the symbolism of colour in producing specially acute forms of racial differences in my native country.

Gradually I became more and more appalled by the collective failures in this regard not only of a single nation but of the cultures of our time, indeed of the whole civilization that had nourished them. The same mechanism, too, trapped smaller groups, from parents and children, husbands and wives, lovers and enemies, down to individuals like myself in our relationships with one another.

Jung and the Story of Our Time, 'The Time and the Space'

Scientists and judges have not the monopoly of laws. Euclid was an intuitive pattern before it became a textbook; Lucretius produced the atom whole out of his heart before it was split in a bomb on Hiroshima. The wholeness and the split, both, are within us.

But we have come dangerously late to this new awareness.

Venture to the Interior, Chapter 23

I myself find it impossible to judge these things [ritual murder in primitive African societies] to be merely murder. In society punishment can, so often, be just a lazy way out of a difficult situation, and at best it is only a half-measure, and society should realize the extent to which it has been accessory to the criminal fact. I do not know how we can be morally justified in hanging and punishing people in Africa for this sort of thing so long as we do so little to change the conditions and circumstances, largely of our creation, that drive them to it. Unfortunately the tendency in all systems is to think that once a crime has been punished society has done its bit. For my part, I can only repeat that to offer the African our faith without the accompaniment of the way of life and opportunity which that faith demands is to offer him no faith at all.

The Dark Eye in Africa, Part III, 'The Discussion'

How naïve . . . There is no limit to violence until the greatest violence of all has subdued the lesser violence.

A Far-Off Place, Chapter 6

Justice

'I quite see that our social system inflicts many injustices on people like Kenon, but I cannot see that it's entirely responsible for their reactions to those injustices. Moreover, your conception of the system is to me, now, an unreal abstraction. I have thought it over a great deal . . . but the more I think of it the less I believe in it. Listen, the unjust man, the selfish man, the cruel man, will act always according to his lights. The system is only a garment round the human heart; it doesn't give the shape to the heart, it takes its own shape from the heart. I agree with you that some garments fit better than others, but yours seems to me not a garment but a straitjacket, which man will have to burst if he is to survive. Under your system the just will still be just, the unjust still unjust, we will be no further forward and you'll have put the world through a period of bloodshed and anarchy in vain. Your enemy and mine in this country is not the system but the heart of every white man. You can't legislate a man's heart away.'

'So you would just let the white people in this country go on having too much, and the black people not enough? You would just let –'

'I think it's terribly wrong. But Burgess, Christ knew what you don't when he told the rich man to give up his riches of his own accord. He asked no one to legislate against riches. He placed all the responsibility for his riches and for their renunciation on the rich man himself.'

In a Province, Book III, Chapter 6

He [Christ] was telling a world obsessed with Roman belief in power and physical might that, for the truly contemporary man, the man aware of this 'now' of being, the Old Testament law of cause and effect, of action and re-action, a blow for a blow, and eye for an eye, a tooth for a tooth and so on, could not apply. The full free spirit must not resent an injury but must accept it as an inevitable aspect of reality. Then, though man be forced to wage war for his preservation in the physical world, he will be saved from carrying the battle over into his own heart and mind. In other words inflicted injuries are not to be turned into so-called spiritual causes, for by 'turning the other cheek' we bring to bear on our injury not the hurt side of ourselves, but a fresh, uninjured aspect not hitherto shown.

The Dark Eye in Africa, Part III, 'The Discussion'

You see, I myself haven't much faith in an abstract conception of justice. It seems to me that between the psychological habits of people and their conception of justice there is, or should be, a very close bond. We wouldn't, with a medieval mentality be able to tolerate twentieth-century justice; if were able to, we would abuse it: and it would, of course, be worse the other way round. Yet that's precisely what we're trying to inflict on these people. In their case it's doubly cruel, because we won't allow the black people to enter into the system of living for which our justice was obviously devised. By refusing to do so, we imply that they are psychologically and racially in a different class. Yet we proceed very illogically to inflict our system of justice on them as if they were like ourselves. If we hadn't prevented these people from living like ourselves, I wouldn't hesitate for a moment to punish them. But you see, I feel that indirectly we have a terrible responsibility in cases like these. We forbid them the sort of life their law demands, and give them our law without the sort of life that our law demands.'

In a Province, Book III, Chapter 2

I was to discover that for thousands of years it had been customary in Ethiopia for plaintiff and accused to be shackled together for weeks before they were brought to lawful judgement. It was, of course, a rough justice in a rough age and land, but it always seemed to me to have contained within it the seeds of a really advanced concept, because it sought to compel individuals to accept in the first place responsibility for their grievances against one another and to do everything themselves to contain and resolve their quarrels before society was bothered about them.

First Catch Your Eland, Chapter 1

Compassion leaves an indelible blueprint of the recognition that life so sorely needs between one individual and another; one nation and another; one culture and another.

Jung and the Story of Our Time, 'The Time and the Space'

The gift of compassion in the spirit of man – out of this compassion a great transformation of the pattern of life itself comes out.

'The Creative Pattern in Primitive Africa', Eranos Lectures

Doing Versus Being

Possession is no substitute for being.

The Dark Eye in Africa, Part III, 'The Discussion'

[169]

Unfortunately life in this hour of disintegration has orders only for honouring men for what they do and for the usefulness of the functions they perform.

And I find myself longing for an order whose investment would be introduced by some citation as this, inevitably heraldic in its language since it issues straight from the ancient unrest of the questing heart of man: 'For valour in the field of life, distinguished conduct in the battle of being and steadfastness in defending its quality and texture against aberration and distortion by the prevailing hatred, malice and envy of our collective time, ensuring thereby an example of how devotion to being for sheer being's sake and pursuing it to its own end, is the true glory of life on earth and the unique source of its renewal and increase of meaning and light in the darkness ahead.'

A Mantis Carol, 'Hans Taaibosch at Home'

There seemed to me moments in a desperate time when one had also to do and act on the ordinary everyday human scene. Art and writing, it seemed, ultimately demanded not only expression in their own idiom but also translation into behaviour and action on the part of their begetters. Being and doing, doing and being, for me were profoundly interdependent, particularly in a world where increasingly it seemed to me the 'doers' did not think and the thinkers did not 'do' ... In the Western world to which I belonged, all the stress was on the 'doing' without awareness of the importance to it of the 'being'. Somewhere in this over-balance of contemporary spirit, there appeared to be an increasing loss of meaning through the growing failure to realize how 'being' was in itself primal action, and that at the core of 'being' was a dynamic element of 'becoming' which gave life its quality and from which it derived its values and overall sense of direction. Because of a lack of such 'being', we were constantly in danger of becoming too busy to live.

Yet Being Someone Other, Chapter 6

The human spirit is being served by words, ideas and world concepts that have become totally inadequate for the meaning which it is trying to express and the being which it is trying to create ...

They need to be de-conditioned from associations that do not belong to our age, and to be reassessed in terms of our own living experience in its fullest contemporary meaning. Further, I believe that the ideas that we use and on which we base our actions are unworthy of the being which is clamouring for expression in modern man, It is the bigoted rationalism and fanatic adherence of Western man to outer physical reality and his over-valuation of the demonstrable objective world round about him which the cause of much of his undoing.

The Dark Eye in Africa, Part I, 'The Background'

Chapter Eight

The Inner Journey

This element in man as keeper of the vision of life in all its fullness and triumphant wholeness is ultimately concerned with a journey of a different kind. It is concerned with a journey made not on foot nor by donkey, camel, horse, ox-wagon, ship or aeroplane, but a journey from one state of being to another, a journey of *becoming*. It is the Far Journey of which the great Yu Ching spoke:

> And the deeper secret within the secret:
> The land that is nowhere, that is the true home.

> *The Dark Eye in Africa*, Part III, 'The Discussion'

Long before man become a peasant he was a nomad following the seasons across the earth. I believe there was a time when man's capacity to journey was as vital to him as the air he breathed and the food he ate, and that whole indigenous races of men have perished because foreign civilizations put an end to their freedom of movement ... I believe that this 'sense of journey' within us commands the most profound, powerful and creative energies of man. I believe that the myth which provokes man to a journey flows directly from the unfailing source of life's transcendent aim and today is concerned just as vitally with man's spiritual survival as it once was with his physical survival ... we need a new kind of explorer, a new kind of pathfinder, human beings who, now that the physical world is spread out before us like an open book with the latest geographical mystery solved and the highest mountain climbed, are ready to turn and explore a new dimension. And it is the myth, I believe, that gives us our first clue as to the way into this new-old dimension. That is why it is so important for us to endeavour to relearn its forgotten language so that we can understand its full meaning and relate it to our contemporary selves.

The Dark Eye in Africa, Part III, 'The Discussion'

[*The Odyssey is*] a great journey of individuation ... of which the ultimate lesson of war was the need of man to rediscover the constant feminine in himself. And even that was not all, for having rejoined the island feminine again Odysseus had to do yet another journey to a great continent of reality that would end in sacrifices to all the gods of the Greek world, not just a favoured one and his or her allies, but all the warring gods in heaven, and so find a way of wisdom and greater discrimination beyond.

About Blady, Chapter 5

With Hamlet, man crosses not only for himself but for all men, this long shunned frontier of the spirit, and from there begins years of journeying of another kind.

Testament to the Bushmen, 'The Great Memory'

In *The Tempest* the ending, which makes Dante's *Commedia* and Shakespeare's journey divine, is told, and told as it could only be told, on an island. And what has become a journey of a great and abundant summer of Elizabethan imagination ends in the fulfilment of all four seasons of life.

About Blady, Chapter 6

The World Within

But sometimes still a dream like flame
Burns through my country calm,
And desires without shape or name
Haunt me with vision of jungle and palm.

Lines from 'Dream of Sumatra', *Yet Being Someone Other*, Chapter 4

... there can be no thrust into what is unknown in the external world without being accompanied, if not preceded, by an equal and opposite thrust into the world of the spirit.

Yet Being Someone Other, Chapter 1

[173]

I have flown many times by night. But I have never quite got used to that first moment in the dark when one sits with folded hands, alone, speeding through the air at a pace one cannot feel or adequately imagine. The night looks on steadily, its feet on the earth far below, its head in the stars. It is a solemn moment; sensations you have not felt and thoughts you have not thought since childhood come back to you. You feel yourself then to be really on a journey in the fullest sense of the word; not just a shifting of the body from point to point but a journey that moves through all conceivable dimensions of space and time, and beyond. For a voyage to a destination, wherever it may be, is also a voyage inside oneself; even as a cyclone carries along with it the centre in which it must ultimately come to rest.

Venture to the Interior, Chapter 4

The deepest of all the patterns in the human spirit is one of departure and return, and the journey implicit in between. The life of man is the journey, a voyage such as that of Odysseus, a travel downward into cataclysmic depths like that of Orpheus in search of his lost Eurydice; Dante's wandering through hell and the dark streets of the city of Diss, and the journey of exile inflicted on the first man and his woman Eve from the garden to which they have not yet returned.

There are also the stories of the wanderings of the Israelites from bondage in Egypt in search of a promised land where they could live after the fashion of their own unique monotheistic conception of the divine and its commandments. There are those strange walk-abouts of aborigines in the never-never of Australia, and of my own Stone Age countrymen in the vast wasteland of southern Africa. The same pattern leads to the road which the Sanyassin takes in India; the Tao of China which was both journey and purpose to Lao-Tzu; and the one and only way of Confucius, conceived at the still centre of togetherness in the storm of all our tumultuous being. There is Bunyan's *Pilgrim's Progress* and others far too many to mention which all tend to illustrate how in the beginning man at his best is outward bound only in order to return from across the seven oceans the inward way from where he started and to see the place for the first time, as T. S. Eliot put it in a precise poetic statement.

Jung and the Story of Our Time, 'Point of Total Return'

I had not yet learnt the futility of trying to get rid of my problems by changing the location in which they were inflicted on me.

The Hunter and the Whale, Chapter 12

For the first time the journey communicated something of reality to him. However deceived he had been in point of departure and destination, the heaving ship, the storm, the night and the struggle to make headway felt profoundly and uncompromisingly real. The journey, thank God, was true, possessing with a great and awesome simplicity a reality independent of his own complex and powerful self-deceptions. He didn't know where he was going but he felt that he was on his way.

A strange new consciousness invaded him – a sense that he was dreaming vividly of being awake in the midst of his deepest sleep. Suddenly he felt purified within himself, free of other people's faces, of smells and colours and above all of other people's voices. He felt profoundly grateful that the only sound about him was this mindless, ancient, prehuman music of the storm. One human voice he feared would be enough to wake him and then he and all would drown. For this dream of being awake suddenly was more urgent than the condition of actually being awake. He felt like an explorer who had at last walked into the true unknown and found that the treasure of discovery was the realization that true awareness needs not only the fact, but also the dream of the fact: these are the two vital ends to the journey between. Then in the swelling rhythm of discovery he was conducted to the edge of the world, to the uttermost frontier of tangible, coherent thought, where the exhausted mind and spirit fall down aghast at the view of the purple, unhorizoned distances they still have to travel and where only the humble and contrite, the sore-rejected heart is left to take over the journey to the final pass in the mountains where life itself comes and goes. It was as if in this wild night of wind and water, of uncorrupted and incorruptible darkness he was presented with the first, the aboriginal vision of the universe, brought face to face with the basic material, the raw and irreducible elements of the pre-created world. It was as if his own being had been driven back so far in time that it had emerged in the moment just before Genesis, when the earth was void and without form and darkness upon the face of the deep, and the spirit of God was about to set out moving upon the face of the great waters. It was a moment in himself of sheer nothingness and of absolute darkness.

The Face Beside the Fire, Chapter 17

I was a coward but I had right to fear, for this journey I was contracted to perform without my seeking from birth to death, from past to future, from world without to world within on to world without end, is not possible without love. He who tries to go down into the labyrinthine pit of himself, to travel the swirling, misty netherlands below sea level through which the harsh road to heaven and wholeness runs, is doomed to fail and never see the light where night joins day unless he goes out of love in search of love ... Only awareness, fully extended and humbly maintained, is needed to know that no moment is without love, and no night truly dark. There is provision for all in life.

The Face Beside the Fire, Chapter 22

We live ... in a sunset hour of time and need the light of this moon of Mantis, this feminine Ariadne soul, which conducts the travel-stained prodigal son of man on a labyrinthine journey to the innermost chamber of his spirit where he meets the 'thou that heals'.

The Voice of the Thunder, 'The Great Memory'

I remembered when I discussed this with Jung my own agony as a child when I came to the moment in Mallory when the dying Arthur compelled a relectant Sir Bedivere to return to the waters the great Excalibur – wherein its image had been born. The sword which itself in its extraction from stone, the stone the medieval heart had become, represented so evocatively the awareness of man in action on his quest for wholeness symbolized by the Holy Grail. I was haunted for years by the dismay that the great order of the Round Table had been dispersed and no longer had a Royal Centre around which it could reassemble. It was as if this dispersal and defeat and death of Arthur reflected the dispersal of what was best in the Western spirit and the arrest of its essential quest, story or myth, whatever name served the imagination best of him who reconsidered it, and explained the fragmented and splintered mass formations that had ever since tried to usurp its place. And it was for me, when I encountered this dream of Jung and considered how he proceeded from there, as if the ancient Arthurian call had gone out loud and clear again and Merlin, who had preceded and tutored Arthur, and all the magic of life which had been buried deep with him in his wound for so long had been unsealed. Through Jung the order of a reassembly of all we had of awareness left of this most authentic, specific and urgent quest of Western man was there once more for all to hear and help in the making of a new Round Table for the nourishment of a truly modern spirit.

Jung and the Story of Our Time, 'Errant and Adventure'

The Dream and the Dreamer

Everywhere at all times, in all cultures and races of which we have record, when the greatest meaning, the highest value of life men called their gods, or god, needed renewal and increase through life on earth, it began the process through a dream.

A Mantis Carol, 'Walk-about'

Man is never alone. Acknowledged or unacknowledged, that which dreams through him is always there to support him from within.

Jung and the Story of Our Time, 'The Time and the Space'

In the beginning, St John says, was the Word. I believe that is a way of saying that in the beginning there was meaning. This word, this meaning, according to the Bible was with God and indeed was God. The ancient Chinese said something similar when they defined meaning as that which has always existed through itself. Somehow this meaning demanded also to be lived. As St John puts it again, the word was made flesh. A similar intimation of its beginnings seems to me present in the first spirit of Africa. It is true the Bushmen I had just met in the Kalahari were not very communicative in this respect. I think it needed more time, more trust and patience than I commanded to elicit from them the full image in which

this intimation moves over the mystery of the beginning in their spirit
in search of some conscious thought to contain it, like the first bird
let out of the ark winging over the dark waters of the Old Testament flood for some tangible fact of earth or rock to light upon.
When I pressed them to talk to me about the beginning they seemed
to lose their power of speech, and the only significant answer
was given to me one night by my favourite hunter. Distressed
by my persistence and his inability to satisfy my curiosity, he said:
'But you see, it is very difficult, for always there is a dream
dreaming us.'

It was a pregnant hint. Quite apart from its likeness to the
Shakespearian assertion, 'We are such stuff as dreams are made on',
it confirmed the observation of the Frenchman, who was among the
first to examine the life of primitive people with no feeling of
superiority or abhorrence, that 'the dream is the true God of
primitive man'. Believing as I do that the dream is not a waste
product of the mind expelled through some sewage system of the
spirit but a manifestation of first and abiding meaning, I thought I
should enlarge St John's theme to include the idea that in the
beginning there was a dream. This dream was with God and indeed
was God. Somehow this dream demanded that it should be lived.
As St John might have put it, 'the dream was made flesh'.

The Heart of the Hunter, Chapter 2

I was greatly moved when one of the first men of Africa, a Stone-
Age hunter in a wasteland greater I believe than even the wasteland
in which Jacob dreamt his dream, informed me, 'You know, there
is a dream dreaming us.' To this day I do not know anything to
equal this feeling for what the dreaming process is to life and the
implication that it is enough for creation to appear to us as the
dreaming of a great dream and the unravelling and living of its
meaning.

Jung and the Story of Our Time, 'The Time and the Space'

The lessons I learned in childhood that no one could subject dreams
to his own will or fancy had gone deeply enough to make that clear.
Dreams had a will of steel, and a way of their own in their role as
direct manifestations of this inner objectivity. They were incapable

of falsehood. Only our reading of them was liable to error, and I had an inkling that they, and the prompting of this other objectivity within, were the true sources of mythology, religion, legend and art, seeking and reseeking recognition and expression through our several histories. If denied those by fair means, they sought them by foul. Refused admission at the front door of the spirit, they came in by force or stealth from the rear.

Jung and the Story of Our Time, 'The Time and the Space'

As one who had dreamt a great deal and had been troubled by them ever since he could remember, I already suspected that dreams could not be taken either for granted or at their face value, and that to be naïve about the dreaming process could be even more disastrous for nations than individuals.

Yet Being Someone Other, Chapter 5

For me it all started as a child in the interior of Africa. In the clear light of a certain *esprit d'escalier* that comes to one on the way down from one's own little attic in time, I seem to have had an inborn predisposition towards the area of meaning in which Jung's abundant spirit, unknown to us, was already embattled. I had always had what seemed to my own family and friends an inordinate interest in dreams. I was always dreaming, and dreams, from the beginning, meant something to me that they did not to the grown-up pale-faces of my world. The pink, marshmallow material they were in the minds of governesses trained in the Victorian order of these things became suspect to me at an early age. Even worse was their dismissal as some sort of poor rich trash of the imagination by the hearty male teachers of our extravert society who followed on where wistful spinster ladies left off. They would pass sentence on one's dreaming processes with a phrase that filled me with dismay, 'But my dear boy, it was only a dream.'

That 'but only' of theirs became increasingly discredited when I saw how it was automatically part of their judgement of almost everything that mattered to me as a child. Growing up in the European way began to appear to be not so much a process of growth as a dangerous reduction to a provisional 'but only' state. I feared it accordingly, and so acutely that the fear is still with me, for it is continuously encouraged by the loss of power of increase that I see in men and their societies, because how can there be either growth or renewal in such reductive soil of the human spirit?

My one defence against the condemnation of adults was the effect on me of the dreams themselves. Almost nightly I was reminded, by yet another dream, of their vitality to persist undiminished against the constant opposition of the adult world. Also they would continue to have marked effects on the mood and atmosphere of my days. There was more to dreaming, I suspected, than my elders knew or supposed.

I had, of course, good dreams as well as bad. The number of good may well have exceeded the bad, but I had nightmares enough to prevent me from thinking of dreaming as an altogether comfortable process. The good and the bad seemed part of one indivisible reality which, for all my inability to define or explain it, I could neither ignore nor depend on as a source of comfort.

I soon took this to be axiomatic because, for a period of about a year, I tried hard to fashion dreaming to my own prescription. I would go to bed determined to inflame my sleep with dreams of wonder or fulfilment. But not once was I able to have the slightest influence on the dreams of my sleep. I knew a brief period when I even tried to enlist the help of our Calvinist Almighty in the matter.

Like all children of my world, I was compelled to say my prayers every night before going to sleep, although our evening meal always ended with a long reading from the Bible, an even longer improvised prayer, with all of us kneeling on the hard, polished wooden floor of the dining-room by our rather medieval chairs and their carved frames and high backs, and a final singing of a psalm. Later, an African nurse or senior member of the family was always there to supervise this last ablution of our minds from the stains of the sinful day. They would see to it that one knelt down by one's bed and ran silently through the prescribed formula for invoking divine protection for parents, brothers, sisters, friends, not forgetting a perfunctory plea for one's own redemption from a state of sin – which one did not feel but had been talked into accepting as an inborn element of one's being.

I never minded the occasion and invariably took to my bed afterwards mysteriously relieved and rather startled by how often the long white, home-made candle by the side of my bed would look transformed into a lighthouse poised on the rim of the great sea of African night, lapping at the lip of the shuttered window, and sanctifying my room with a sort of pentecostal glow. I would stare for a moment at the brass rails of my bed rendered gold before glancing up to see candle and flame stand transparent on the glass within the frame which enclosed on the wall above my bed the text, stitched in blue gothic letters on yellow silk, 'The Lord is my shepherd, I shall not want.' After that, I could have no doubt of finding safe harbour in sleep, and in sleep the dream I had secretly placed on my prayer list. But no such dream ever came.

There followed some months of agonizing questioning and self-examination when I woke up so often, to prod myself on to greater dream exertion, that I got up in the mornings looking exhausted and had my parents thoroughly worried. But somehow, I made my peace with the fact that I myself could not fabricate dreams. Far from lowering the process in my estimation it increased my respect for the dream, since I concluded that with a will and a way all its own it was greater than both I and prayer combined.

By this time my obsession had become common knowledge. In so affectionate a family, even so large a one as ours, it was astonishing how one's most secret thoughts and aspirations were enticed from one. In particular, one's sisters seemed to have a special nose for divining secrets and then spreading them around. If they were found to be at a tangent to the family norm, one instantly became the subject of endless teasing. I would try hard to fall back on a previously prepared position (as military strategists would say), and take refuge in a secrecy I should never have abandoned. I no longer confessed my dreams or fantasies inspired by dreams to anyone. But the damage had been done and inevitably I was nick-named, 'Joseph the Dreamer' . . .

I was protected too from hubris by the fact that the dreams of Joseph, themselves, did not impress me as much as perhaps they ought to have done. I was never over-fond of the dream spectacle of the sheaves of corn, as proxies of Joseph's brethren, bowing their yellow heads obsequiously before the one that represented his dreaming self, and could well understand why it was regarded as an egotistical presumption that had to be resisted. But, all in all, my reaction to Joseph's dreams, of course, was purely instinctive and I could not possibly tell, as perhaps I can today, that what really limited their appeal was that they appeared over-confined to a kind of fortune-telling role, largely contrived to help Biblical man in his struggle for physical survival. That, of course, was not to be despised. Nothing could be more natural than that the dreaming process should have a vested interest in the survival of the vulnerable flesh and blood which have to live the dreams that so mysteriously impel them. But once a particular battle was won there appeared some uneasy truce in an endless campaign as, for instance, after the flood and famine, fire and brimstone which destroyed the cities of the plain, after which man is brought back starkly over and over again to the real business of living, namely the task of living a life of increasing meaning as the only answer to the problem which provoked the very act of creation in the beginning.

Jung and the Story of Our Time, 'The Time and the Space'

The mere action of lifting your feet from the ground, getting into bed and turning off the light, releases the mind, the spirit, from routine considerations. Strange flowerings of what has been, of what can be, hang over you like clouds horizoned by the Orient. Your ears catch the sound of something which you are not accustomed to call reality. The world trembles like a million-stringed guitar. Some unknown thought from an unfathomed deep bursts the surface of the mind like a phosphorescent octopus the water of a moonless sea.

In a Province, Book II, Chapter 5

The impact of dreams on everyday life which had perturbed my imagination for so long could no more be dismissed as 'fantasy'. They were, on the contrary, increasingly broadened by Jung's empirical demonstration of their validity as facts of natural science. As I saw it, neither psychiatry nor his enlargement of the field of psychology were his major achievements. They were by-products of the discovery and evaluation of an as yet unmeasured potential that followed his breakthrough into this great new world within. It was as momentous as the breakthrough into the nature of the atom. Again the fact that both coincided in time suddenly seemed significant.

Indeed it is almost as if the synchronicity of the two developments imply that they are concerned with two aspects of the same reality. Perhaps even the atom, nuclear in its fission, could be regarded as a physical metaphor of the 'inscape' of man, nuclear in fission of a conscious and unconscious self. Relative to the position from which we view them, one can be seen utterly from within, the other only made visible from without.

The relationship between spirit and matter, world within and world without, is transcendental and incapable of total expression in non-transcendental terms. These two great objectives to which we are subject play on us like some great symphony of music which we cannot describe save through its effect on us. We are condemned to know them in part and only through their consequences in us, even though they circumscribe us in full. Yet this much seems certain. Less and less can we maintain that there is a cast-iron division between the inner and outer worlds. Today even the most rational of scientists consider the possibilities of their being aspects of one and the same greater whole. I myself never doubted that the physical world is spirit seen from without; the spirit is the world viewed from within.

It does not surprise me that in the final analysis, at the point where our dreams vanish over the rim of sleep, we meet matter receding fast over the horizon and, under the most powerful electron microscope, behaving less like solid, predictable material but more as the swift changing texture of living thought. We pass from one to the other like Alice in Wonderland through a looking glass, to find that the objective mystery which faces us macrocosmically in the night skies above, confronts us microcosmically in reverse. In the depths of our own mind, beyond those 'cliffs of fall frightful, sheer, no-man-fathomed' of which Hopkins wrote, symbols, images, patterns of meaning with all the immense energies at their disposal, are constellated and in orbit and strangely akin to the minuscule solar systems, planets, Milky Ways, comets, nebulae and black holes of anti-matter, dynamic in the heart of the physical atom. How could two such discoveries coming at the same desperate moment in time, therefore, not be another of those strange affirmations of the symmetry of meaning?

But immediately one faces the common misconception and cause of one of the commonest errors in contemporary thinking regarding Jung. Jung's breakthrough as a result of his descent into this Dantesque underworld was a result of his over-riding concern for consciousness in man. Metaphorically, he was concerned with making fire for greater light out of the darkness of the mind; and to determine among other things what it was in man that so often arose to extinguish such little light as he possessed.

Great as is the mystery of so vast an unconscious area in life there is a yet greater mystery involved. There is the mystery of consciousness and beyond that the ultimate wonder of how and for what purpose these two-in-one are directed. The mystery is not lessened because it is articulate. The light the fire throws does not diminish the aboriginal mystery because of its power to illuminate some of the night. On the contrary, the mystery grows with the growth of consciousness. Consciousness could not have the importance it possesses for life, nor could it have survived the onslaught which is symbolized in the Flood of the Old Testament, and made visible and active in all the wars, disasters, revolutions, social and individual tragedies inflicted on the human race, if in some way consciousness had not had the support of the collective unconscious. All that is unconscious in life must aspire to consciousness. Consciousness is meaningful, I imagine, precisely because in some way it serves the greatest longing of the collective unconscious. It is, as it were, the deepest dream of greater spirit in this underworld of life. It is only when consciousness betrays the longing and the dream which gives it birth, that it is overwhelmed and temporarily destroyed. Temporarily, I suggest, because always, hitherto, the dream and the longing have never failed to return, and consciousness been refashioned. Yet there is a lesson here as portentous as it is difficult to declare.

The mystery and the unknown before and after, are not the synonyms we may take them to be. Mystery includes the known as well as the unknown; the ordinary as well as the extraordinary. Once the feeling of mystery abandons our travel-stained senses in contemplation of the same well-worn scene, we have ceased, in some vital sense, to know what we are observing. What that mystery is, is beyond verbal definition. We know only that its effect on us is either positive or negative. It is, perhaps, most creatively, the feeling that in the midst of our own partial knowing and experience of life there is the presence of a something far greater than man can comprehend. Reality, no matter how widened and heightened our perceptions, never ceases to be an infinite mystery. Again, Shakespeare expresses it better than anyone else when he makes the doomed Lear say to Cordelia, 'We shall take upon us the mystery of things and be God's spies.' In other words, awareness of the mystery of things acknowledged and revered, though inexpressible and utterly non-rational, is also a vital form of knowing which enables the human spirit to pass through the defence lines of what he knows, and enter the territory of an embattled unknown like a spy to prepare the way for the mobilized forms of consciousness to follow and so extend the area of his awareness. And it is in all these senses that this ever-recurrent process of the dream, the longing in its keeping and the consciousness which emerges from it, is one of the most moving and life-giving aspects of the mystery that motivates our brittle lives.

In this great abysmal underworld, to which Freud had opened the gate and through which Jung had passed and continued to become the first to penetrate it in depth, the dream and its longing were never permanently discouraged. They rose phoenix-like from the burnt-out ashes of a conscious expression which had failed its unconscious motivations and soared, again and again, to compel life anew for another effort at greater consciousness. It is perhaps not odd that Jung had a phoenix in his family coat of arms, and that he was so young, both in person and name, the youngest and most childlike wise old man that one could meet, as if to leave no doubt that he was uniquely charged to make what was oldest in life young and new again. In this manner he was the very first great explorer in the twentieth-century way. And to understand what he was and accomplished and the immense hidden distances he travelled, I myself go back not only to what others close to him told me over the years but most of all to the little he told me about his own beginnings and the feelings it evoked in me. Without these feelings and the impact of the man, such knowledge and statistics as the world already possesses could not have lived as they still live and shine for me like a fire of my own in the African night.

Jung and the Story of Our Time, 'The Man and the Place'

Even now I have only to close my senses to see in the darkness within a ladder pitched on the stony ground of a great wasteland and reaching to a star-packed heaven, with the urgent traffic of angels phosphorent upon it . . . All this made the coming of the dream appear to me to be as fateful for life within as the coming of fire for life on earth without . . . Up to this moment, ever since the expulsion from the Garden, the life of Biblical man had been a singularly one-sided affair. It was a progression ordered entirely by command and the direct voice of God . . . Man himself had no direct say in the matter . . . He had but to fear and obey or face the most catastrophic consequences. With Jacob's dream, however, all this suddenly changed and the whole relationship between creator and created became reappraised.

The traffic of the spirit which had been so uncompromisingly from above to below, now was suddenly transformed into a two-way affair also possible from below to above . . . It is as if creator and created, through this dream, are being joined in an increasing act of partnership. Indeed, it almost seems as if the dream has taken charge both of God and man and made them, however disparate the degree of their relationship, servants of a common purpose.

Jung and the Story of our Time, 'The Time and the Space'

C. G. Jung

[Jung] believed that the spirit was all important – and that the physical world could be the spirit seen from without. Jung had so much to do and was so intuitive, he very quickly knew if a fork in the road was a genuine choice of main road or a sort of side-track. So he did not have to go far down for his intuitive sense to say, 'Ah, this is not for me. I must follow my own road.' But he was terribly insistent on this – that work, earning, sacrifice in a contemporary way – all were necessary. That is why he was not surprised when people did not queue up to take on his psychology. He did not offer instant redemption. His approach calls for the hardest of all human tasks, the task of individuation. It presupposes the hardest road man can travel and there is no other way. The true road is a hard road.

A Walk with a White Bushman

The essence of Jung's message, then, is that as far as the future was foreseeable, the highest task of man is the old religious task of redemption of Evil that he called the shadow. As shadow, Evil was not absolute and final but redeemable, and through its challenge to be redeemed an instrument of the enlargement of human awareness.

Jung and the Story of Our Time, 'Point of Total Return'

Consciousness imposes upon the individual a choice, and this is the point. You come to a moment in life when what you have chosen consciously and worked at consciously has lost its power of increase – and perhaps all the rest of your life should be spent in working on what you did not choose before, for what has been sacrificed has returned, dagger in hand, to sacrifice the sacrificer. That is where the darkness lives, and you must bring it up into consciousness as well and as fastidiously as you can. Then you achieve what Jung called 'wholeness'. A whole individual who has explored not just half his possibilities but all of his possibilities, as it were. That is the highest and most urgent task of the individual, his truly religious challenge – the wholeness which, we should never forget, is synonymous with 'holiness': to be whole is to be holy. And that is why Christ was the great healer, because he made what was partial in the life and spirit of man, whole.

A Walk with a White Bushman

'I don't want anybody to be a Jungian,' Jung told me, 'I want people above all to be themselves. As for "isms", they are the viruses of our day, and responsible for greater disasters than any medieval plague or pest has ever been. Should I be found one day only to have created another "ism" then I will have failed in all I tried to do.'

Jung and the Story of Our Time, 'Prologue'

We have knowledge enough of [Jung] and his ideas but, beyond the shrinking circle of those who knew him, little imaginative, rounded record of the dynamic, life-giving feeling that emanated from him.

What was of overwhelming consequence to me was that as we sat there talking, something was communicated to me of what Jung was in himself, rather than out of his ideas. In this process the feeling of isolation and loneliness in a vital area of myself which had haunted me all those years vanished. I was no longer alone. I had company of a noble order. For the first time in my life I had a neighbour in the inmost part of myself. I was also having an elementary lesson in the fact that men, women, ideas and the causes which are singularly our own, are often those which we most brutally reject. Perhaps there is something in all of us that demands a 'journey to Damascus' of our own before we can discover in a single, blinding, decisive flash that light which we are, in the innermost nature of ourselves, contracted to seek.

Jung certainly was a great and inspired neighbour. He had a genius for propinquity. He was companion to all sorts and conditions of men and women from the most despised and rejected to those overcome with vertigo from the intellectual heights they had achieved. He is a neighbour to millions that are yet to be born. His gift for propinquity brought him near to all manner of men and women. From deeply disturbed spirits shut away in some asylum to some humble negro barber in New Orleans; the 'Mountain Lake' of an almost vanished American Indian entity; a Hindu guru; just a despised and persecuted primitive or Zürich lake-side cellarman – they understood and felt near to him when some of the great minds of his own day dismissed him. I personally found that he gave me the feeling that there could be a valid meaning to this loneliness regarding Africa and also this other 'dreaming' area of myself which I had carried about with me for forty years. He performed precisely the same service for countless others.

Jung and the Story of Our Time, 'The Man and the Place'

When Jung's storm-battered book *Answer to Job* first appeared, he had a most moving and tender correspondence with a white nun in a convent in the Black Forest of Germany. She found that, for the first time, someone had enabled her to see meaning in the concept of the Trinity. Shut out for so long by her doubt of a vital concept of the faith to which she subscribed, she had suffered a form of loneliness of guilt that made her feel almost untouchable in her community. But long before this correspondence was ended, she saw herself again as part of a living human procession. She was, as the Kalahari Bushmen say, 'walking again with the moon and stars'.

Then there was the doctor with a practice in a remote mountain district of Switzerland who asked Jung to see a simple girl of the hills whom he thought was going insane. Jung saw her and realized at once that she had neither the intelligence nor need for a sophisticated and intellectually demanding analytical treatment. He talked to her quietly in his study and came to the conclusion that all she suffered from was the fact that her community, in a sudden enthusiasm for what was thought to be modern and progressive, had poured scorn on all the simple beliefs, ideas, customs and interests which were natural to her. Her own natural state, her primitive self, had lost such honour with herself and others that her heart wilted because of a lack of incentive in the kind of prospect life held out for her.

Accordingly he got her to talk to him at length about all the things she had enjoyed and loved as a child. As she talked, almost at once he saw a flicker of interest glow. He found himself so excited by this quickening of the spirit of a despised self, that he joined in the singing of her nursery songs and her renderings of simple mountain ballads. He even danced with her in his library, and at times took her on his knee and rocked her in his arms, undeterred by any thought of how ridiculous if not preposterous would be the picture of him in the eyes of orthodox medical and psychiatric practitioners.

At the end of a few days the girl was fully restored to a state of honour with herself and he sent her off in high spirits to her home. She never again regressed.

Jung and the Story of Our Time, 'The Man and the Place'

[Jung's] language which could be just as earthy as it was poetic, when he was roused in this profound regard was worthy of an inspired peasant, and words like 'shitbags' and 'pisspots' would roll from his lips in sentences of crushing correction.

Jung and the Story of Our Time, 'Point of Total Return'

Modern men have forgotten the art of growing old. They have devalued it into an inferior state that they see as the decline and fall of the human spirit. They see life merely as an orchard full of bright, thrusting young trees and forget that they have still to bear fruit which has to be harvested. Jung's old age was old in the classical sense, where the fruit of his experience was gathered, stored and evaluated. It was not decline or fading away but a state of growth into death and beyond.

Jung and the Story of Our Time, 'Point of Total Return'

I said goodbye to Jung with so much of this and more in turmoil within myself. As always with that innate sense of good manners the French call *politesse de cœur*, he came down the path leading to the gate with me. He stood there for a moment, leaning perhaps more heavily than usual on his stick, and waved goodbye saying, in his schoolboy English, 'I'll be seeing you.'

But some weeks later Jung was dead. I do not know the medical diagnosis of the immediate cause and in a sense I really do not need to know, because it is irrelevant. I know that he was dead because he had done his work and his life had come to its natural end . . .

The afternoon on which Jung died, a great thunderstorm raged over his house at Küsnacht, as if nature itself were mobilized to acknowledge the event. Just about the time of his death lightning struck his favourite tree in the garden.

One of the earliest rituals to reconcile men to the death of those dearest to them was to burn not only their bodies but all their most precious belongings with them. They did this so that, through the fire which brought light, what was imperishable in matter could be released from the perishable to accompany on the journey beyond the spirit freed from bondage, however loving, in flesh and blood. The wood that makes the fire, the body that nourishes the flame of the spirit burns out, but fire and spirit flame and flare on. It is almost as if nature itself sent the lightning to perform this task for Jung. But not only did this happen in nature. It was as if in the dreaming and visionary unconscious of numbers who had known him, an awareness like a kind of witnessing of a great ship going down appeared to draw all sort of portents and visions towards the vortex of his death like flotsam and jetsam on the sea marking the place of a titanic sinking.

I myself had an experience of this which I have long hesitated to make public. I had sailed from Africa profoundly distressed by the condition of my native country. I was obsessed with forebodings of apocalyptic disaster. I did not recognize what my own people had become and they did not recognize me. As a result, the sea and ships, which have always given me one of my greatest feelings of belonging and rest, utterly failed me on this occasion. I could not sleep. Even the strongest of sleeping draughts were of no use to me.

And then one afternoon alone in my cabin, worn out and hovering between waking and sleeping out of exhaustion, I suddenly had a vision of myself in a deep, dark valley in avalanche country, among steep, snow-covered mountains. I was filled with a foreknowledge of imminent disaster. I knew that even raising my voice in the world of this vision could bring down the bulging avalanches upon me. Suddenly, at the far end of the valley on one Matterhorn peak of my vision, still caught in the light of the sun, Jung appeared. He stood there briefly, as I had seen him some weeks before at the gate, at the end of the garden of his house, then waved his hand at me and, called out, 'I'll be seeing you.' Then he vanished down the far side of the mountain.

Instantly I fell asleep and slept the whole evening and night through. I woke next morning just as the sun was rising, and as I pushed aside the curtains of the porthole of my cabin, I saw a great, white albatross gliding by; the sun on fire on its wings. As it glided by it turned its head and looked straight at me. I had done that voyage countless times before and such a thing had never happened to me, and I had a feeling as if some tremendous ritual had been performed. Hardly had I got back into bed when my steward appeared with a tray of tea and fruit and, as he always did, the ship's radio news. I opened it casually. The first item I saw was the announcement that Jung had died the previous afternoon at his home in Zürich. Taking into consideration the time, the latitude and longitude of the ship's position, it was clear that my dream, or vision, had come to me at the moment of his death.

Jung and the Story of Our Time, 'Point of Total Return'

Jung was possessed by a capacity for love so great that it included also a love of all that life until now rejected, reviled, and persecuted. In all this he was more than a psychological or scientific phenomenon; he was to my mind one of the greatest religious phenomena the world has ever experienced. Until this central fact of his work and character is grasped and admitted, the full meaning and implication of Jung for the future of life is missed. But once this fact is grasped and admitted, the life of the individual who had experienced it can never be the same again, as I am certain the life of our time can never be the same again because of Jung.

Jung and the Story of Our Time, 'Point of Total Return'

Chapter Nine

The Artist

===

The Living Word

The word that was at the beginning and shall be at the end is a living word. The living word and the living truth are always more than statistics and facts. Neither can be imprisoned in any particular expression of themselves, however valid and creative, but must move on as soon as that phase of themselves is fulfilled. The concepts, cultures, whole civilizations, indeed, are not terminals, but wayside camps, pitched at sunset and broken at dawn so that they can travel on again.

The Voice of the Thunder, 'The Great Memory'

I lived among a people for whom the word was the main means of communication. They did not write much and could barely read. Everything really depended on the word, the living word, the spoken word, not the artificial, the hacked-out word, but the word meant to be for ever. The sign of a well-brought-up person among my native countrymen was a person who spoke well. You were really not thought much of among the black and coloured people I grew up with, unless you were well-spoken. That did not just mean that you could talk fluently – they were too quick at picking up mere rhetoric or braggarts or boasters – but that you could use the word in a way that moved people, that changed people. It was always wonderful to me, in the evenings sitting and listening to them talking, to observe how they found the right words for the occasion, and how, when the only possible word was found, there came the smack of satisfaction, the joy that it had been spoken, and it instantly became an achievement for everybody sitting there.

My life has since taken me far away from such moments but not before they had made their point. So I have been uneasily aware, particularly since the war and the arrival of television and the new kinds of newspapers, that the importance of the living word, the right, the only word, is overlooked. The word is, consciously or unconsciously, under attack and in decline. Yet nothing else can replace it.

Just think of the word, the depth of the word: it goes back over the horizon of our beginnings, and God alone knows where it comes from. Even the animals have forms of sound that are their word. It is the earliest form of conscious communication in life. 'The Word was made flesh' means it was made conscious, and to live and be lived. This kind of word is what life is about.

A Walk with a White Bushman

One can listen to words, poetry above all, and one is aware of this immense, almost magical evocation of meaning, of ancient meaning that just comes along with the words as part of the package. So one cannot just define all words rationally and use them purely rationally. All the dimensions of meaning tend to have a part in their impact. And the right word will not only touch you rationally, it will also touch your heart, it will touch you emotionally. Your eyes, your ears, your sense of smell, your intuition, everything comes into the greatest word. Altogether words form a system of communication which is as profound, subtle, proven and experienced as life itself. And in a sense it is life and gives life. Without it, life as we have known it is inconceivable.

A Walk with a White Bushman

Much of my life has been occupied with the written word, but also with the spoken word. And I have had a feeling, coming towards the end of my life; I have been deeply disturbed because I have not been able to write more. I have had to talk more, which I do not enjoy. And I have begun to think that perhaps this is wrong of me and that I must realize there is a moment when only the living word will do, the unpremeditated word, the word which speaks also for the words which have not yet been formed, the word which has really some connection with this unexpressed not-yet world of infinite meaning, which is clamouring for flesh and blood to live it. And that, particularly in moments of world crisis, the clearly spoken, controlled living word is far more important than the written word.

A Walk with a White Bushman

I have always had a keen sense of obligation to the life of my time which did not seem to me discharged by sticking to writing alone.

About Blady, Chapter 2

I believed that, in life as in writing, one's material must not be sought in some pure mountain source of the spirit but from what is nearest to mind and hand, even if it were something apparently discarded and insignificant in the dust around one's feet.

Journey Into Russia, 'Introduction'

In moments of crisis, I myself have never greatly trusted words.

The Face Beside the Fire, Chapter 16

What moves me very deeply about primitive peoples is that they still attach an enormous importance to a certain kind of communication which we have lost; and that is that they allow the being of the person they are with to communicate with more than words. They seem to let the soul of the other person – or the animal – communicate by the way it expresses itself, in the look and in the bearing, in the tone and in the voice. They allow that part of communication to play an enormous role; whereas we in the West tend to let words play an excessive role. We forget to listen to the tone and the expression which are used, and these are vital because we tend to use words in a fraudulent manner. Words demand to be treated with great truth. We feel it is such a terrible crime in the West to counterfeit money; but it should be a worse crime to counterfeit words. We see it in the newspapers and we see it amongst politicians particularly, who say things they really do not mean, or things they do not even understand. The word was in the beginning, and, if it is to be at the end, exacts all we have of reverence and respect.

A Walk with a White Bushman

Seed Stories

Everything in life is a story. The story of a man is in the soul and its own perception. It provides us with our sense of wonder. It provides us with the sense of living mystery in life. And it helps to heighten our sensitivities, our perceptions, our awareness. And it carries us on. With a story you go on a journey in time and space, in life and creation, always travelling.

A Walk with a White Bushman

The history of art and literature . . . contains as many examples of persons who have succumbed before the perils encountered in the world within as those who have been overwhelmed by their difficulties in the world without . . . There is, for instance, the uncomfortable example of Rimbaud, who, though a poet of genius, found the implications of genius more than he could bear and took on the perils of gun-running in one of the most dangerous parts of Africa as a more attractive alternative. Yet before he turned a deaf ear to the profound voice of his natural calling, he had shaped a vision of reality which increased the range of poetry for good. One may regret his desertion, but surely no one who cares for poetry can read 'Le Bateau Ivre' and 'Les Illuminations', for example, without some understanding of the power of temptation, and an inkling of how exposed and vulnerable the ordered personality is to the forces of this world that the artist carries within him.

The suicide of Van Gogh is another instance. We owe it to him that our senses are aware of the physical world in a way not previously possible (except perhaps by the long-forgotten child in all of us when the urgent vision is not yet tamed and imprisoned in the clichés of the adult world). But because of Van Gogh, cypresses, almond blossom, cornfields, sunflowers, bridges, wicker chairs and even trains are seen through eyes made young and timeless again and our senses are recharged with the original wonder of things. Here was not only genius but also high courage. Yet nothing so well gives one the measure of these inner forces as the fact that they were able to destroy both courage and genius.

Introduction to William Plomer, *Turbott Wolfe*

'Why' . . . is a severely limited question, as the child discovers from the moment it begins to talk. It produces limited answers, limited as a rule to the mechanics and laws of the world, universe and life of man. But the human heart and mind come dishearteningly quickly to their frontiers and need something greater to carry on beyond the last 'why'. This beyond is the all-encompassing universe of what the Chinese called Tao and a Zen Buddhist friend, in despair over the rationalist premises native to Western man, tried to make me understand as a newly-graduated man by calling 'the great togetherness' and adding, 'in the great togetherness there are no "whys", only "thuses", and you just have to accept, as the only authentic raw material of your spirit, your own "thus" which is always so.' In and out of these great togethernesses it came to appear to me that the story brings us a sense of this unique 'so' that is to be the seed of becoming in ourselves during the time which is our lot.

This is what gives the artist in the story-teller his meaning and justification to go on telling his story, and sustains him, despite a lack of material reward or recognition, in poverty and hunger. Even though his work falls on stony ground and deaf ears or is trodden under the indifferent feet of the proliferating generations too busy to live in their frantic search for the joys and hopes of gaining the honours of the plausible world about them, this radar of the story never fails him. He does not even try to know but, through an inborn acceptance of the demands of the gift which entered him at birth, spins his story in the loom of his imagination. The life in him knows that once a story is truly told, the art which this mysterious gift places at his disposal will, when the time is ready – and the readiness is all – find listeners to take it in; their lives will be enlarged and the life even of the deaf and dumb around them will never be the same again.

The Voice of the Thunder, 'The Great Memory'

The Zen that held their Shinto-rooted imaginations was non-rational, unconceptualized and a growth in the Japanese spirit, and it sprouted from seeds of stories like parables regarding the conduct and example of centuries of Zen masters and their pupils. And it came over me that the story could be so important in that regard because, if truly told, it had the seeds of new being in it. None of us, it struck me then, could take such a story into our imaginations without being changed by it. That was the urge which forced the Masters of Zen to resist the written word and pass on in endless anecdotes and stories from lip to lips of living men, alive and dynamic in their search for enlightenment. For the first time I realized that this was precisely what Christ had done. Although he could confound Pharisees and scholars in the Temple of temples with his learning, he too avoided the written word in delivering the message which was the 'end unto which he had been born'. He left the writing to others, and conveyed to his disciples and the world the meaning of his coming only through example and the living word of the living God with whom it had been in the beginning. He refused to pen it down in unchanging sentences that would start the process of special pleading for absolutes that men call dogma and doctrine. How blind I had been not to notice the significance before of so obvious a fact in the life of the greatest source of enlightenment in Christendom! And why could not so great a community of seeking as evidenced there be pooled, and all made to enrich rather than divide one another?

Yet Being Someone Other, Chapter 5

The not inconsiderable group of people, so absorbed that they did not notice our arrival, were there at the feet of a man sitting on a yellow mat talking in a low, clear voice. He was dressed in a golden kimono, held with a broad sash woven of green and red round the middle. It was a far more abundant garment than usual, and lay with ample folds around him that overruled any shape or movement of his body within, and fell wide to the ground to disguise even the way he sat. In this sense he was more like a monument of singular authority rather than the man himself. This authority was immeasurably increased by the head and face above the dress. It was the face of an old man with features of a cast so old that it seemed beyond measure of antiquity that I possessed regarding the history of Japan. He looked, in fact, like one of those philosophers, statesmen, poets or resolved servants of the earliest emperors of China, serving, in exile from the people they loved and all that they valued, on the frontier of some remote province among the barbaric subjects of their imperial masters. They did so with such absolute commitment that some of the most moving and healing poetry of classical China before its age of 'troubles' came from their philosophical brush to convey a quality which seemed personified in the man now talking with such hypnotic power to the little gathering. His skin was like an ancient parchment, covered with innumerable creases and lines as of sensitive writing describing a long record of complex experience of life, and so exacting metamorphosis of its hurt, injury, conflict and, perhaps even most demanding, the pull of its pleasures. It was the face, indeed, of someone who had made his final peace with chance and circumstance, and so could speak without impediment or interruption because the words that came to him were not so much his own as those of finalities and necessities of life speaking through him. And so, as if to complete the authenticity of the image that came to me, he had a long, thin, grey beard as in the earliest paintings of the pioneer sages of China, while the hands that emerged from the wide sleeves of his coat were elegant, the fingers long, palms broad and used to illustrate his meaning, eloquent not in terms of the words they accompanied so much as of the rhythm of a spirit conducting a sacred rite. Somehow I seemed to know him and his function before Mr Tajima whispered to me, 'He is a travelling and professional story-teller.'

Yet Being Someone Other, Chapter 5

I became apprehensive about the decline of the story in its most relevant and contemporary form, and its reduction to more and more archaic expressions in the cold, brutal sensation and action-dominated fiction starved of soliloquy and inward vision. Stories were increasingly being strung along on thin, arbitrary threads of a bleak curiosity without a twist of fantasy, feeling and wonder in their making, or, worst of all, reduced to adroit and nimble paper-chases of intellect. They were written computer-wise without regard for humanity and its flesh and blood to give them life, as if all were mind – and the metamorphic spirit had no part in it. It struck me as a symptom of a deep and alarming sickness in the heart of our time, a loss of soul as the primitive companions of my boyhood would have called it, and as such an erosion of the power of increase and renewal that we and our societies so desperately needed. Where, I wondered with increasing dismay, had all the stories gone? Why this decay of the great and meaningful orchestration of the story that had occurred everywhere in the nineteenth and early twentieth centuries? What made eminent critics say complacently and with an assumption of ultimate authority, 'The novel is dead', as if it were some kind of archaic technology of the imagination, to be superseded by something more up to date? I knew writers with imaginations so bankrupt that they no longer gave birth to the characters of their stories but went to research them in the world about them. There was no metamorphosis of fiction, which is art, but rather sociological essays on people without a breath of invention or fantasy to give life to them.

The Voice of the Thunder, 'The Great Memory'

The world of fairytale and folklore proclaims with irrefutable accuracy that no matter how many evil feminine forces and wicked masculine ones in the shapes of ugly sisters, witches, giants, uncles, stepfathers and stepmothers combine against creation on earth, somewhere always there is something built into life to counter them: a small, often despised something, a mere Tom Thumb, a crumpled old man, a humble, simple peasant couple like Baucis and Philemon, or even just a being of potential nobility disguised as a repulsive toad.

The Voice of the Thunder, 'The Great Memory'

I myself, in my own small way in south-east Asia and all over Africa, had tried in vain to achieve a more merciful settlement of our debt to life. I had tried for some fifty years through my writing to prevent petrification and judgement according to the letter of archaic law in a court of fate whose appointed officers were executioners without love, and disaster without human bonds. How could men still doubt that disaster and suffering were the terrible physicians summoned by life when all other more gentle means of healing them had failed?

Yet Being Someone Other, Chapter 7

The Artist

It was as if I were looking at it with my eyes opened to a wider vision, as happens when one sees a landscape, no matter how familiar, after confrontation with a rendering of it by a new, great and inspired painter, and is humbled and somewhat outraged by the realization of how small a shift of position in our wilful senses it took to make accessible such unsuspected riches of shape, colour and rhythm in what had appeared an exhausted view for so long.

The Voice of the Thunder, 'The Great Memory'

There was the moment when she had done her work on his head as well as she could, and, despite an intense dissatisfaction at what was still left out, could use those words that, for an artist conscious of all the other possibilities and subtleties of interpretation and expression shut out in the finality of any given form, are as much a sentence of death as a certificate of birth: 'I have finished.'

A Mantis Carol, 'Mantis Follows Through'

He thought Rembrandt's self-portraits, and particularly the portraits of his old age, the greatest pictures ever painted. We found him several times with the large book of Rembrandt reproductions open on his knee, a glass of brandy by his side, staring with searching concentration at Rembrandt's last self-portrait, rather as I have since seen condemned people look at their own reflections before being taken out to their execution. One day, a little drunk, he exclaimed:

'See that! If ever you children want to know what a man who does 'what he would not' looks like, here is one! If you want to know what it feels like to be old and to look and look at yourself in a glass darkly and ask, 'What the hell have I been about?' and to get no answer, except to be told to go on and on looking, here it is.'

The Face Beside the Fire, Chapter 4

'I am an old man now and not since my early youth have I been so uplifted by an exhibition. Please do not think me patronizing if I say that you have a very great talent, a very profound gift for painting,

[201]

which is all the more reason why I feel bound to raise my aged voice before the confused clamour of blind and misleading although well-deserved praise explodes around your ears.

'Monsieur, I feel compelled to remind you of the grave and onerous obligations a gift like yours imposes. Oh! I do trust, Monsieur, that you will not regard it lightly. I have seen nearly three generations of painters come and go but none to whom paint has been so native, so much their own aboriginal idiom, as with you. You think, you feel, you wake and sleep in paint, and I hope you will not overlook the significance of such unanimity. All my life I have seen people painting with tired unsleeping eyes propped open by brittle theories of bright, determined minds. But you, Monsieur, so it seemed to me today, by some miracle were born free of mental despotism, and may well in time bring back to painting the sleep and the dreams it sorely needs. Therefore, I repeat, Monsieur, a gift like yours is a solemn responsibility. It is not yours so much as a great and difficult trust confided to you on behalf of life.

'Above all, Monsieur, I pray you, do not neglect the sane and wise and healing discipline of self-portraiture. It is an ancient practice that has long fallen in disrepute but if I may advise you, I would recommend that in your inevitable moments of confusion and doubt, you sit down quietly and look into yourself with those far-seeing, undogmatic eyes of yours and paint yourself as truly as you painted these African animals, these black hunters and sheepshearers, whose darkness reverberates with the tread of the ultimate sun like the sound of a horn in the silence of the great woods, these southern interiors sullen with sunlight and these London rooftops gay with soot and rust even in their autumnal mist and fog. If that is too much to ask of yourself, go to some friend whom you respect and trust and ask him to do a portrait of you and borrow his eyes to read the magnetic compass within yourself. Whatever happens do not neglect what is the natural and only sure way for a person like yourself of increasing his knowledge of himself. For believe me, Monsieur, if you dedicate yourself truly to your natural calling, all the self-knowledge in the world will not come amiss.'

The Face Beside the Fire, Chapter 10

David was beginning to paint in a new way. The outside world seemed suddenly to have ceased to exist for him. His back was determinedly turned on life as we normally see and experience it. He who until now had loved the ceaseless traffic of light, colour, sound and smells, the world charged with meaning and beauty, suddenly rejected it all, and began to paint only a strange world within. I have said 'a' and not 'the' deliberately for had it been the whole of the world within I would not have been so worried. After all, the world within and the world without are equally valid although neither of them in isolation is ultimately adequate. It is possible for a nature to be dedicated to all of either without damage to its integrity. But David's new world was only a fragment, a carefully selected portion of the immense within.

The world he was painting was centred entirely in his head. It gave me the impression that his nature, feeling itself threatened from within, had withdrawn itself to where it felt strongest and would be most accessible to external support; but in the process it had abandoned all its defences to the enemy. In three years his painting had become the painting of a man in desperate retreat, of a person holding on to life not by instinctive love but merely by a conscious and determined effort of the will and the mind.

And the images that crowded into his pictures clearly showed it. They had no colour or solid, rounded shape to them, no muscle and bone, but were so cold, thin, unfelt and miasmic that they drifted like the ghosts of unborn and miscarried children across his canvases. No human body had any honour with this new David. From the chin downwards the body had ceased to have meaning; arms, legs, hands and feet were perfunctorily added, and often the ribs and spine were shown through a wide-open chest, like the columns of a chapel in front of a deserted and crumbling altar.

But if the shapes in David's pictures lacked recognizable bodies, they were never short of heads. Two, three and even four heads on one thin neck and one brittle, mist-dissolving body were not uncommon. Many faces had two or three rows of eyes, one mouth and jaw in front and another in reserve, and one noble, high brow stacked upon another. This obsession with the head, as if a multiplicity of these could make up for the utter and total rejection of what was below, was so marked that I could find a parallel for it only in the remote and legendary past, and I realized sadly that David had not only rejected the world without but also the world of his own urgent time. He had ceased to be contemporary; had ceased to meet the demands proper to his age and its time context and had gone archaic. I felt the only people who could welcome this David and his work with understanding and sympathy were those Greeks for whom the hydra-headed monster was a living reality.

The sense of danger and unrecognized distress that went with all these multi-headed designs was truly alarming. One saw those colourless phantom figures fleeing in flames through streets, pursued always by some nameless thing out of sight, or else standing on the edge of bridges with broken arches, one row of eyes focused one way, the other row another, staring down into dark, unrippled waters at dead and drowning female faces staring expressionlessly upwards. But where was that inner richness of colour and shape which life welcomes into the heart of our being? Oh, it was very sad and most bitter. Finally, I saw the portrait of a man with a most moving, sensitive, wide-eyed face, and a noble head slightly bowed with infinite resignation. The head was full-face and was unexpectedly real, although it was supported on the left and the right by its own profiles. The body was a phantom shape composed of the dispersing smoke of a burnt-out fire. Out of the corner of each of the beautiful, tragic eyes, a tear like a Pacific pearl with a sad, submarine stain on it, was falling. This painting was called 'The Exile' and the moment I saw it, I understood.

I was looking at the new photography, the photography of the great and threatened world within. What David was doing was to copy with photographic and unerring exactitude his own state of mind and spirit. He was constructing an Admiralty chart of the troubled seas of his own being. It confirmed every fear I had. I looked at 'The Exile' closely and saw that the features were David's. At last, he had done a portrait of himself, as that wise old Frenchman had so long ago suggested. But he had left it dangerously, perhaps fatally, late.

The Face Beside the Fire, Chapter 14

The great cathartic role of tragedy in life and art, and the reclamation of human suffering in the discovery of its position in the progression of universal meaning, seems for the moment to have been abolished.

In so far as it is acknowledged in art anyway, it is more and more as a kind of sick joke played by life on man, if not a meaningless farce. It is as if the human spirit is increasingly in the grip of an age of ice and cold, impersonal indifference in command of its values. The free exercise of fantasy which is the imagination unsevered from its instinctive roots at play, has gone from literature and art . . . The visual arts more and more have withdrawn from the objective without, severed its links with its counterpart within and see and portray in this dark averted dimension the symptoms of anger, rebellion and dissociation caused by stubborn neglect of our natural spirit. D'Annunzio's resounding objection to the science of his day, because it presupposed a corpse, could be applied to the immense, laborious exercise of dissection which occupies so much of the spirit of our time and prevents it from a renewal and reintegration of its wounded, fragmented self.

Jung and the Story of Our Time, 'Epilogue'

But what held my attention still with the shock of discovery was the painting that looked down at us from the centre of what was left of the wall and dome of the cave. Heavy as were the shadows, and seeing it only darkly against the sharp morning light, it was yet so distinct and filled with fire of its own colour that every detail stood out with a burning clarity. In the focus of the painting, scarlet against the gold of the stone, was an enormous eland bull standing sideways, his massive body charged with masculine power and his noble head looking as if he had only that moment been disturbed in his grazing. He was painted as only a Bushman, who had a deep identification with the eland, could have painted him. Moreover, it seemed that he had been painted at a period before the Bushman's serenity was threatened, for the look of calm and trustful inquiry on the eland's face was complete. I was greatly moved because it seemed to me that this was the look with which not only the eland but the whole of the life of Africa must have regarded us when first we landed there. On the left of the bull, also deep in scarlet, was a tall female giraffe with an elegant Modigliani neck. With the tenderness of a solicitous mother she was looking past the eland towards a baby giraffe standing shyly in the right of the picture. In the same righthand corner of the canvas below them the artist had signed this painting on the high wall with a firm impress of the palms of both hands, fingers extended and upright. The signature was marked so gaily and spontaneously that it brought an instant smile to my face. It looked so young and fresh that it mocked my recollection that rock paintings signed in this manner are among the oldest in the world.

The Lost World of the Kalahari, Chapter 8

One also should not forget that there is a sense in which Christ was an artist: Van Gogh, in one of his letters to his brother Theo, said something to the effect: 'All other forms of art pale into insignificance compared with the art of Christ. We paint on canvas but Christ was an artist in flesh and blood . . .' It comes back to what I have always felt, that it was not for nothing that for the Greeks and the Romans art was a divine process and the function of art was a religious function; that the true artist is following, whether he knows it or not, Christ's injunction to be guided by the guide he left behind, which was the Holy Ghost. Goethe made an interesting observation. He said, 'All art loses meaning and becomes merely repetitive when it loses contact with its religious motivation.'

A Walk with a White Bushman

Art, for me, became increasingly a manifestation of pentecostal spirit, seeking to make men aware of a greater reality. It introduced the seed of a greater becoming in the midst of our being: and out of this element of becoming we derived our senses of meaning and belonging. I saw art as a magic mirror making visible what is invisible in us and the life of our time. An instrument also for making what is oldest in the human spirit contemporary and new. It was an unfailing source of increasing human awareness, and by such increase enabled life to renew itself in greater and more authoritative expressions of itself. Without art truth was not whole.

Jung and the Story of Our Time, 'The Time and the Space'

Sometimes I think beauty is the bravest thing on earth. It goes on day after day, in spite of all the ugliness men bring to it.

The Hunter and the Whale, Chapter 13

Chapter Ten

Life and Love

═══

The Mysterious Business of Life

At heart life is utterly mysterious and in consequence is a matter for natural faith and trust. Without this essential acceptance of mystery, our consciousness is deprived of a vital proportion of reality and tends to be excessive and arrogant in its claims. We need a sense of wonder, for it is part of our wholeness and keeps us humble and our minds in position.

The Dark Eye in Africa, Part III, 'The Discussion'

I believe that my own life established some small but undeniable and imperial facts: namely that every life is extraordinary; that the 'average man' is a statistical abstraction and does not exist; and that every single one of us – not excluding the disabled, maimed, blind, deaf, dumb and the bearers of unbearable suffering – matters to a Creation that has barely begun.

Yet Being Someone Other, Chapter 7

Great beginnings tend to have the shape of the dwarf and the uniform of the clown.

The Hunter and the Whale, Chapter 9

'Perhaps what life intends to be great it first makes small, so small that it can be almost imperceptible . . . P'raps that's where we all go wrong. We're too impressed by what is great, established in the world around us to notice that bulk and greatness have already lost the power of increase and are doomed to die . . . I think it's the last and the least we notice and care for within ourselves which is often destined to be first and most.'

The Face Beside the Fire, Chapter 16

The good, true and real in life not only have no use for secrecy but shun it like the devil. It is a subtle, diabolic and corrosive poison which, unless utterly rejected, ultimately eats its way into every cell of our being.

The Face Beside the Fire, Chapter 14

The art of living . . . is nothing if it does not consist of being sensible on completely non-sensible grounds.

Story Like the Wind, Chapter 9

There is nothing more dangerous for man in the bush than regular habits.

A Story Like the Wind, Chapter 9

Never try to go ahead of your spoor. Many a man has died because he has not observed the discipline of the spoor to the end.

A Story Like the Wind, Chapter 5

'But what good is a long view to us whose lives are conceived in terms of a short view? If we try to look further than the life that is in us, it merely lands us in confusion, in a vague speculation which is only too easy since the reality that must qualify it does not yet exist. Isn't it better to look around our feet, there where we can see clearest, not there where we can see furthest? If we look at the steps, won't the miles and the years take care of themselves? Anyway, I am going to begin there. I'm going to begin by minding my own step. Each one must take heed for himself, and the system will in the end take heed for itself. If the system perpetuates a colour prejudice, we can counteract it by refusing to admit a colour prejudice in our own lives, we can live as if no colour prejudice existed. If we are too rich we can counteract riches by leading a simple life and helping the poor. I am tired of people who still point me only to a cross in Palestine, tired of people who are always telling me to keep my eyes on the horizon, looking for a justice which never comes. I don't know if I want justice, lest in justice being done to others justice should be done to me. It is not justice I need, but forgiveness. Never again shall I reject, or not recognize, affection offered me, but take it and go on alone with my love. That's all; no more . . . I shall mind my own step.'

In a Province, Book III, Chapter 6

'You allow yourself to feel sorry only because otherwise your essential indifference would be intolerable to you. No pity is worth the name of pity unless it has the courage of the actions that pity demands.'

In a Province, Book II, Chapter 4

Manners are an age-old condition of the civilized mind, in order to have a system of behaviour which prevents human contact from sliding into chaos and old night. The primitive peoples of Africa that I have known have wonderful manners and the most courteous and orderly forms of debate. One of the most significant things for me in Dante's great journey down into Hell and up into Heaven was that in Hell there was an absence of good manners; when he emerged and arrived in Purgatory he was amazed how grace and courtesy between the spirits he encountered were already present, and increased with a breathtaking and inspiring acceleration as he neared Paradise.

A Walk with a White Bushman

[Mori] declared he was first of all going to teach me how to fall without doing myself injury in the process. He then said that, as in life, one had first to learn how to fall before one could learn how to get up and rise; first master the how of losing properly before one could be worthy of winning.

Yet Being Someone Other, Chapter 4

He appeared incapable of being frustrated, and seemed to regard 'setbacks' in life as an experienced climber recognizes false summits on the way to the top of a mountain.

Yet Being Someone Other, Chapter 4

I took a liking to him at once. It is not difficult to like people provided they have something in their lives that they themselves like. Liking begets liking. The difficult people are the great critics, the ones who cannot find anything in life to like.

Venture to the Interior, Chapter 10

No life, however humble, was ever without universal importance if it truly followed its own natural gift, even if it was only to plough a straight furrow and plant potatoes well.

Yet Being Someone Other, Chapter 7

As Hamlet put it so heartrendingly to himself: 'The readiness is all.' If one is truly ready within oneself and prepared to commit one's readiness without question to the deed that follows naturally on it, one finds life and circumstance surprisingly armed and ready at one's side.

The Lost World of the Kalahari, Chapter 4

'It is late! Take up again the individual adventure before it is too late and assert your own, your true, unique and basic differences. Your love of life depends on your living your differences and your wholeness in love. Without love and wholeness there is no security. Walk out of your mindmade Kremlins before life stands still in you as it does in bees and ants which can repeat only themselves. Live your difference for love of the increasing wholeness it brings, and you will have adventure such as the world has never seen. Have done with loveless, substitute begetting. Live out your own nature fully and do not pile on the generations to come, who already have loads of their own heavy enough, the burden you shirked of unravelling your secret nature and letting out your imprisoned and unlived self.'

The Face Beside the Fire, Chapter 22

One of the most difficult problems for me in life has always been to draw a distinction between fear and wishful thinking on the one hand and valid intuition on the other.

The Night of the New Moon, 'Story'

Intuition is, I believe, a natural capacity in all living things to live around the corners of the future.

Yet Being Someone Other, Chapter 4

The battle of the universe is made specific for us in the small and has to be fought out not only in heroic issues, but in trivial series of choices during our daily round.

The Hunter and the Whale, Chapter 12

I have never . . . taken salt for granted. I felt that for the first time I had an inkling of the meaning of that question in the New Testament which like all truly profound questions answers itself by implying a greater question: 'If the salt should lose its savour wherewith will ye put it back again?' . . . The gift of life is always worth the cost, whatever that cost may be.

First Catch Your Eland, Chapter 1

Nothing that is ever done is ever wasted or without effect on life. Nothing is ever so insignificant as to be unimportant. Everything in life matters and ultimately has a place, an impact and a meaning.

A Far-Off Place, Chapter 15

Though we can cheat and defeat ourselves we cannot cheat and defeat life.

The Face Beside the Fire, Chapter 7

The problems of life, the problems of the universe, the problems of man, are our most precious possessions because they are the raw materials of our redemption.

A Walk with a White Bushman

This shrill, brittle, self-important life of today is by comparison a graveyard where the living are dead and the dead are alive and talking in the still, small, clear voice of a love and trust in life that we have for the moment lost . . .

All on earth and in the universe were still members and family of the early race seeking comfort and warmth through the long, cold

night before the dawning of individual consciousness in a togetherness which still gnaws like an unappeasable homesickness at the
base of the human heart.

The Voice of the Thunder, 'The Great Memory'

This, then, was a certainty which has never left me since that
moment: life was greater than non-life, meaning more powerful than
meaninglessness, and all were bound irresistibly from a half-way to
a full house of love.

Yet Being Someone Other, Chapter 7

All life is just an imperfect effort towards answering the perfect
question.

The Hunter and the Whale, Chapter 8

I think one's whole life is a search, is a matter of reunion as Dante
sought it, with God, a reunion with one's origin. I always feel that
origin and destination are one; they are the same thing in the human
spirit, and the whole of life consists of making your way back to
where you came from and becoming reunited with it in a greater
awareness than when you left it; by then adding it to your own
awareness, you become part of cosmic awareness.

A Walk with a White Bushman

Masculine, Feminine and the Foursome Spirit

There is room for both, for Ariel and Caliban, for Cain and Abel,
there room for all, without murder, at the centre, in the heart,
without circumference . . .

For there, in the heart, man's own dark aboriginal courage makes
him free, his humbleness before the mystery of his being brings
awareness, awareness makes him whole, and wholeness gives him
love . . . Give him a horse, give him a spear and bring out the
dragon!

Venture to the Interior, Chapter 21

There are, I know, human beings either doomed or blessed to a way of life which deprives them of any of the normal indulgences and privileges of their communities. It is almost as if they are charged with a role that sets them apart and makes them incapable of joining in the society of men. They are, as it were, victims of a kind of Ancient Mariner compulsion of the spirit, which makes them incapable of participation in the round of life which is symbolized in its essentials by the church of collective humanity. It is not that such men do not feel human in themselves and seek to shun the company of their own kind. If once known and understood . . . it is clear that the longing within them to be part of the ordinary community of man is greater than that of any of those who daily take for granted such belonging.

Yet Being Someone Other, Chapter 3

I have always been appalled by St Paul's attitude to sex and women. He was in large measure responsible for organized Christianity's lack of recognition of the sexual values of the spirit, and its profound dismissal of the importance both of the woman in life and in the spirit of man. This was a tendency already encouraged in The Old Testament and its dedication to a masculine patriarchal concept of God.

Jung and the Story of Our Time, 'Errant and Adventure'

. . . the vast complex of the consequence of a compulsive suppression of sex in the mind and customs of man was so great that one could easily see why, as Freud implied, it could appear as the villain in almost every piece of human folly and individual and cultural derangement. Even the Victorian dancing, just becoming fashionable in our late-Edwardian colonial day, was regarded as sinful. A young girl I knew, for instance, was badly beaten with a length of rope by her eldest brother because she had taken part in an impromptu dance in a house where she happened to be staying. Woman's place was so much confined to the home, kitchen and nurseries, that one of my own sisters had sermons preached against her in our local church because she had had the presumption to become one of the first of her sex to go to a university and take a degree.

Obviously, in such a world, this aspect of Freud's approach had to have a certain compelling validity. Yet for me it failed because, ultimately, sex remained a part and not all, nor, indeed, even the greatest of the sources of life's energies.

Jung and the Story of Our Time, 'The Time and the Space'

The underground stresses caused by this elevation of the masculine, however necessary, and the general lack of recognition of the importance of the feminine, caused the great war of the Amazons which came near to man's undoing – and that pattern too . . . was strangely contemporary, for I recognized all over the place, particularly in the places of European man, a kind of gang warfare raging between the angry and rejected feminine and the men of power and establishment. I could name many of them and give chapter and verse of their work and their histories, and show how the rejection has been so deep that they denied even their own feminine nature, just as the Amazons did, and pursued an ersatz masculinity instead. Happily there has been as yet no repeat of an all-out war, because there are too many other signs of a healing totality, a foursome at work in the spirit of man. I refer to the feminine in the man and the masculine in the woman, no longer denied either by the man or the woman but two twosomes making a fourfold spirit with a fourfold vision of life. And that, too, I am certain is where . . . the rounding of the square of ourselves is to happen.

About Blady, Chapter 5

I was predisposed to notice in prison a strange kind of longing among the Japanese for the moon; and out of this longing a kind of frustration and a kind of rage over the frustration which added to the power of this very deep longing . . . And I often wondered if there were a rearrangement, a reversal, of the poles in the Japanese spirit, with the moon a sort of implied masculine, and their sun a great feminine . . . For the Germans too the moon is masculine and the sun is feminine and these things are signposts of the spirit; they and we should perhaps not think, so much as wonder, aloud about such things.

A Walk with a White Bushman

Her belief in the unending continuity and flow of life from before and beyond any rhyme, reason, idea or temporary arrest of it, was so deep ... that it appeared to be not a form of belief so much as an irrefutable kind of knowledge built into the heart of that woman. Accordingly she despised those women who because of the terrible world situation proclaimed that they would bear no more children to suffer as they had suffered. Life was a woman's answer to the enemies of life, she said. Men like his Australians might have to fight death with death just as, she understood, in Australia they fought bush fires with fire. That was a man's answer to the death about now and she'd respected it. But a woman could only answer death with more life. Yet could a man respect the answer from the woman irrespective of the form wherein it was given, just as she respected and accepted the brutal necessity of the man's?

The Seed and the Sower, 'The Sword and the Doll'

Men had a terrible tendency to institutionalize life. Fear of life, born from their own wilful estrangement from it, made men build fortresses to hold what they had chosen to select from life. Instead of striving to make permanent the passing forms and shapes of meaning, it would be more creative if they entrusted themselves to the natural processes of change and so refused to become ensnared in surface patterns.

The Seed and the Sower, 'The Sword and the Doll'

[David and Alis watched the sunset from their boat] ... they felt infinitely privileged as if they had just been presented with the fundamental symbol of the master pattern wherein opposites lost themselves in some greater meaning.

The Face Beside the Fire, Chapter 18

Although it is in the nature of the masculine to possess the will and armour, it needs the feminine to evoke the love of the whole that will give it the employment of meaning in life once called knightly, so that on occasions such as this, when those elements of masculine and feminine meet, the imagination immediately experiences the transformation which was once called chivalrous.

A Mantis Carol, 'The Carol'

'Life's made us keepers of the authentic image, the original blue-prints of each other, and there's no escape from this charge. You, the woman, have to teach your male to be male; and the man his female to be woman ... O my beloved ... help me to be my full self and I'll reward you with a life in which you need never submit to compromise.'

The Face Beside the Fire, Chapter 20

Ever since she could remember she'd known that some day someone would say just that thing to her. She'd nursed that knowledge against all the experience of her world. In the midst of a life of deliberate planning she'd clung to the irrational knowledge that one day from a far country, from a wild and perilous shore in a snarling and foaming sea, someone whom she did not know and yet would know instantly would make his way to her through great danger, recognize her instantly, and brushing the banal crowd aside take her by the hand and say: 'Come!' And at once she would leave whatever she was doing, however urgent, and go. She had held on to this blind knowledge until even she had begun to lose heart; and reason, affection and loyalty had forced a compromise upon her, a denial of her true faith: yet even then faith had not died. Through the paralysis of compromise this dream had stayed alive. If her life were to have all its full meaning and become open-eyed and truly alive, compromise had to be killed and the last ghost of it exorcised from her heart.

So, the moment she saw David she'd recognized him. He'd walked straight into this image burning in the darkness of her being like a soldier into armour made ready for him.

The Face Beside the Fire, Chapter 17

I have never been able to believe that a woman's task in life is limited to her children. I can quite well conceive that in my mother, as with more and more women of our own day, there is an urge to creativeness which lies underneath and deeper, above and beyond the begetting of children. These women have a contract with life itself, which is not discharged by the mere procreation of their species. Men recognize and try to honour this contract in themselves as a matter of course. Their contribution to life vibrates with their passionate rebellion against the narrowly conceived idea that would restrict their role to that of protectors and feeders of women and children. They do not acknowledge and respect the same thing so readily in women. Perhaps until they do the world will not see the full creative relationship that life intends there should be between men and women.

Venture to the Interior, Chapter 1

It was her first clear annunciation of the role in which women are compelled at one and the same time to be both mistress and mother to their men.

A Far-Off Place, Chapter 7

For a moment she looked intently and searchingly at herself in the mirror. The clear, nostalgic sun of an African winter was just beginning to clear the tree-tops, to come through the wide window, to shed along the edges of the carpet and round her tall graceful figure, a delicate, silvery glow, so subtle and intimate, that it seemed to emanate as much from within her as from without. She felt as if she was looking not at her reflection but at a portrait of herself, in which some great artist had portrayed a personal defeat so great and yet so heroically and gracefully borne that it had become almost a form of victory. She lifted a hand to her heart, or rather to the heart of the person she saw in the mirror, in a gesture of the most delicate and compassionate understanding, and at that moment the door of her bedroom flew open and David rushed in, almost breathless with excitement, crying, 'Oh, Mummy, Mummy! what's it? Klara says . . .' and then he too saw her reflection in the mirror, stopped suddenly, stood silently gaping at his mother's graceful back and her luminous reflection beyond, and said, 'Golly!'

Mary had not turned for she could see quite clearly behind her own reflection the open door and David standing in it, his eager face first flushed and excited, and then dissolved in an instant trance of wonder.

Suddenly she felt loth to leave their reflection in the mirror and wished she could perpetuate the moment, for perhaps if they could but stand there long enough, some answer would be born to flush the meaningless inarticulate yesterdays with the meaning of this new today. She felt more real, more alive in that reflection of herself than she had done for years. Her son's unfeigned admiration, vivid and true with the healing integrity of the spontaneous, made her feel strangely fulfilled and reassured her that what she saw in the quicksilver frame was no illusion of her poignant mind. But, once she'd turned her back on this illumination of herself she knew she would be again in the familiar room and life she had known so well these thirty years and more. She longed to throw herself in the arms of the woman she saw in front of her, to weep and to weep long on that medieval shoulder and ask forgiveness . . .

The Face Beside the Fire, Chapter 2

Marriage

My father was still alive and a lawyer much in demand. As a politician and statesman he was away a great deal and she never failed to accompany him, because, great and natural mother as she was, she knew that for all the assurance and authority with which he moved in the world, there was a neglected child in him that needed mothering, even more than her own children did.

The Voice of the Thunder, 'The Great Memory'

It was not that she felt no grief at all over Albert's death. A woman could not live with a man of Albert's quality for thirty years, bear him seven children and then not feel sad at his dying. But the grief she felt was human and general, rather than personal and particular. Her inmost self was hardly darkened by grief. On the contrary part of her deepest being experienced such a wild, barbaric upsurge of relief that it could find no frank and undisguised place in her conscious Christian thinking, in the high-principled conception of herself by which she had lived and been upheld these thirty years. She could look the beautiful widow of a distinguished man, dignified and noble in grief for all the world to see and admire, and from which her daylight self too could take heart. But she was only technically a widow. She was in terms of the fundamental values of life and of her own special being, not a bereaved wife but the virgin mother of seven. Somewhere far down within her the drums had started to beat again.

The children, the servants, even the dogs and the cats in the household knew with instant intuition that some profound restraint had suddenly been abolished in Mary, and instinctively they readjusted themselves accordingly. With the inevitable exception of Anna Maria and David, they fell overnight into easier, more spontaneous relationships with their mother and with one another.

The Face Beside the Fire, Chapter 4

He had told her plainly he could only go into marriage with her as a friend. At the time it had sounded so reasonable, even dignified, that he thought it would be almost easy. But he soon found that there were other sides to his nature that took a different view. His body, for instance, was most crudely, obstinately and blindly difficult on this issue. It did not like being touched or fondled by Helena. No matter how much David's mind and initial affection objected to this behaviour, his body continued to shrink from Helena. Time and again he was startled and dismayed by the violence with which this impermanent physical substance of his being rose into rebellion, and its refusal to be convinced and guided by his own unselfish motivations. The only time when it was more or less tolerant of physical contact with Helena was when it was soothed by drink.

The Face Beside the Fire, Chapter 14

Slowly she is poisoning Albert so that she can be free for you. No, you needn't be alarmed, the police will never know. This poison Mary uses is found in no chemist's book of dangerous drugs. It is unrecognized and irrecognizable in the world of science and reason. It's an imponderable pollen of a deadly nightshade. Every night when Albert is asleep, it enters his being to corrode his will and desire to live. It is a poison brewed from all the words, the delicate, tender, burning trivialities and petty endearments she's never used – but would so constantly have spoken if she'd truly loved him. Despise them not, these little sounds – they're as necessary to the human heart as golden bees to flowers, by taste of honey unmade, provoked to fly the traffic of love from cup to cup otherwise condemned to die narcissus-bound to one still reflection in their own deep scented pools. Make no mistake: Albert's tired rejected heart hungrily draws in the poison of this sweet neglect through his dreaming brain.

The Face Beside the Fire, Chapter 22

What went on in the Denysse home during those eighteen months was a demonstration of the terrible truth that there are no panders, procurers and pimps so cunning and irresistible as those parents who themselves have not experienced love.

The Face Beside the Fire, Chapter 19

At this time Alis had only one real weapon for use: the idea of marriage had never presented itself to her as a career. She saw it as the one free, supreme, equal and opposite relationship . . . an adventure of two free and coincident individuals.

The Face Beside the Fire, Chapter 19

Outside the last of the shelters sat two of the oldest people I have ever seen. They were Nxou's grandparents and the skins of both were so creased and stained with life, weather, and time that they might have been dark brown parchment covered with some close Oriental script. Both had serene expressions on their faces and they looked continually from one to the other as if in constant need of reassurance that the miracle of being together after so many years was indeed still real. They seemed to have grown old in the right way, they and their spirit being contained within their age as naturally as a nut is enclosed within a shell, and only when fully ripened falling obediently to the need for a renewal of life.

The Lost World of the Kalahari, Chapter 9

Home

My home was as pure a structure of love as simple, unpretentious flesh and blood could make it. But there are so many houses of the mind which are not homes and fortresses, but cages and prisons of the living spirit. These prisons have long, winding corridors and deep cells and dungeons from which one must escape unless . . . one is to become one's own gaoler. Indeed, this breaking down of prison doors, this riding forth to build one more warming fire against the storm and greater darknesses, is perhaps one of the more truly heroic tasks of life, for which the enduring spirit is allied to our frail and impermanent flesh and blood. For without it, life might so easily stand still and fail itself. It might fail because by standing still it forfeits the great, blessed, uncomfortable but heroic privilege of life which is to create beyond our immediate natures.

The Face Beside the Fire, Chapter 7

It was the 'Una Casa Portuguese' sung so often and well by Amalia Rodrigues . . . Yes, she would sing, in a Portuguese house there is always bread and wine on the table, and no matter who knocked on the door he was asked in to sit at the table. For in a Portuguese home, no matter how poor, the real wealth was in the capacity for giving. Four whitewashed walls, a smell of rosemary, some yellow grapes, geraniums and roses in the garden and a painting of the blessed St Joseph on the wall, that and a promise of spring and love under the sun, was a Portuguese home for her.

First Catch Your Eland, Chapter 2

Families

Alis and her father between them had achieved a most unusual relationship. It was founded really on Alis's uncanny understanding of her father. She was the pivot on which the relationship turned, she was the responsible partner and he relied on her. It was as if she alone had understood that this gallant and distinguished officer, this leader of men and captain of ships, had never really grown up and was at heart still a lone small boy, bullied by himself, his career and life, and in constant need of reassurance and simple, protective, unexacting affection. Alis not only understood it but in her immediate, unquestioning way lived her understanding. Her stepmother might be his wife, but Alis was mother to the unfulfilled child in him, and he turned all the more to Alis for feelings before and beyond resolute living.

The Face Beside the Fire, Chapter 19

Little that was new and creative could come out now from that family relationship. It could add to its own massive quantity but its creative qualities were exhausted. Like actors who had learnt their parts its members could now only continue to repeat their lines endlessly whilst getting relentlessly older. Their audiences alone could be renewed and refreshed, unless, of course, someone in the family could break free.

But breaking free is not just a matter of walking out of one's home and slamming the door behind one. One does not walk out so easily from the house, the solid and cunningly fortified building, the labyrinthine courtyard that the family has built in the mind, spirit and emotions, in the very sinews, nerves and reflexes of its members. It may not even always be desirable that one should do so.

The Face Beside the Fire, Chapter 7

We make a great mistake when we think that people whose lives have been intimately woven into our own, cease to influence us when they die. While they are living they are to us, as Albert was to David, many things. But with death, change and colour are sealed off. The quintessential thing that they have been in our lives is fixed and stabilized for good. All the rest is discarded. The dead become part of the dynamics of our spirit, of the basic symbolism of our minds. They join the infinite ranks of the past, as vast as the hosts of the future, and so much greater than our own little huddle of people in the present. The dead become allied as it were to the gods themselves and walk in company with the favourites of gods, sail on the seas of our spirit from the beginning to the end of our time or else sit immobile and dark with frustrated love and hatred on some twilit and receding foreshore of our being.

The Face Beside the Fire, Chapter 4

Being Young

I have always been amazed by the fact that at the moment of birth
the child still belongs to all the life that has ever been and not to the
moment so young in time in which we all appear so briefly. We
forget that it is our own life on earth that is so painfully new. What
we bring into it at birth is already as old as time. Our own progress
from there on is an act of increasing separation from that organic
and idiomatic antiquity of our being at our earthly beginning. To me
no child at birth is so young nor so poignant and unarmed as is the
boy or girl born into their own contemporary selves in adolescence.
This is particularly true now that all the aids designed by a wise and
infinitely experienced nature in rules and ritual of initiation for these
occasions have been universally discarded by our rational selves.

Jung and the Story of Our Time, 'The Lake and the River'

A baby an hour old is older, to me, than any adolescent. Babies
seem to be born with all antiquity present and active in them . . .
The adult world only gradually converts the currency of their
antiquity into the inflated coinage of the present until, by the time
they reach adolescence, they find the values of their inborn antiquity debased. They have come, as it were, to a market place
where their ancient exchange is no longer valid.

This is the moment of their own and personal birth, in which
they face a distinctive future inwardly naked and curiously
ashamed. All that seems left of their antiquity is a vast indefinable
nostalgia.

The Hunter and the Whale, Chapter 8

'Women and children, children and women,' David exploded,
'there seems to be nothing else in the world . . . wherever you go
you find there's either a woman or a child, or both, setting a trap
to get you back into the nursery.'

The Face Beside the Fire, Chapter 16

The world is over-peopled with child-mothers and boy-fathers and
their infant children . . . children, children everywhere and not a

grown-up mind and mature emotion in an adult body. Just children in grown-up bodies begetting beings whose adult causes their baby selves refuse to further. Life has begun to miss out a whole generation in its chain: the grown-up link between infant and child has vanished and a formless, stifling oblivion of wet baby-love, a damp mist of nursery emotion is taking the mature edge off the world, rusting through the all-weather steel in us.

The Face Beside the Fire, Chapter 19

This was perhaps one of the greatest burdens of being young; one was always expected to take, and so rarely thought to be in a position of ever wanting, and needing, to give as well. And what one had to give, even when accepted, once measured in the scales of deliberate values of the grown-up world, appeared trivial.

A Story Like the Wind, Chapter 7

'It would be quite easy for me to tell you what I think. But I'm not going to do so because it would be very wrong of me. The question is one which ultimately only you can answer for yourself. You must consult with your own mind and heart for they alone can tell you both what you can and should do. You don't need someone else's advice. In fact if your instincts seem reluctant to give you a clear answer at the moment, it may mean that already too many people and things have interfered between you and them. Your mother has thrust a man's decision on you. You are young but not too young for it. You must plough your life with your own plough. My plough might appear better than yours and I might lend it you for a bit, but in the end you will have to use your own. It is what life has given you, and you must work your lands accordingly.'

The Face Beside the Fire, Chapter 8

'You've no right to be contemplating your navel at sixteen, your vision should be focused a little lower down. You should be writing sonnets to the moon or to somebody's eyebrow.'

In a Province, Book I, Chapter 2

But before leaving, the young woman, standing there in the half-light of her new and desperate youngness with tears falling down her cheeks, took courage from her despair, stamped her foot at her mother and cried repeatedly: 'I wish I was dead! I wish I was dead!' The nature of her cry was unmistakable. The technique is as old as life itself. Wherever there is powerlessness, oppression and deep-rooted fear, human beings make themselves the subjects of wishes they dare not inflict openly on those who cause their fear and impotence. Since the wish is too urgent and too powerful to be repressed its involuntary begetters are forced to parade themselves also as its victims.

The Face Beside the Fire, Chapter 7

Love, the Aboriginal Tracker

Love . . . transcends all and is the light of darkness that leads man and God to the final wisdom.

A Walk with a White Bushman

There was no challenge, however great, reckless or cataclysmic in its onslaught, that a spirit in full possession of love could not overcome.

A Mantis Carol, 'The Carol'

Once exposed to the experience of love, there was no room for past or present hatred left in him, and space only for a growing disposition towards sweetness and yet more love. It was proof of how love was the only source of a spirit incapable of corruption either by worldly power or suffering.

A Mantis Carol, 'The Carol'

The spirit of man is nomad, his blood bedouin, and love is the aboriginal tracker on the faded desert spoor of his lost self.

A Walk with a White Bushman

People . . . still sow out of their love of the oppressed the seeds of a terrible hate. Life is bent low with hate. But take heart. For here, where your footsteps disappear, so near that if you stretched out

[226]

your hands you could almost feel them, come the feet of the generations that trample the dim future and there may be love at their side.

In a Province, final words

If there is one telling image inherited from the past that causes much fatal, cynical and ironical misunderstanding it is the image of the blindness of love. If there is one thing love is not, it is blind. If it possesses a blindness at all, it is a blindness to the man and the mind-made blindnesses of life; to the dead-ends, the culs-de-sac and hopelessnesses of our being. In all else it is clear and far-sighted as the sun. When the world and judgement say: 'This is the end,' love alone can see the way out. It is the aboriginal tracker, the African bushman on the faded desert spoor within us, and its unfailing quarry is always the light.

The Face Beside the Fire, Chapter 7

For how often it happens, in the lives of people, that a purely human interest immediately creates a corresponding concentration in the field of ideas. Here you see a man very fond of a woman and there a woman very fond of a man, create out of their love for one another attitudes of mind totally incompatible with the former trend of their lives. This feeling for another becomes, indeed, a rallying point for interests and ideas which have hitherto been scorned, and soon what had first possessed little more than position and no size, snowballs into an avalanche which threatens to overwhelm the old self.

In a Province, Book I, Chapter 13

From that moment the night became peculiarly their own . . . He had never before experienced a nature in the physical world so packed as was that island with events of fire and earthquake, of upsurge of plants and volcanoes, of cloud, thunder, lightning and rain in the sky, and of the unending music of the small first things of life, celebrating with scraping legs, beating wings, and brilliant little voices the various urges of creation minutely entrusted to each of them. Yet that night was even more eventful than any crowded moment he had lived through, and each event within it seemed

[227]

designed to bless and make the two of them more meaningful in each other's arms. There were times when they were both so stirred by their nearness to each other and to all other living, singing, flashing and shining creatures that they made love close to tears, until finally, utterly resolved, they fell into sleep as if they had all life before them.

The Seed and the Sower, 'The Sword and the Doll'

It was amazing once he had believed he understood her silence how alive and near to him she had become again. He could hardly feel closer to her than he was now . . . It was as if she had been standing beside him whispering the words he was to use. There was not a day that passed wherein he did not hear her voice again in the wind, not a year wherein he did not see her face in the spring and witness her fulfilled in the summer.

The Seed and the Sower, 'The Sword and the Doll'

We fool ourselves in the most pathetic and dangerous manner when we think we can really have secrets from the people we love. All we can do is to deny them awareness of this thing which lames the free movement of our spirit: but we can have no secrets from our inner life. The submerged knowledge is passed on in the most indirect and destructive way by its influence on our actions, by the impediment it causes in our being, and by all the subtle withdrawals, abstentions and negations it produces in our living contacts. The secret is known as surely as an astronomer knows the position and nature of some black midnight star which, although beyond the range of his strongest telescope, is accurately charted from its effect on the visible constellations in its vicinity.

The Face Beside the Fire, Chapter 1

In François's world, unlike the world of Luciana's Italian godmother, where affection takes the form of exaggerating the stature of its subject, the more one loved a person the smaller one made it in one's feelings. One elaborates this fact because it was an integral element of François's character, derived from the Bushman influences of old Koba, since what distinguished the Bushman spirit so singularly from others was its uncompromising rejection of the physically great in favour of the small as if, long before the poet Blake, it had discovered infinity in the grains of sand of the desert that was its last home on earth.

A Story like the Wind, Chapter 8

Of all man's inborn dispositions there is none more heroic than the love in him. Everything else accepts defeat and dies, but love will fight no-love every inch of the way. And if love be denied natural expression as it had been to this old man, then it will bind itself to an animal, or a bird, or to trees, flowers, a patch of earth or even the shaping of a stone. I myself in the darkness of my cell outside Harbin had loved a rat and shared my little rice with him.

Flamingo Feather, Chapter 7

The great hunger, of course, is the hunger for love, and I am certain now that the point of Hans Taaibosch's apparently irrelevant appearance in your world was to bear witness in his obscure way to the reality and power of love.

A Mantis Carol, 'The Carol'

In bringing Hans Taaibosch's vicarious message of love to the [Kalahari] desert from a great city [New York] that knew it not, it was as if with the storm clouds of summer standing like monuments and towers and battlements of marble so high in the trembling blue above it, I saw a certainty of promise that the garden in the beginning, no matter how far lost behind us now, could be recovered through love and the desert we had made of it redeemed. So, when after the night the first rain fell, that rain which is for ever the image of love in action, the immense, scorched, Cinderella earth, so full of the great hunger, conceived and within days was transformed with new life of grass, flowers and budding thorn, and resounded with the drumming of bees making honey and the singing of birds building nests, I thought I had never seen a greater statement of beauty in my own round of life on earth. And I knew as never before that there was no greater beauty possible in nature or man than that of the uncared for and rejected, rediscovered and redeemed for growth through love.

A Mantis Carol 'Strange Jerusalem'

'I can't speak for the others, only for myself,' she answered without hesitation and unusual assurance. 'It is quite simple. I just loved him for himself.'

Of course I accepted that implicitly. Yet I had to question whether she had not overlooked this ambivalent principle in life we had talked about so much – this dimension in which we were both ourselves and another, both friend and stranger, brother and enemy, 'I' and 'thou', or, perhaps better still in the cooler language of physics, 'mirror' and 'reflection' – this paradoxical organization of all being and things going so deep into the core of even the most inert of substances that, on the last horizons where its infinitesimal constituents were no longer discernible visually but manifest only through the effect of their behaviour on the nuclear constellation of their matter, the sun of their tiny contribution to our physical reality sank into the night still, reflecting and reflected. So that for all of us, Hans Taaibosch was not only himself but also a mirror in which there was also reflection of ourselves.

A Mantis Carol, 'The Carol'

I hoped she would realize how here least of all I used the term love in any sentimental, loose or lush a state. I was thinking here above all of love as the act of the knowledge of the totality to come, not a cerebral knowing but the emotion of a knowing before the fact of it, charged with awareness of all the life that had ever been, was and could be. It demanded therefore also that we should know ourselves as it knew us in the full term of our origin and destination. It demanded that we should make knowing and accepting responsibility for all of ourselves, without fear or favour for any part of ourselves, the foremost and most urgent of our tasks. In return it would do the rest.

A Mantis Carol, 'The Carol'

I was aware of another level which I had not yet considered; the gratitude to life which comes flooding in over one as one experiences again how pervasive and always near is this mystery of love as though it were delegate in the blood and bone of ourselves. For such a gratitude was flooding me unsolicited from within, giving me so intense a feeling of belonging and participation in the movement and activity of the stars that I was dazzled with the light as of certain knowledge. I had an emotion of knowing beyond doubt how, long before we were thought of or conceived and the dancing stars made, already all was loved, and that however provisional or inadequate the shape in which it was expressed at any given moment in time, despite the apparent ruthlessness of the inevitable processes of dissolution involved, all would be as carefully, lovingly and tenderly unshaped, the stars unmade and the universe dismantled as in their fashioning at the beginning, since in the instant of undoing, unmaking and dismantling, all would be reborn and remade into a greater expression of the love that is our origin and destination.

A Mantis Carol, 'Strange Jerusalem'

Love, this improbable calling for wholeness in life, had to be experienced first in loneliness and isolation by a single heart and lived out in the small round of one unique life, however powerless and absurd it may appear to itself, before the great impersonal and arrogant collective spirit of our time would be moved to imitate it. That was always how real change in history began; one heart truly turned in the direction of wholeness and the movements of life and the universe itself conformed in due course. Just as physics found the greatest source of energy today in the smallest unit of matter, the atom, so the smallest unit of man, the individual atom, nuclear in this division between the Jacob and Esau in himself but contained in love, was the greatest force of change in human societies.

The symbol and the images in which this greater self pursued us were always more than any dogma, theory or imagination could express. The answers it sought had to be lived before they could be known . . . For creation was growth, slow, patient, enduring and endless. There were no short cuts to it. The idea that there were intellectual, wilful, short cuts to any real change for the better was one cause of the barbarism and violence increasingly in command of the spirit of our time. The longest way round was the shortest way to creative change, and such a change possible only as a process of growth in keeping with the law of time which I had already defined also as the patience of love. I would even go so far as to say that the future of human life depended on the rate at which such individual examples could be achieved, made manifest and multiplied.

A Mantis Carol, 'The Carol'

Job, after all, suffered his fate, not because he was rejected and unrewarded by life and God but precisely because he was the most loved and exemplary of the Creator's servants on earth. So that one had to accept that, in essence, his tragedy was tragedy in the midst of exceptional privilege.

About Blady, Chapter 3

Love is a mystery and ultimately, for us men especially, it is a feminine mystery for our guide, our way to it, is always through the great objective feminine. I have always said that as a natural scientist Jung made the journey which Dante undertook as a poet in *The Divine Comedy*. At the end of both journeys, as they both were in the presence of God, they experience what all the traffic and travail of life and creation has been about – this love, which for Dante joins intellect and feeling and reveals itself as that which 'moves the sun and the moon and all the other stars' and for Jung it is the divine gift of God to man, the awesome freedom to choose between truth and error. Dante's guide was a beautiful feminine face – Jung's the rejected, the despised, the suppressed, the metaphorically 'dirty and ugly and averted face of woman'. By looking for the meaning in the fantasies of a certain permanently alienated Miss Miller, or of Babette, committed to an asylum whom Freud dismissed as an 'ugly old woman', as well as in the lives of hundreds of others, he was led into and safely through the depths of his own hell, to become, like Dante, a freeman of creation and, as Dante had done, reintegrated for the future the scattered and neglected, trampled and bruised fragments of the life of our disintegrated time.

This was Jung's ultimate achievement that, like Dante, he achieved a condition within himself of a total objective love. The totality is proved in that it included the ugly as well as the beautiful. Dante followed a beautiful feminine face, and that is perhaps the easy way for a man; but Jung followed the face of a woman of whom Freud said he could not understand how Jung could waste his time with such a disagreeable person. That is one measure of the innate distance between the two men. Jung thought that to understand was 'beauty' of a transcendent kind because from the beginning his nature had so predisposed him that he had to live his life in love, in search of a cosmogonic love that included all, and I for one believe he found it not only for himself but for us all and showed us the way and means to do likewise for ourselves and our time.

Now also in the same chapter Jung refers to St Paul, who wrote, 'When I was a child I spake as a child, I understood as a child, I thought as a child: but when I became a man I put away childish things.' And that seemed so true because as a boy I knew that one day, very soon, I too would have to put away childish things. And this concept of love, of which a lot of people have a sentimental idea, is to me not sentimental but the most heroic of all concepts, because it is a call to battle.

A Walk with a White Bushman

Chapter Eleven

The Wonder and the Mystery

——

Great as is the mystery of so vast an unconscious area in life there is yet greater mystery involved. There is the mystery of consciousness and beyond that the ultimate wonder of how and for what purpose these two-in-one are directed. The mystery is not lessened because it is articulate. The light the fire throws does not diminish the aboriginal mystery because of its power to illuminate some of the night. On the contrary, the mystery grows with the growth of consciousness. (. . .)

The mystery and the unknown before and after, are not the synonyms we may take them to be. Mystery includes the known as well as the unknown; the ordinary as well as the extraordinary. Once the feeling of mystery abandons our travel-stained senses in contemplation of the same well-worn scene, we have ceased, in some vital sense, to know what we are observing. What that mystery is, is beyond verbal definition. We know only that its effect on us is either positive or negative. It is perhaps, most creatively, the feeling that in the midst of our own partial knowing and experience of life there is the presence of a something far greater than man can comprehend. Reality, no matter how widened and heightened our perceptions, never ceases to be an infinite mystery.

Jung and the Story of Our Time, 'The Man and the Place'

The Capacity for Wonder

Until we considered man, on his journey from the cradle to the grave, with the sort of feelings evoked in us by the sight of a star shooting out of the dark into the dark, we knew him – and ourselves – only in the briefest and least of all his parts . . . To me it was clear and of the most urgent practical importance to turn back to what we had left of the capacity for wonder; only reverence for life could deliver us from our inhumanity in Africa, and from the cataclysm of violence awaiting us at the end of our present road.

The Heart of the Hunter, Chapter 9

It is a law of the universe, it is a law like the law of gravity. Faith yields only to faith; faith begets, succeeds and replaces faith. Faith creates, all else destroys. Nothing else works. Our bright and glittering knowing by day induces an equal and opposite unknowing by night. But faith is knowing both ways:

It is the not-yet in the now,
The taste of fruit that does not yet exist,
Hanging the blossom on the bough.

Venture to the Interior, Chapter 4

Some instinct has prevented me from ever finding coincidences accidental. I had come gradually to think of them as manifestations of some cosmic law of which we are inadequately aware, confirming, among many other things, the extent to which one's own life was obedient to an overwhelming universal pattern.

A Mantis Carol, 'The Coming of Rantis'

The ancient Chinese believed that coincidences are not accidental but manifestations of a profound law of life of which we are inadequately aware. They hold that time possesses a character of its own which colours what happens at any given moment anywhere in the world. This, they maintain, we dismiss as 'sheer coincidence'. The German conception of *Zeitgeist* is, I expect, the nearest European parallel and more acceptable to our normal way of thinking.

I can only say in support of the Chinese belief that I have noticed that, when one renounces an established order and the protection of prescribed patterns of behaviour and, out of a longing for new meaning, commits oneself to an uncertain future like a fish to the sea, then 'coincidences' crowd fast in on one like the salvoes of stars shooting out of the night in southern Africa towards the close of the year. Coincidences, at these times, do not appear capricious and extraneous, but rather signs of confirmation that one has found again the rhythm and swing of the authentic sea of life.

Introduction to William Plomer, *Turbott Wolfe*

Each one of us is aware of far more than he can ever express. We all know more than we allow ourselves to know because of a certain cowardice in face of the inexpressible, and fear of accepting its effect on us as guide to the nature of its reality.

A Mantis Carol, 'Preamble'

The knight of La Mancha and his peasant follower ride on in all of us from our first classic rose-pink dawn to our last romantic twilight. For the knight and the peasant are not two separate people but one. The knight riding in search of a fit cause for his dedicated and heroic spirit is symbol of the aboriginal myth in us seeking flesh and blood to make it a living reality; the peasant following grumbling behind is our physical worldly self which clings to the myth for without its spirit his life has no meaning.

The Dark Eye in Africa, Part III, 'The Discussion'

I was allowed to attend a victory parade, as it were, of all the life that has ever been. I saw all that has ever been come streaming through the long lanes and corridors of my blood, through their arch of admiralty, round the inner square and then straight down past my own white lighted Hall. Out of the darkness that preceded Genesis and flood, it began with a glimmer and a worm of the unformed earth in love with the light to come. Yes! a worm with a lantern, a glow-worm with phosphorescent uniform, marched proudly at the head, and behind came great streams of being protozoic and prehistoric. Nothing was excluded and everything included, their small fires of being clearly lit, tended and well beloved. This, it was said, is the true, the noble heroic and unique crusade of the love of life. For look, among them not a brain but only matter tentatively and awkwardly assembled. Yet remark on their bearing and the trust with which they hurl themselves into the uncomprehended battle. Ah! tears of love and gratitude burned in my eyes at so urgently moving and life-confiding a sight. To feel, at last, the burden that they carry for me in my own blood, to know at every second several of these reflected in white corpuscle and scarlet cell are dying unflinchingly in battle for my all, to know that giant lizard and lion as well as unicorn came after, and were hurled too into similar struggle and defence of the totality of all. I was allowed, too, to see the first man and registered the seismographic thrill of the marching column at the appearance of so skilled and complex a champion. I was allowed to speak to him and I touched his skin riddled with snake bite, his shoulder pierced by mastodon's spike, his skull deep-scarred with sabre-tooth's claw. And as reverently and tenderly I took his hand shaking with marshy malarial fever, I was moved to pity him by the evidence of such dread and unending war. But he would have none of it. He looked me fearless in the eye and in a voice that boomed like a drum in his stomach said: 'Brother, it was worth it. Whatever they tell you, add this, it was worth it.'

I spoke to a Bushman half-eaten by a lion in the Kalahari, his only vessel a brittle ostrich egg with red and black triangles painted neatly on it, now broken and sand scattered. He looked in my grey eyes with the brown eyes of a people at dusk, slanted to bridge a chasm behind the face of a dying member of a dying and vanishing race. He too, my dying nomad brother, said: 'Add, add quick before I go, "it was worth it." ' I spoke to an aborigine in the bight of the great gulf. Tattooed with dung he said: 'I vanish, but it was worth it.' In New Guinea, I met a Stone Age Papuan, his black skin sheened with green after centuries in the jungle between basin and fall of water and spurting volcano, and he too said: 'Doubt it not, it was worth it.' Everyone said, 'Lovely gift of a life that we blindly trust burns with such loving fire in the dark that at any price, no matter how great, it is worth it.'

Yes, they all agreed and utterly convinced me, so that I can never doubt again. I wept when the great procession came to an end, for one and all, great and small – I loved them all. Yes, even to the worm that brought up the rear, with shaded night light and a nurse's white, in its dress concealing a phial of the drug of the greater sleep made with a touch of the hand of God's great, good night.

The Face Beside the Fire, Chapter 22

Religion

With Goethe I believe that the essence of religion is creation in man. As he said, 'Man is only creative when he is truly religious; without religion he merely becomes repetitive and imitative' . . . Religion is . . . the longing in the human being which encourages him to create beyond himself a new, greater expression of life and human personality.

The Heart of the Hunter, Chapter 13

Religion is not religion unless it keeps burning bright in the dark hour the idea of life as journey begun in the physical world and continued on into another world of 'becoming'. Religion is not religion unless it heals the dividing wound inflicted between these two levels of being and becoming. If the devil rules man by dividing himself against himself, God rules by uniting us within ourselves.

The Dark Eye in Africa, Part III, 'The Discussion'

'Little Cousin, always remember in Africa that what we Europeans call superstition, is just the wrong explanation for the right truth. It is, in fact, an attempt to draw attention to mysterious facts and laws of nature which Eureopeans ignore because they cannot explain them with their brains.'

A Story Like the Wind, Chapter 7

The valid role of the exercise of reason, which is so legitimate a part of the elements which constitute our greater awareness, has become inflated until it is a form of tyranny and superstition in this time wherein we live, and has grown so totally out of proportion that sooner or later fate, as our ancestors called it, will discipline it, and confine it to its ration with the three other instinctive faculties that constitute the full range of consciousness.

About Blady, Chapter 5

What had started as wars of religion in Europe, became converted into upheavals like the French and Russian revolutions. One of the main targets of the instigators of violent change was always religion.

Jung and the Story of Our Time, 'The Time and the Space'

Even the church (whose task it was to heal, as its New Testament master had come to heal) was itself as sick as the rest of the institutions charged with the duty of nourishing the spirit of man. It had utterly forgotten that it should draw as close, if not closer, to the sinner as to the sinned against.

Yet Being Someone Other, Chapter 7

I had only to look into my own life to realize how, ever since my childhood, the church into which I was born and all the other churches I had encountered, far from promoting the natural interest I believe I have always had in religion, seemed to come down like an iron curtain between me and my own religious feelings. This reaction was something that came about despite itself. I tried hard to like the church. I fought my natural reaction away from it for years because of the history and cultural conditioning of my family, the example of parents I loved, and the precepts of friends and masters I respected. Also I acknowledged the need for churches and religious institutions in the collective life of man. I was born profoundly biased their way. Wherever I went in the world I took great comfort in looking not only at Christian churches but also entering the temples of countries as far away as Ceylon, India and Japan. Indeed, any ground consecrated by pagan, Hindu, Buddhist or Christian in the name of their gods had similar numinous effects . . .

The trouble for me only began when I joined congregations in such places and was compelled to listen to the priests and their utterances. Instantly I was dismayed, and whatever there had been of God in the church or temple fled. Fortunately, I never fell into the error of looking upon organized religion and the aboriginal hunger in the spirit of men that we call religion as completely the same thing. However organized creed came between me and religion: between me and the New Testament and the utterances of St Paul, particularly in his thirteenth chapter of his second Letter to the Corinthians, which I still find one of the greatest utterances of the spirit ever penned. I knew that the churches tried to serve what was most important and vital for the continuation of the human spirit. But did that make them more adequate for the unacknowledged and desperate religious necessities of my time? Could it perhaps be another form of religion? For it was another of those prison perceptions that became axiomatic to me; only religion could take the place of religion. Religion, I was convinced, could not be pinned down to one final dogmatic interpretation, nor even to one final revelation. The Book of Revelations already was final proof for me that the Bible ended with the drawbridge of the Christian citadel let down and the road open once more for the spirit of man to travel to the end of time with a renewing and infinitely renewable capacity for fresh religious experience and revelation.

Jung and the Story of Our Time, 'The Time and the Space'

I have lots of Jewish friends. When I talk to them I am aware of the fact that I can talk to them in a way in which I cannot talk to other people, and they respond in kind. When you think of the history of the Jews, their suffering from their period of bondage onwards to their massacre in millions by Hitler, I find it most impressive how unsoured and unembittered on the whole they have been, how creative, what a source of art, fun and gaiety they have retained. Above all, they have proved what is of the greatest importance to the future: that you can remain a coherent and integrated people even when deprived of country, worldly power and native language, as long as you retain a common faith in your religion, God and his word.

A Walk with a White Bushman

Jung had been impressed by the fact that invariably among the many people who swarmed to him as patients, he found at the core of their neurosis a sense of insecurity. This unease coincided with a loss of faith; a loss of the quintessential requisites of personal religious experience. He found that he seldom succeeded in what for want of a better word is called 'a cure', without enabling the patient to recover his lost capacity for religious experience. Subsequently a purely psychiatric approach to the problems of life could no longer satisfy him. In any case he had always been aware of the vitally interdependent roles of science and religion. The interest of psychiatry itself compelled him to know that it was not enough to reassemble the fragments of the shattered spirit among the men and women of his day and put them together into some sort of working order. He had at the same time to restore to them a sense of overall direction, a feeling of meaning. The process of reassembly, the re-integration itself indeed, was impossible without bringing back to his patients a feeling that they were instruments of meaning, however remote.

Healing the sick without a re-quickening of religion, as he put it to me, was 'just not on'. He used the word 'heal' in the sense of 'making whole'. This indivisible concept of life was symbolized by the finding of the Holy Grail, the transcendental vessel (*graille* was an old Provençal word for a vessel) wherein the spirit, with all its apparent self-contradiction, could be poured and contained.

This approach made Jung an inspired healer in the ancient, classical sense, and inevitably compelled him to reach out in his work more and more towards grasping what greater end healing itself served. Even more urgent than the work of trying to heal became the search for what constituted the 'wholeness' that was the condition of 'holiness'. As if from the moment of his first glimpse of this vast unconscious objective within, he saw the mentally deranged, and even the least disturbed of his patients, afflicted with the sickness of an entire age and culture. He saw us all, as it were, as guinea-pigs in a vast laboratory of time. And he knew that the only valid answers could be answers extracted under the knife of the great vivisectionist of 'meaning'.

Jung and the Story of Our Time, 'Errant and Adventure'

Christianity

I have often felt that it is as if there has been only one modern man and we crucified him two thousand years ago. We still have to make his example truly modern in ourselves and be individual and specific in terms of the totality of our own natures, as he was. This is the way we have to go. But we now have to do our own leading. We have not to wait on masters; we do not have to wait for foolproof spiritual exercises; we can go to people and seek what they seek, but we cannot do it wholly their way and be stereotypes of one another. Like the leaves on the trees, we are compelled to be each our own way, again and again. We have, for this, to turn inwards – to look into ourselves; look in this container which is our soul; look and listen in to it and all its hunches – incredible, silly, stupid as they may appear to be. It might tell us to make fools of ourselves in the eyes of our established selves but, however improbable, just listen, just give it a chance in yourself, particularly at this moment when everything is increasingly impersonal. Until you have listened in to that thing which is dreaming through you, in other words answered the knock on the door in the dark, and discovered your estranged self, you will not be able to lift this moment in time, in which we are all imprisoned, back again on to a level where the great act of creation is going on, whether we heed it or not. We can join in with increased awareness, thanks to the Creator's evolution, or stay out. If we stay out we perish; if we join in, we live for ever.

A Walk with a White Bushman

Europe has made a terrible kind of spiritual totalitarianism out of Christianity. It has regarded all other gods and forms of religion as lesser breeds without the laws and commandments of the one and only God it professes to worship. The word 'pagan' for the vast religious dimension of other cultures and peoples may, at its best, be allowed to rise to a certain instinctive form of nobility but is normally denied the dignity of being anything except superstitious and falsely religious.

The Voice of the Thunder, 'The Other Journey'

Contemporary man does not realize what the coming of Christ meant, and will fail it in a blind imitation of what Christ himself was. I think for me one of the most profound things Jung ever said was that human beings believe that they have to live their lives as if they were mere imitations and copies of the life of Christ, whereas if they truly sought the meaning of the coming of Christ, they would realize that they had to live their own seeking lives, their portion of the Holy Spirit of imagination which is in their keeping, their own true selves – just as Christ had lived himself without deviation, in a way that had never been seen before, to the end for which he had been born.

A Walk with a White Bushman

Surely the most precious value implicit in the coming of Christ and the New Testament was that of an individual capable of taking upon himself the great universals and making them specific in his own imagination and being.

Jung and the Story of Our Time, 'The Time and the Space'

Perhaps the only thing to do was to trust one's bad as much as one's good fortune. Could not what seemed to be so inexplicably bad today turn out years later to have been a stroke of good fortune and both be part of a meaningful whole amounting to something which was greater even than the sum of their parts?

In fact I found it of help to admonish my own impatient thinking by adapting a famous New Testament observation and contemplating the probability that the children of this world might well be luckier in their own generation than the children of the light. Perhaps this is what we all unconsciously implied when we said that so and so or such and such were 'lucky devils'. Who, after all, had ever spoken of 'lucky angels'? The matter, I felt, could not be disposed of on all levels until one had faced also the awful question: 'Who was the more fortunate, Barabbas or Christ?'

The Hunter and the Whale, Chapter 1

Recognition of what it lacks is one of the most dynamic forces in the human spirit. Realization of our greater selves comes first through the recognition of what we are not. That, I suggested, is the significance in the Sermon on the Mount of the enigmatic 'blessed are the poor in spirit': only the spirit that recognizes itself to be poor, through what it is not, has any promise of increase. We are beggars always to what we were meant to be. It is the failure to recognize this that bars the way and crucifies the new man in us. That was the meaning of the cry: 'Father, forgive them, for they know not what they do.' We are a people, indeed an age, in a dark cloud of unknowing of this kind.

The Heart of the Hunter, Chapter 9

The Milky Way was superb, more like a track densely strewn with daisies than its usual blur of misty light. Orion, Vance's old hunter, club erect, jewelled belt tucked tightly into his slim waist, seemed to be prancing like a buck negro to the throbbing of the drum. Castor and Pollux, the heavenly twins, Alfa Centauri, Sirius, the watch-dog at that dark entrance through the Milky Way into the greater night beyond; our own Jupiter, Mars and the inevitable Plough were all there, spear, bow, arrows and blade in hand. And away to the south where lay the Nyika, the land of tomorrow, a dark, pointed peak cut deep into the night. It was a night so clear that I had no difficulty in recognizing the full line of the great head of Chelinda. Immediately over it hung the Southern Cross.

As a Cross, I know it is not perfect. It is not symmetrical. But to love only perfection is just another way of hating life, for life is not perfect. And now, as I looked at the Cross, it seemed to hang over the proud, sullen head of Chelinda like a legendary blade, a crusader's jewelled sword, or the great Excalibur itself, held reverently in prayer against the lip and brow of the night. It made of the darkness a wayside altar, a chapel at which the undubbed soul might come for its final vigil and dedicate a sword to the quest for a single grail. It was itself a Sword-of-all-such-Swords; but also it was a cross held over a world old in time, but new in the European heart.

And what does that mean? What does any cross mean? These shapes of crosses litter our horizons from birth to the grave, but do we know what they mean? Out of what tender wood, by what great carpenter, are they nailed?

We must shut our eyes and turn them inwards, we must look far down into that split between night and day in ourselves until our head reels with the depth of it, and then we must ask: 'How can I bridge this self? How cross from one side to the other?' If we then allow that question to become the desire for its own answer, and that desire to become a bridge across the chasm, then, and only then, from high above on this far peak of our conscious self, on this summit so far above the snow-line of time, in this cold, sharp, selected moment, clearly and distinctly we shall see a cross. A gulf bridged makes a cross; a split defeated is a cross.

A longing for wholeness presupposes a cross, at the foundations of our being, in the heart of our quivering, throbbing, tender, lovely, lovelorn flesh and blood, and we carry it with us wherever we journey on, on unto all the dimensions of space, time, unfulfilled love, and Being-to-be. That is sign enough.

After that the drum can cease from drumming, the beating and troubled heart have rest. In the midnight hour of the crashing darkness, on the other side of the night behind the cross of stars, noon is being born.

Venture to the Interior, Chapter 23

Truth and the Method of the Rose

There has perhaps never been a moment when the importance of 'being' is so neglected in the general preoccupation with 'doing', and when there is no realization, at heart, of the unfolding of the human spirit which truth demands. The truth yields to nothing except growth: it has no method which does not correspond to the 'method of the rose' – which is but to grow.

About Blady, Chapter 1

I am reminded of something Jung said to me not long before he died. He said that the truth needs scientific expression; it needs religious expression and artistic expression. It needs the poet and the musician. And even then, he said, you only express part of it.

'Wilderness – A Way of Truth', Essay

One of the most pathetic things about us human beings is our touching belief that there are times when the truth is not good enough for us; that it can and must be improved upon. We have to be utterly broken before we can realize that it is impossible to better the truth. It is the very truth we deny which so tenderly and forgivingly picks up the fragments and puts them together again.

Venture to the Interior, Chapter 15

Without argument I left it at that, feeling it was best in the worst of circumstances to let the worst be the worst as quickly as possible. Often in my life I have found that the one thing that can save is the thing which appears most to threaten. In peace and war I have found that frequently, naked and unashamed, one has to go down into what one most fears and in that process, from some-where beyond all conscious expectation, comes a saving flicker of light and energy that even if it does not produce the courage of a hero at any rate enables a trembling mortal to take one step further.

The Lost World of the Kalahari, Chapter 7

No imagination has yet been great enough to invent improvements to the truth. Truth, however terrible, carries within itself its own strange comfort for the misery it is so often compelled to inflict on behalf of life.

A Story Like the Wind, Chapter 5

Human beings, he [Mopani] stressed, always knew more than they allowed themselves to know. One of the things they never knew clearly enough was the power they possessed of overcoming prob-lems . . . Provided men looked them straight in the face, stood fast and directed their imaginations truly to the centre they would find their strength.

A Story Like the Wind, Chapter 5

Our Sister Grief

I felt that here the grief, the capacity for grasping suffering through participation – something to which our age seems increasingly impervious and incapable of accomplishing – was like what my black countrymen so movingly called 'the stringing of beads'. In this ancient and beautiful Bantu metaphor, each tear of sorrow shed is a jewel that has to be strung on an unbroken thread of feeling into a necklace, which one can thereafter wear as an ornament of grace around the image of one's spirit, and so prepare the way for the final metaphor: 'Let in our sister, Grief, who should always have a place by our fire.'

About Blady, Chapter 3

Always I ask myself the question: where did Prometheus go? And always I feel that he, relieved of his special form of suffering and immortal chains, is moving onwards in the spirit of man, and where he and the spirit of man will go cannot be known until the purpose for which the fire was lit is one day understood.

About Blady, Chapter 5

In the dark night of soul only the lonely speaking to the lonely can be companion to the other.

Jung and the Story of Our Time, 'The Time and the Space'

Illness gives one a licence, a generosity and often a pity for oneself, that in a precariously organized being can have the most disconcerting results. It brings the individual face to face with a purely individual problem. He may have long lost sight of himself in the social pattern, but in illness his eyes are turned inwards. He is struggling with a condition that primarily can annihilate or change only himself. And that private inward world which has hitherto seen in the balance of his actions merely an attempt to silence or to crush it, finds in this struggle which he wages, not for abstractions it cannot understand but for himself, the hope that he is changed from an enemy into an ally. It brings to his attention doubts, desires, memories which his actions have long since ignored, and clamours for a wider share in the future life he is to lead.

In a Province, Book I, Chapter I

It was . . . a decisive factor as an ingredient of the raw material of greater being which suffering and disaster become when they are accepted and endured without evasion.

A Far-Off Place, Chapter 6

All my reading of history and experience of art and literature left me with an acute impression of how vital an element tuberculosis was in the climate of life and time behind us. Great as the role of plagues and illnesses had been, with their names – the Black Death, leprosy, and so on – attached like sinister labels to desperate stretches of time, tuberculosis added a new and subtler element to the nature of the disease, because its role was such that one could hardly tell where it began and ended as a state of mind or a state of body, since through its working in human life and imagination these two things seemed from the beginning present and inter-changeable. As far as I was concerned, it seemed almost the perfect sickness to qualify as the chosen instrument of an inflexible, in-scrutable and implacable fate.

About Blady, Chapter 2

Happiness for me is health in its most complete state just as a sense of beauty is its awareness and love its fulfilment.

The Face Beside the Fire, Chapter 1

Once suffering had a meaning whose imagery could be recognized and named, it could, I believed, be made welcome and endured. And this new meaning was not only inaccessible to rational and verbal expression but superseded it through the power and glory of the symbols and images which had served its predecessors in the wounded and vanished past . . . all symbols and images that seek, night and morning, to enlarge our daytime awareness and to open wide the gates that bar the way to the future, once they have served their turn they too sink back into the dreaming unconscious of man, where all is refreshed, transfigured and restored to new life. Though many a symbol inevitably had to vanish and give way, the progression of meaning that they served never ceased, and produced other forms and shapes to take their place and continue the campaign in a more contemporary manner against the loss of meaning which would deprive life itself of purpose and leave it defenceless. The wood may burn out but the fire flames on, and somewhere beyond those dancing stars, floodlit as for a night of universal celebration, there was a universe and a life that was profoundly seasonal and needed both fall and winter in the spirit of man and its symbols for the great resurrection of spring and summer, for another thrust of meaning.

Yet Being Someone Other, Chapter 7

The important thing for me was to think of Job and the immense dimension of suffering with which it was concerned as the orchestration of a great symphony of meaning. To take it literally would be to destroy all entrance to a great and imperative unknown to which it was pointing, and the question gradually arose, why those who were nearest and most loyal and most obedient to the exactions of the patterns of creation in life were called upon to realize that their Creator, in so far as he could be spoken of in an image accessible to us, was also a profoundly suffering Creator, and that the love of which he himself was a subject demanded that those he loved should be taken into an ever closer partnership where flesh and blood would have to endure not only the joy of helping to bring more light in the darkness that was in the beginning, but also the suffering of the everlasting battle for more light out of chaos and old night. Only those who were nearest and dearest to him would not be destroyed but enriched by a glimpse of the great and terrible enormities of creation which would have been unendurable at all levels if they were not part of a cosmic battle for life subjected to the love where feeling and intellect truly join, or what Dante called 'the love that moves the sun and the other stars'.

About Blady, Chapter 3

The sadness in you is no longer without a name and has found its voice. When sorrow finds a name and a voice, it is like the lightning you see calling and the thunder speaking after it saying that soon the rain will fall on you again.

A Far-Off Place, Chapter 12

Chiron [one of the Centaurs] was the earliest and most complete personification of perhaps the greatest element in life, which contains great goodness and great suffering simultaneously, so that in their totality they make more than their sum. They make the two and two of the four . . . mysteriously into a five.

For me this potential of fulfilment, which brings to creation something which was not there before, was realised and made accessible in the minds of human beings, so that the gods and all living things were emancipated from outworn aspects of creation in an overwhelming movement of metamorphosis, of which death was as natural and creative a part as birth; where birth, as it were, seen from without, was an exit, and death . . . an entrance into a universe of new meaning.

About Blady, Chapter 6

The first sign of happiness in the human heart is a desire to share with one and all; share food, jokes, laughter, tears, conversation, news, space, sympathy, consideration and everything that could be imagined.

Yet Being Someone Other, Chapter 5

I respect happiness as I respect nothing else and though I detest the popular concept 'duty', if I had to allocate one duty to humanity I would allocate, with the highest possible priority, the duty of the individual to achieve happiness. But few people will agree with me. They not only no longer know what happiness is but also have no faith in its being a practicable possibility. In so far as they are aware of it they confuse happiness with some of its lesser parts like pleasure and gratification and would not begin to understand, for instance, that happiness which loves the great necessities of life like a bride. Happiness does not exclude unhappiness but merely discovers and preserves its meaning. The foolless Lear who could say at the moment when he and Cordelia were about to be thrust back into prison: 'We shall be God's spies and take upon us the mystery of things,' was happier, in the true sense, than Lear the king on his throne giving kingdoms away with a right royal hand.

The Face Beside the Fire, Chapter 1

King Death

Death knows no king, it is its own king.

A Story Like the Wind, Matabele saying, Chapter 5

Death needs no outside assistance to make it dramatic. It is in itself, in its own dark night, so charged with drama that although we see it constantly around us we never get used to it, and although we know it makes no exceptions, we never fail to be shaken and surprised when it visits anyone close to us.

The Face Beside the Fire, Chapter 3

Death is not something that happens at the end of our life. It is imprisonment in one moment of time, confinement in one sharp uncompromising deed or aspect of ourselves. Death is exclusion from renewal of our present-day selves.

The Seed and the Sower, Chapter 5

'Death', he [van Bredepoel] would say, 'is always with us. It's one of the biggest commonplaces of life. Everyone expects death, and yet when it does come, everyone is horrified. It's because they have not faced the problem squarely, that they are horrified, and being horrified, overwhelmed. No system of life can ever be satisfactory unless it has an answer for the problem death poses, unless it can oppose a feeling of spiritual security to our sense of death.'

In a Province, Chapter 2

I found myself thinking of how, on the Hindu island of Bali one night, I had watched an aristocratic funeral as one of the great equatorial sunsets made grand opera of the hour. The dead aristocrat's body had been placed on top of a tower of dead wood and the tower securely lashed to a big raft, and the timing, as the final ritual demanded, was in harmony with the tides of the sea and the raft launched as the tide turned and the placid water full of opal sky withdrew out to sea. The priest waded after the raft until the water was up to his shoulders and set the pile alight. He joined us all standing silent on the shore and we watched this tower of fire go slowly out to sea. The light left the sky: it became dark. The stars came out, and still the fire flickered in flame further and further out to sea. I do not remember how long it took but I do know that suddenly somewhere behind us a bantam cockerel crowed and the fire vanished and we all made slowly for home.

About Blady, Chapter 1

This glossy black and white snapshot of him still as a laughing warrior, proved none the less how ready almost to the point of nonchalance he was to end his life not with a whimper but a bang of joy, implying after the most terrible of yesterdays that the gift of life no matter how problematical, painful or exacting was always worth it.

Bitterness, resentment, hatred at the end over what life has given one, I believe, is defeat; gratitude despite all, victory.

A Mantis Carol, 'Hans Taaibosch at Home'

As I put the telephone down, an image of the story of Charlie's [Charles Douglas-Home] end, which had been trying to form itself from the moment I left the hospital, became clear and I saw it as I have often seen life towards the end, like one of those torrents which, in its last descent towards the sea, finds on the golden beaches sand enough to pause and form a reluctant lagoon and builds up slowly water enough to mirror heaven before breaking through the final bar and joining the Homeric white horses of the sea.

About Blady, Chapter 3

Albert [Michaeljohn] looked calmer, and more at peace. In retrospect I am tempted to say that he looked happier than I had ever seen him look alive. The dissatisfaction on his handsome features, the angry flush of the war within that suffused his living face had gone. He looked like a not ignoble monument of himself, as if in the moment of dying he had rediscovered his original innocence, as if every line and expression in his face had been determined to re-affirm for the last time, before they dissolved the initial design from which Albert and the world had worked so industriously and intelligently to estrange them.

The Face Beside the Fire, Chapter 3

Edward [the son of an old friend] was dying the Edward way . . . a continuation of something everlasting wherein all that was happening to him was a form of supreme privilege.

About Blady, Chapter 3

I was telephoned by my son John, who asked me if he could see me urgently. When he came he told me about a recurrent dream which perturbed him so much that he sometimes doubted his own sanity. With slight variations the dream was, as so many of the most significant dreams are, short and to the point. He was somewhere by the sea, watching the rising of an equinoctial tide, and wanted to turn about and run from it but felt himself fixed in that position and could not turn for all his trying. So paralysed, in dream after dream he would see a black head emerge from the phosphorescent swell and 'insinuating waves' of an ocean heaving through its own motivation and not because of any wind or other disturbance. The head turned towards him and slowly, with immense deliberation, began to come closer until an enormous black African elephant bull stepped through the swell and began to move remorselessly towards him; and always, at this point, he awoke in terror . . .

I had to ask: 'But what did you associate with this elephant to make you afraid?'

'I knew', he said, 'it was not just a normal elephant. It was an elephant bent only on uprooting trees.'

. . . I began to wonder if my son might not be far more seriously ill than the doctors whom he had been seeing for some years thought he was, and whether, coupled with the vivid association with a great uprooter of trees, it was not telling us that this is where a life as we know it finishes, where the tree is uprooted and the story comes to an end . . .

A week or so before the end my son, in great pain, had insisted on taking me to his favourite little church at Binsey, which was close to where he lived in Oxford . . . As we came out of the church and looked on the day again, my son said: 'This is where, if I am to die, I would love to be buried . . .

I took heart from this 'if', and we walked slowly back, in an afternoon clear-cut and cold but full of a long yellow sunlight, so dense and sweet that the birds beginning to home seemed not to fly through it so much as to be swimming in a kind of honey. Then he spoke again: 'You remember that dream I brought to you nearly six years ago? I know now that that was the precise moment the cancer entered my body.'

The brief moment of relief brought on by his 'if' passed swiftly . . .

I asked of myself . . . how would I deal with the unselving when the person who walked tall beside me, his shadow lengthening in the sinking sun, was gone, and the uprooting of the tree of which he had dreamt six years before was fulfilled, and the book ended? What then?

I have seen so much of death and dying and have even lived alone under what appeared to be an irrevocable sentence of death, but there was something new about this kind of dying, as if it were carrying deeply encoded within the process an urgent message, desperately trying to tell us something 'most immediate', as we had labelled messages of the greatest priority in the war behind us. Of course we knew, deeply, that his dying would be unique, and he could not be nearer to it at that moment than I had been to my own, so strangely deferred. I knew the country he was entering, as it were, from just across the border, within sight of customs and immigration. I was the last of seven brothers and had lost both father and mother and four sisters and, of course, had lost many, many others dear to me. I was, in a sense, as well prepared as a human being can be, yet I felt lost and unarmed, except for a kind of still but insistent voice from beyond the furthest star whispering: 'Ask and ask, again and again, until it speaks. Importune until door or window flies open and reveals some intimation of meaning that will transform and redeem.'

About Blady, Chapter 3

When a Bushman in the Kalahari dies he is buried in the red sand in his skin blanket, face to the east with his bow and quiver and spear at hand, and beside him an ostrich egg full of water for the long journey. Then crying bitterly his companions pile the wood high at the foot of the grave and light a great fire.

When I asked the reason for this they said: 'Don't you know it is dark where he is going and he needs the light of the fire to show him the way to the day that is beyond.'

'The Creative Pattern in Primitive Africa', Eranos Lectures

Xhabbo sighed a profound sigh of fulfilment as he declared quietly: 'Xhabbo knew that the stars who hide in light as other things hide in darkness were there to see all today. For the stars do fall in this manner when our hearts fall down. The time when the stars also fall down is while the stars feel that our hearts fall over, because those who had been walking upright, leaving their footprints in the sand, have fallen over on to their sides. Therefore the stars fall down on account of them, knowing the time when men die and that they must, falling, go to tell other people that a bad thing has happened at another place.'

A Story Like the Wind, Chapter 11

I became, if you like, a haunted person. Yes, I know the meaning of ghosts. And we who discount them do so only because we look for them in the wrong dimension. We think of them as a return of the bodily dead from their graves. But these dead have no need to return to life, for they are not the dead. As I see it, what has once given life to the spirit can never again be dead in the dimension of the spirit. So we mistake the shadow for the substance; confuse the reflection and the reality. Ghosts do not follow physical death, but rather they precede life. The only death the spirit recognizes is the denial of birth to that which strives to be born: those realities in ourselves that we have not allowed to live. The real ghost is a strange, persistent beggar at a narrow door asking to be born; asking, again and again, for admission at the gateway of our lives. Such ghosts I had, and thus, beyond all reason, I continued to be haunted.

The Seed and the Sower, Chapter 4

It was . . . the anniversary of the dropping of the first atom bomb on Hiroshima, and the young American interviewer was extracting, with skill and delicacy, from the little old Japanese gentleman his experience of that great and terrible day.

He was, he said, a doctor. Both he and his wife were Christians. He was at work in his surgery and his wife was in the Japanese equivalent of a drawing-room, sitting at her harmonium. He could hear her playing a Christian hymn – no, he no longer remembered which particular hymn it was because his mind was on medical things and he heard it only in snatches. In any case, the shock of the horror that followed had been so great that to this day he found it difficult if not impossible to remember what had happened immediately before. Besides she had not been at the harmonium long when the bomb fell. She and his four children in other parts of their house were killed instantly; he, miraculously, was spared.

He said this with a nervous sort of smile, which I doubt if anybody else who noticed it understood, but which moved me almost to tears. It was the kind of smile which comes almost by reflex to the Japanese, who attach so much importance to good manners, in order that it should lighten for others the impact of the news of any personal tragedy which they may have had to impart . . .

I began by trying to reassure the Japanese doctor . . . that I wanted to tell him something which I hoped would help him to make his peace with the tragedy of Hiroshima even more effectively than with his obvious magnanimity he had already done . . .

General Penney [Lord Mountbatten's Director of Intelligence] had assured me that, among the staff records captured at Terauchi's headquarters, evidence was found of plans to kill all the prisoners and internees when the invasion of south-east Asia began in earnest. I begged the doctor, therefore, to accept that, terrible as the dropping of the two atom bombs had been, his wife and the many thousands who died with her had died in order to save the lives of many hundreds of thousands more. I had tried to speak to him in this way not only for myself but for thousands thus saved, and would like him to know how we would be forever in his wife's debt as well as that of her fellow victims.

Those of us who had survived like him and myself could only discharge our debt by looking as deeply and as honestly as we could into the various contributions we had made to this disaster. The war and the bomb, after all, had started in ourselves before they struck in the world without, and we had to look as never before into our own small individual lives and the context of our various nations. We who were saved seemed to me charged by life itself to live in such a way now that no atom bomb could ever be dropped again, and war need never again be called in, as it had been throughout recorded history, as the terrible healer of one-sidedness and loss of soul in man. Could I through him thus presume to acknowledge my debt of life to his wife and beg him to believe she had not died in vain? . . . he bowed to me . . .

Hissing between his teeth as the old-fashioned Japanese used to do when moved, he came out of his bow to say: 'Would you please be so kind as to allow me to thank you for a remarkable thought.'

He added to that, after a pause, the traditional farewell of the Japanese, which in itself reflects much of their spirit charged so heavily with provision of fate: the Sayonara that just means: 'If it must be.'

The Night of the New Moon, Prologue, 'A Remarkable Thought',

I certainly think that the lesson we learned from Hiroshima and Nagasaki could be used for the good of mankind . . . There is an enormous symbolic importance in the fact that the source of this destructive energy was nuclear — that it came from the atom — because it shows that the greatest energy in the physical world is in the smallest unit . . . Just as the source of power, transforming power, in human society is in the smallest unit of human society, which is the individual. The individual is the atom of society and therefore these two symbols are in a sense complementary. What is most threatening and destructive in human society today is the human being who is split in his own nucleus: it is fission in the modern soul which makes nuclear fission so dangerous — he is a split atom. He has got to heal himself, make himself whole.

A Walk with a White Bushman

Death has always seemed to me one of the greatest moments of truth, when all that is false and imprecise in life is erased . . .

Yet Being Someone Other, Chapter 7

[257]

The Wonder and the Mystery

All I believe I know is an experience, a mystery that is not mysterious-ness but a life-giving wonder, a something which alone gives food to the greatest of all natural hungers, a hunger which is a fact even for the atheist, no matter how much he denies it the food that it demands.

Everything that one tries to do beyond that dimishes, but I think what one should work at is one's relationship with God, this overwhelming 'is-ness'. What is the impact of God on me or the thought and feeling of God to me? What does it mean for my life, what does it mean for the life of my time? Once I start groping in that way great energies begin to flow into me. And this is a fact. All civilizations, from the oldest to the newest, they could not do without this. One of the strangest ideas ever conceived is the idea that religion is the opium of the people, because religion is a call to battle: it's a call to fight in life as you've never fought before. The idea of God is very uncomfortable because again it increases your responsibility. If there is no God, there is no point in being respons-ible – it's just chaos and eternal night. But if there is one, it is harder and yet more bearable because in Him is the dimension really where it all begins . . . But even there, where man and god-image meet, and we are most whole, there is yet more.

A Walk with a White Bushman

I lay back on the grass: the mountain seemed to take a firm, a friendly grip of my back. It, too, felt unbelievably near and sustaining. It seemed as if through me and through its great, strong heart, and right down to the centre of the earth, ran the axis on which the wide world turned through space and time. I had a vision of the universe and myself, in which circumference was reduced to a mere mathematical abstraction, and in which all was Centre; one great unfailing Centre, and myself, in the heart of Africa, in the heart of the Centre.

Venture to the Interior, Chapter 21

We are no longer sufficiently aware of the importance of what we do not know – the living experience both before and beyond the transitory knowledge of the moment . . . Less and less does [modern man] permit himself, or perhaps it would be more accurate to say less and less is he capable of committing himself body and soul to the working, to the fire of the creative experiment that is continually seeking to inflame him and to fill his little life with great objective meaning.

We are facing a situation, in fact, which the primitive world knew only too well. It is the moment about which a grey-haired and lean old Zulu witch-doctor and prophet called Shembe spoke to me in 1927 . . . I begged him to speak of the first spirit of the Zulu nation – Umkulun-kulu – 'the great one'. He shook his beautiful old head with its metal ring of wisdom around the crown, and said sadly: 'We do not speak of Umkulunkulu any longer. The praise names of the Great One are forgotten. People now talk only of the things that are useful to them.'

'The Creative Pattern in Primitive Africa', Eranos Lectures

I have never had a definition of God but I just have a tremendous feeling and a sense of direction, of creation in that area, which I know is real, and this is the most important thing in me. I trust it completely. I have always known it somehow, and it has not got less with time; it has got stronger. So that in a sense one knows, one knows through experience: and I think it is just that people have this area in them but sometimes it gets cut off. Human beings know far more than they allow themselves to know: there is a kind of knowledge of life which they reject, although it is born into them: it is built into them. But in their rational selves they shy like frightened horses away from a God who is not the source of opium for people but a reawakening and renewal of creation and a transcending of the forces and nuclear energies in the human soul. The task of using creatively the nuclear power in the atom without will never be completed without first containing and transcending the nuclear power within the heart and soul of the individual atom: these two discoveries, atom without and atom within, are aspects of one another in the sum of the same greater thing. To know this and assume individual responsibility for their effects in our own lives is to be modern; to know only one and not the other is to be partial and archaic and a danger to creation.

A Walk with a White Bushman

'Laurens Jan', [my grandfather] told me at last, 'I know that we all are always in the hollow of the hand of the Lord, but it must be awful to feel his fingers moving underneath one as they seem to do at sea.'

Yet Being Someone Other, Chapter 2

There is in the world around us not a form of life, not a stone, not a crystal, not a plant, not the smallest insect or the greatest beast that walks on the earth or swims in the ocean, not the moss which is perhaps the first and most moving image of the need of the organic for the inorganic in the life of plants and grass, conquering and clinging to the stone it has conquered, that is not synchronised in every detail and limited to an equal something within; and that life and creation in itself is the synchronicity, all paradox and polarity transcended in a great acausal moment with which creation as we know it began and moves on . . .

This can be illustrated not so much in words as through their happening. To take the commonest of examples, as the dawn, red in the morning, or the sunset in flames at night, stir their synchronised partner in the world within and confront the ego with their full synchronistic reality, they become mythological events of extreme and overwhelming significance, and the poor old ego, which for so long has thought of itself as author of all that there is in the human spirit of poetry, music, art, song, the praise and the story, is overwhelmed by so great a presumption and inclined to fall on its knees in an attitude of what it inadequately calls prayer, realizing the smallness of its role in these mythological matters, and realizing too that all such invention and creativity have come out of this double environment like birds winging out of the blue, particularly, as in my own case, like the honey-guide for our African selves to be set on a way of the spirit to the honey which is the ultimate symbol of Eros.

The Voice of the Thunder, 'The Other Journey'

I have often thought that the most important issue of our time is how we overcome evil without becoming another form of evil in the process.

A Walk with a White Bushman

The New Testament exhorted us not to resist evil because all men tend to become what they oppose – and what follows logically is that ultimately the dark and dishonoured self triumphs. Proud, angry and undefeated, the rejected forces mass in the shadow of the unconscious, knife in hand, demanding revenge. The answer, as Jung saw it, was to enthrone good and evil side by side in the service of the master pattern – not opposing or resisting evil but transforming and redeeming it.

Jung and the Story of Our Time, 'Point of Total Return'

The day [W. H. Bleek] died the little colony of Bushmen he had established around his house, so that he could study their language and write down their stories, were heartbroken. So were his children, and at sunset they all gathered in his great African kitchen to find comfort in one another's company. Suddenly an owl appeared, fluttering at the kitchen window, and hooted loudly. Bleek's children were all terrified, but the Bushmen started dancing and clapping their hands, singing, 'He has arrived! He has arrived!'

A Walk with a White Bushman

There is a story about this individual quest which the Stone Age people in the desert tell and it is, in some way, a natural parable to me. It is the story of the young man and the lion. They say there was a great young hunter, perhaps the greatest they had ever known. Now the hunter is an interesting figure, because he carries a symbolic charge. He is not only the hunter in the world without, who seeks food for the body; he also represents in the human imagination that aspect of man seeking new meaning in the jungle of his time. One day when this hunter was on his way to the water, a lion, which was also on its way to the water, attacked him. This happened because for a moment he had ceased to be fully aware. It is interesting that this is the fatal sin, that fate always acts through our lack of awareness. It is also interesting that both were on their way to water, because waters in the desert are places of magic; they are places where the desert is transformed and new life grows. Here, as in the Bible and most myths and legends, water carries an image of new being, of new life. It is as if the story is saying: both the lion and the man are in search of a new form of life.

The lion seizes the young man, but, being very thirsty, it says, 'Well, I won't eat him at once.' The young man knows that his only hope is to pretend he is dead. So the lion carries him off to a thorn tree and pushes him into the fork of the tree. The thorns stick deep into the skin of this young man, but he knows that he must not show his pain. None the less, the pain is so severe that through his closed eyelids tears start to run down his cheeks.

Then an extraordinary thing happens: the lion starts to lick the tears of the young man, and instantly the situation changes. It is a marvellous moment of revelation, right at the beginning in the mind of the first man, of the role of tenderness, of gentleness and of compassion in life. The lion feels changed and says, 'This young man whose tears I've licked is my man for ever.' And the lion goes slowly over the hill to the water, deep in thought.

The moment the lion is gone, the young man jumps up and runs back to his community. The community, because they are very fond of him, jump up in alarm and ask, 'What has happened?'

He tells them the story and they say, 'Well, don't worry. We'll defend you against the lion.'

But he replies, 'You won't be able to defend me against the lion, because it has licked my tears and will insist on coming for me.'

Nevertheless, they wrap him in all the hides and skins they can find, and prepare for battle. The hide and skins are, of course, symbols. They put him back into a collective attitude, a collective state of mind.

I would like to emphasize at this point the importance of the lion. The lion, not only in the imagination of first man, but even in our day, is not the king of beasts for nothing. It is so chosen because, of all forms of animal life, it is the most many sided, the most highly differentiated. It is powerful. It is swift. It is strong. It can see as well by night as by day. Its senses of smell and hearing are very good. It is very intelligent, and it doesn't abuse this formidable combination of powers. It has a sense of proportion, and does not kill except for food. (This latter is a well-known fact in countries where lions have not deteriorated as a result of being hunted and tormented continually by tourists.) Above all, the lion is fundamentally the cat that walks alone. In other words, the lion is the individual; it is the symbol of the instinctive and royal individual self.

In the story, looking for a man to eat is a way of acquiring new being, because primitive man believed that whatever you ate, you became. So it is in certain symbolism of today. In taking communion, for instance, in taking the bread and wine, one partakes of Christ's flesh and blood in order to become like Christ. Similarly, at another level, the lion, by eating a man, seeks to become man, to be also human. This is what the story is saying to us. The greatest, the most formidable combination of instincts in the command of life demands an individual man, demands also to be lived individually.

But the young man runs away from this fate. It is too much for him, and the community agrees with him. They try to protect him. In a minute, however, the lion appears. They do everything they can to kill it, but they fail. The lion simply lets it be known, 'I've come for him whose tears I've licked and I shall not go away until I've got him.'

At last, the young man says, 'Look, it's no good. The lion will kill all of you.' He makes them take the skins off him – he undoes the collective attitude to the problem – and he falls in front of the lion. The lion then falls upon him, and the story tells us that both in that moment die.

The fate of lion and man would seem to indicate that, although primitive man feels that the attainment of the self must come about, although this is what life is for, it is not fully possible as yet. It is still to be achieved sometime in the future. None the less, it is something for which we must earnestly begin to strive. Never before has it been so important to rediscover this natural pattern in ourselves, to withdraw from the collective values, or lack of values, of our time, and to find ourselves in our unique, historical, specific and individual way.

A Testament to The Wilderness, 'Appointment with a Rhinoceros', Essay

I am certain that if only man could increase his awareness and renew his relationship with this whole pattern in himself, which theologians call 'God', all the feeling of helplessness would go.

May I illustrate it from something . . . that happened to me in the last war? I was standing at nightfall looking out of my prison. It was what I believed to be my last night alive, and I had fully accepted that I would be executed by the Japanese in the morning. An enormous thunderstorm had broken outside and the heavy rain – which always, in my drought-conditioned African senses, brings feelings of relief and music – was falling. The lightning and the thunder were almost continuous. I thought I had never seen lightning more beautiful – it was almost as if I were in the workshop of creation where lightning is made – and it was so charged and intense that it seemed to overflow its own zig-zag thrust at the jungle and come more like a great stream of fire out of the sky and make a delta of flame in the black. But there were also great purple sheets of lightning in between, that swept like archangelic wings over my prison. But it was the thunder which meant most of all. I had never heard the voice so loud, so clear and so magisterial. And suddenly, quite unbidden, a great feeling of relief came over me. 'That's it!' I thought. 'The Japanese are ultimately not in overall command. There is witness of a power greater than man which, in the end, will decide all.'

I express it very badly because the experience was totally beyond the capacity of words and is one of the most overwhelming emotions I have ever experienced; and in that moment all anxiety left me and I was, in the deepest sense of the words, no more troubled. Through nature outside I had been reconnected with a kind of powerhouse inside myself of which I had been unaware.

A Walk with a White Bushman

Even Job, the archetype in symbol of a pioneer in the world of the spirit, after all the eloquence that flowed between him and his comforters, between him and the suffering which threated his integrity, had to 'lay his hand upon his mouth' and, in the act of confessing his defeat, the knowledge came to him: 'my redeemer liveth'. And at that moment, emptied of words, of all argument, of all resistance and attempts to deal purely out of himself with his suffering, into this terrible vacant place within himself there moved something for which I can only borrow the old theological word: grace. A process of metamorphosis immediately took over . . . and all that Job had lost, and more – even in a wordly sense – was returned to him.

There is admission in all this of a dynamic known unknown, a knowledge that belongs utterly to the future, and yet is magnetic in the present in the area where the world within and without meet and are interwoven.

About Blady, Chapter 3

I had to turn astronomer and prowl among the known and visible stars and their neighbours, watching their activity and places of congregation where at some inner sanctuary of the universe the mystery of things is being transformed into a kind of living wonder. And so, by following a pattern in and out of time before and beyond the here and now, one discovers one's own specific sense of meaning . . .

About Blady, Chapter 1

I had once seen on a master television screen at the Space Centre in the United States of America . . . a superb and unbelievably detailed view of the earth as seen moments before man first set foot on the moon . . .

It is impossible to convey, and I shall not be so foolish as to attempt it, how moved I was by that view of so tiny a speck of dust as the 'earth' taking on itself the mystery of the universe; and, despite all its own divisions, conflicts and suffering, compelling men to combine and set out once again to make the great 'unknown' that begot it, and us who inhabit it, known, as already we were known to it. . . . it seemed to me that a great shift in design and regrouping of energies had taken place, and already provided man with a physical and tangible perspective of the essential unity of his native earth; and how in the travel and exploration and resumption of the quest for wholeness and life once symbolized in a legend of a Holy Grail, he would see his departure not from a specific place, town or country but as from an earth at one, and the unique, beloved and infinitely heroic home of the life and family of a man whose frontier was no longer to be found on any man-made map or chart, but beyond that undiscovered beach on which the swell of the seas of the night was breaking . . . into the foam and spray of the 'milky way'. In so far as he still had obligations and feelings of citizenship, I felt that it would be as citizen of the earth;

certain that this master pattern within him would always have need of him, never leave his spirit unemployed, but give it increasingly work of ever greater meaning to do.

Yet Being Someone Other, Chapter 7

The dream is the keeper of the wonder . . . It is there that we must go to 'take upon ourselves the mystery of things as if we were God's spies'. The first time I came across this great cry which would deliver Lear from imprisonment in his own anguish, not by removing his suffering, but by giving it a new meaning, the word spies troubled me greatly . . . Now I realized it could not have been more apt. Intimation of the new meaning to be lived never comes by battalions but in single spies. It comes as an improbable summons in some lonely, seemingly ill-equiped and often suffering individual heart, operating far ahead of the armies of new life, like a spy behind the lines of the totalitarian spirit of its day. The mystery we must take upon ourselves in order to free our arrested being is that of the first things of life, which our twentieth-century civilization puts last . . . if we are to enter the kingdom.

The Heart of the Hunter, Chapter 10

Ultimately all endings are happy endings. The human comedy finally is divine.

About Blady, Chapter 3

'Wind and the spirit, earth and being, rain and doing, lightning and awareness imperative, thunder and the word, seed and sower, all are one: and it is necessary only for man to ask for his seed to be chosen and to pray for the sower within to sow it through the deed and act of himself, and then the harvest for all will be golden and great.'

The Seed and the Sower, 'Christmas Morning'

Bibliography

———

WORKS BY LAURENS VAN DER POST

Sources for the extracts in this anthology are given as chapter number or part titles, which are applicable to all the various editions of the works, whereas page numbers might be specific only to one edition. Listed here are the English language editions of the works of Laurens van der Post, and, additionally, his introductions to other works, and his essays and lectures which are quoted in this anthology.

In a Province, London, The Hogarth Press, 1934; Penguin Books, 1984. New York, William Morrow, 1965.

Venture to the Interior, London, The Hogarth Press, 1952; Penguin Books, 1957. New York, William Morrow 1951; Harcourt Brace 1980.

The Face Beside the Fire, London, The Hogarth Press, 1953. New York, William Morrow, 1953.

Flamingo Feather, London, The Hogarth Press, 1955; Penguin Books, 1965. New York, William Morrow, 1955.

The Dark Eye in Africa, London, The Hogarth Press, 1955. Braamfontein, South Africa, Lowry Publishers. New York, William Morrow, 1955.

The Lost World of the Kalahari, London, The Hogarth Press, 1958; Penguin Books, 1962. New York, William Morrow, 1958; Harcourt Brace, 1979.

The Heart of the Hunter, London, The Hogarth Press, 1961; Penguin Books, 1965. New York, William Morrow, 1961; Harcourt Brace, 1980.

The Seed and the Sower, London, The Hogarth Press, 1963; Penguin Books, 1966. New York, William Morrow, 1963.

Journey Into Russia, London, The Hogarth Press, 1964; Penguin Books, 1965. New York [entitled *A View of All the Russias*], William Morrow, 1964.

BIBLIOGRAPHY

The Hunter and the Whale, London, The Hogarth Press, 1967; Penguin Books, 1970. New York, William Morrow, 1967.

The Night of the New Moon, London, The Hogarth Press, 1970; Penguin Books, 1977. New York [entitled *The Prisoner and the Bomb*], William Morrow, 1970.

A Story Like the Wind, London, The Hogarth Press, 1972; Penguin Books, 1974. New York, William Morrow, 1972; Harcourt Brace, 1978.

A Far-Off Place, London, The Hogarth Press, 1974; Penguin Books, 1976. New York, William Morrow, 1974; Harcourt Brace, 1978.

A Mantis Carol, London, The Hogarth Press, 1975; Penguin Books, 1989. New York, William Morrow, 1976.

Jung and the Story of Our Time, London, The Hogarth Press, 1976; Penguin Books, 1978. New York, Pantheon Books, 1975; Vintage Books, 1976.

First Catch Your Eland, London, The Hogarth Press, 1977. New York, William Morrow, 1978.

Yet Being Someone Other, London, The Hogarth Press, 1982; Penguin Books, 1984. New York, William Morrow, 1983.

A Walk with a White Bushman, London, Chatto & Windus, 1986; Penguin Books, 1988. New York, William Morrow, 1987.

The Lost World of the Kalahari, illustrated edition with photographs by David Coulson and a new Epilogue by the author, London, Chatto & Windus, 1988. New York, William Morrow, 1988.

About Blady: A Pattern out of Time, London, Chatto & Windus, 1991; Penguin Books, 1993. New York, William Morrow, 1992; Harcourt Brace, 1993.

The Voice of the Thunder, London, Chatto & Windus, 1993. New York, William Morrow, 1994.

OTHER WRITINGS BY LAURENS VAN DER POST

Introduction to *Turbott Wolfe* by William Plomer, London, The Hogarth Press, 1965.

Introduction to *Progress Without Loss of Soul* by Theodor Abt, Bern, Switzerland, Hallwag AG, 1983, translated by Boris L. Matthews, Illinois, Chiron Publications, 1988.

'Wilderness – The Way Ahead', essay, Scotland, The Findhorn Press and Wisconsin, The Lorian Press, 1984.

'Wilderness – A Way of Truth' and 'Wilderness – Appointment with a Rhinoceros', essays, Scotland, The Findhorn Press, and in *The Wilderness Within*, Festschrift for Dr C.A. Meier, Switzerland, Daimon Verlag.

BIBLIOGRAPHY

'Our Mother Which Art in Earth', address, with interview by Robert Hinshaw, Scotland, The Findhorn Press and Switzerland, Daimon Verlag, 1991.

'The Creative Pattern in Primitive Africa', Eranos Lectures, The Eranos Foundation, Ascona, Switzerland, 1956, and Dallas, Spring Publications, 1957.

Letter to Hiroaki Mori, 1989.